Understanding Sociology Through Fiction

Understanding Sociology Through Fiction

Myles L. Clowers
Professor of Social Sciences
San Diego City College

Steven H. Mori
Professor of Sociology
San Diego City College

McGraw-Hill Book Company

New York St. Louis San Francisco Auckland Bogotá
Düsseldorf Johannesburg London Madrid Mexico
Montreal New Delhi Panama Paris São Paulo
Singapore Sydney Tokyo Toronto

This book was set in Times Roman by National ShareGraphics, Inc. The editors were Lyle Linder and Barry Benjamin; the cover was designed by J. E. O'Connor; the cover illustration was done by Thomas Lulebitch; the production supervisor was Charles Hess.
R. R. Donnelley & Sons Company was printer and binder.

Understanding Sociology Through Fiction

1 2 3 4 5 6 7 8 9 0   D O D O   7 8 3 2 1 0 9 8 7 6

See Acknowledgments on pages 222–223. Copyrights included on this page by reference.

Library of Congress Cataloging in Publication Data

Main entry under title
Understanding sociology through fiction.
    1. Sociology—Literary collections. I. Clowers,
Myles L. II. Mori, Steven H.
PN6071.S53U5   301   76–9108
ISBN 0–07–011452–8 pbk.

*To Nancy, Steven, and Lisa Mori
and Shirley, Nadine, and Laura Miller—
with love*

Contents

Preface

Since the beginning of time, men and women have been social creatures. Be it in the form of a large or small group, people have banded together for protection, survival, and companionship. To understand this phenomenon, the study of society or sociology came into being.

In trying to obtain some degree of understanding about the nature of society, sociologists have employed various techniques and methods, and certainly the use of literature has not been overlooked. The plays of Shakespeare, the novels of Dickens, and the poetry of Bob Dylan have, in some ways, contributed to the discipline. These are people who know their fellow human beings in an intuitive way, and thus their conclusions are sometimes quite valid. The novelist has been and will continue to be a source of information for students of sociology.

Our purpose in writing *Understanding Sociology through Fiction* is to take these observations by fiction writers and use them to demonstrate key sociological concepts. It is not our intent to replace the conventional sociology textbook but merely to supplement it in a more interesting and readable fashion. While fiction is not necessarily better than nonfiction in achieving an understanding of sociology, it can motivate a student in a way that most traditional texts do not. This not only gives more relevance to the educational process but it also allows the student to relate his or her personal experiences with the characters depicted in the selections. Fiction, for these reasons, can be an extremely effective supplement to a nonfictional text.

The most difficult task in putting a book of this kind together is the choice of the selections. After sorting through many novels and short stories, we gave priority to those excerpts that were academically sound and relevant to the topic. Additionally, we wanted to make sure that the selections were of high literary quality and would stimulate the reader into doing some personal inquiry. We believe that we have accomplished our goal.

The structure of the book follows that of a traditional sociology text. Each chapter begins with a brief condensation of the topic, and the selections are introduced with an essay that focuses the reader's attention on the concept and gives some informational background about the characters and the plot. At the conclusion of each selection there is a question that will provoke the reader's thoughts about the topic of the selection.

As with any project, this book is not the work of two people; many colleagues and friends have contributed advice, ideas, and inspiration. Our debt to them is great, and there is no proper way in which we can thank them. However, it is to our loved ones that we owe the greatest debt for their patience and, most importantly, their love.

Myles L. Clowers
Steven H. Mori

Understanding Sociology Through Fiction

Chapter 1

The Human Group

Human beings are social animals who live together in groups. This behavior is not usual from other animals, but what does distinguish man is the physical endowment of a complex brain. This has allowed him to create a system of symbols that is used by him to construct various social structures for the purpose of survival.

Two of the more important concepts that sociologists have created in order to predict social interaction are those of status and role. The term *status* refers to "a position in a network of social relations" while *role* can be conceived of as "the proper mode of social behavior for the person who occupies a certain status." Thus, as William Shakespeare shows in the soliloquy from *As You Like It,* each age or role brings about a different status and is open for interpretation to the person who is in that position. Status and role, then, vary according to the person who occupies them.

Given the varying nature of role and status, interaction among people will differ, and these interactions can be classified into four categories: cooperation, conflict, competition, and exchange. Cooperation can be considered as people or groups who act together in order to promote a common interest, while conflict is where there is a struggle among people for some commonly prized object or value. Competition is a kind of cooperative conflict in which the parties agree beforehand on some predetermined rules. Exchange is a process in which one person behaves in such a manner toward another for the purpose of receiving a reward. In the selection from William Golding, *Lord of the Flies*, all four aspects of social interaction are demonstrated.

As You Like It

William Shakespeare

Although sociologists were the ones that formulated the concepts of status and role, these ideas did not escape the attention of humankind's greatest dramatist, William Shakespeare. In this brief soliloquy from the play *As You Like It,* Shakespeare outlines the key aspects of status and role.

All the world's a stage,

And all the men and women merely players;
They have their exits and their entrances,
And one man in his time plays many parts,
His acts being seven ages. . . . At first the infant,
Mewling and puking in the nurse's arms:
Then the whining school-boy, with his satchel
And shining morning face, creeping like snail
Unwillingly to school: and then the lover,
Sighing like furnace, with a woeful ballad
Made to his mistress' eyebrow: then a soldier,
Full of strange oaths and bearded like the pard,
Jealous in honour, sudden and quick in quarrel,
Seeking the bubble reputation
Even in the cannon's mouth: and then the justice,
In fair round belly with good capon line,
With eyes severe and beard of formal cut,
Full of wise saws and modern instances,
And so he plays his part. . . . The sixth age shifts
Into the lean and slippered pantaloon,
With spectacles on nose and pouch on side,
His youthful hose, well saved, a world too wide
For his shrunk shank, and his big manly voice,
Turning again toward childish treble, pipes,
And whistles in his sound. . . . Last scene of all,
That ends this strange eventful history,
Is second childishness, and mere oblivion,
Sans teeth, sans eyes, sans taste, sans everything.

QUESTION

What roles are you involved in, and why do you present yourself in the way that you do?

William Shakespeare, *As You Like It,* 1623

Lord of the Flies

Willian Golding

The novel by William Golding, *Lord of the Flies,* presents an example of all four types of social interaction: cooperation, conflict, competition, and exchange. The book is about a group of young boys who are isolated on a small island. Quickly, they organize their energies for the purpose of survival (cooperation). Gradually, the group splits into two different bands: one wanting to keep things like they were in the boys' previous society and one desiring a different life-style (conflict). Competition among the two group leaders, Jack and Ralph, takes place in order to gain a position of leadership. The interaction of exchange is also shown in the sharing of the pig.

The first rhythm that they became used to was the slow swing from dawn to quick dusk. They accepted the pleasures of morning, the bright sun, the whelming sea and sweet air, as a time when play was good and life so full that hope was not necessary and therefore forgotten. Toward noon, as the floods of light fell more nearly to the perpendicular, the stark colors of the morning were smoothed in pearl and opalesence; and the heat—as though the impending sun's height gave it momentum—became a blow that they ducked, running to the shade and lying there, perhaps even sleeping.

Strange things happened at midday. The glittering sea rose up, moved apart in planes of blatant impossibility; the coral reef and the few stunted palms that clung to the more elevated parts would float up into the sky, would quiver, be plucked apart, run like raindrops on a wire or be repeated as in an odd succession of mirrors. Sometimes land loomed where there was no land and flicked out like a bubble as the children watched. Piggy discounted all this learnedly as a "mirage"; and since no boy could reach even the reef over the stretch of water where the snapping sharks waited, they grew accustomed to these mysteries and ignored them, just as they ignored the miraculous, throbbing stars. At midday the illusions merged into the sky and there the sun gazed down like an angry eye. Then, at the end of the afternoon, the mirage subsided and the horizon became level and blue and clipped as the sun declined. That was another time of comparative coolness but menaced by the coming of the dark. When the sun sank, darkness dropped on the island like an extinguisher and soon the shelters were full of restlessness, under the remote stars.

Nevertheless, the northern European tradition of work, play, and food right through the day, made it impossible for them to adjust themselves wholly to this new rhythm. The littlun Percival had early crawled into a shelter and stayed there for two days, talking, singing, and crying, till they thought him batty and were faintly amused. Ever since then he and been peaked, red-eyed, and miserable; a littlun who played little and cried often.

The smaller boys were known now by the generic title of "littluns." The decrease in size, from Ralph down, was gradual; and though there was a dubious region inhabited by Simon and Robert and Maurice, nevertheless no one had any difficulty in recognizing biguns at one end and littluns at the other. The undoubted littluns, those aged about six, led a quite distinct, and at the same time intense, life of their own. They ate most of the day, picking fruit where they could reach it and not particular about ripeness and quality. They were used now to stomach-aches and a sort of chronic diarrhoea. They suffered untold terrors in the dark and huddled together for comfort. Apart from food and sleep, they found time for play, aimless and trivial, in the white sand by the bright water. They cried for their mothers much less often than might have been expected; they were very brown, and filthily dirty. They obeyed the summons of the conch, partly because Ralph blew it, and he was big enough to be a link with the adult world of authority; and partly because they enjoyed the entertainment of the assemblies. But otherwise they seldom bothered with the biguns and their passionately emotional and corporate life was their own.

They had built castles in the sand at the bar of the little river. These castles were about one foot high and were decorated with shells, withered flowers, and interesting stones. Round the castles was a complex of marks, tracks, walls, railway lines, that were of significance only if inspected with the eye at beach-level. The littluns played here, if not happily at least with absorbed attention; and often as many as three of them would play the same game together.

Three were playing here now. Henry was the biggest of them. He was also a distant relative of that other boy whose mulberry-marked face had not been seen since the evening of the great fire; but he was not old enough to understand this, and if he had been told that the other boy had gone home in an aircraft, he would have accepted the statement without fuss or disbelief.

Henry was a bit of a leader this afternoon, because the other two were Percival and Johnny, the smallest boys on the island. Percival was mouse-colored and had not been very attractive even to his mother; Johnny was well built, with fair hair and a natural belligerence. Just now he was being obedient because he was interested; and the three children, kneeling in the sand, were at peace.

Roger and Maurice came out of the forest. They were relieved from duty at the fire and had come down for a swim. Roger led the way straight through the castles, kicking them over, burying the flowers, scattering the chosen stones. Maurice followed, laughing, and added to the destruction. The three littluns paused in their game and looked up. As it happened, the particular marks in which they were interested had not been touched, so they made no protest. Only Percival began to whimper with an eyeful of sand and Maurice hurried away. In his other life Maurice had received chastisement for filling a younger eye with sand. Now, though there was no parent to let fall a heavy hand, Maurice still felt the unease of wrongdoing. At the back of his mind formed the uncertain outlines of an excuse. He muttered something about a swim and broke into a trot.

Roger remained, watching the littluns. He was not noticeably darker than when he had dropped in, but the shock of black hair, down his nape and low on his forehead, seemed to suit his gloomy face and made what had seemed at first an unsociable remoteness into something forbidding. Percival finished his whimper and went on playing, for the tears had washed the sand away. Johnny watched him with china-blue eyes; then began to fling up sand in a shower, and presently Percival was crying again.

When Henry tired of his play and wandered off along the beach, Roger followed him, keeping beneath the palms and drifting casually in the same direction. Henry walked at a distance from the palms and the shade because he was too young to keep himself out of the sun. He went down the beach and busied himself at the water's edge. The great Pacific tide was coming in and every few seconds the relatively still water of the lagoon heaved forwards an inch. There were creatures that lived in this last fling of the sea, tiny transparencies that came questing in with the water over the hot, dry sand. With impalpable organs of sense they examined this new field. Perhaps food had appeared where at the last incursion there had been none; bird droppings, insect perhaps, any of the strewn detritus of landward life. Like a myriad of tiny teeth in a saw, the transparencies came scavenging over the beach.

This was facinating to Henry. He poked about with a bit of stick, that itself was wave-worn and whitened and a vagrant, and tried to control the motions of the scavengers. He made little runnels that the tide filled and tried to crowd them with creatures. He became absorbed beyond mere happiness as he felt himself exercising control over living things. He talked to them, urging them, ordering them. Driven back by the tide, his footprints became bays in which they were trapped and gave him the illusion of mastery. He squatted on his hams at the water's edge, bowed, with a shock of hair falling over his forehead and past his eyes, and the afternoon sun emptied down invisible arrows.

Roger waited too. At first he had hidden behind a great palm; but Henry's absorption with the transparencies was so obvious that at last he stood out in full view. He looked along the beach. Percival had gone off, crying, and Johnny was left in triumphant possession of the castles. He sat there, crooning to himself and throwing sand at an imaginary Percival. Beyond him, Roger could see the platform and the glints of spray where Ralph and Simon and Piggy and Maurice were diving in the pool. He listened carefully but could only just hear them.

A sudden breeze shook the fringe of palm trees, so that the fronds tossed and fluttered. Sixty feet above Roger, several nuts, fibrous lumps as big as rugby balls, were loosed from their stems. They fell about him with a series of hard thumps and he was not touched. Roger did not consider his escape, but looked from the nuts to Henry and back again.

The subsoil beneath the palm trees was a raised beach, and generations of palms had worked loose in this the stones that had lain on the sands of another shore. Roger stooped, picked up a stone, aimed, and threw it at Henry—threw it to miss. The stone, that token of preposterous time, bounced five yards to Henry's right and fell in the water. Roger gathered a handful of stones and began to throw them. Yet there was a space round Henry, perhaps six yards in diameter, into which he dare not throw. Here, invisible yet strong, was the taboo of the old life. Round the squatting child was the protection of parents and school and policemen and the law. Roger's arm was conditioned by a civilization that knew nothing of him and was in ruins.

Henry was surprised by the plopping sounds in the water. He abandoned the noiseless transparencies and pointed at the center of the spreading rings like a setter. This side and that the stones fell, and Henry turned obediently but always too late to see the stones in the air. At last he saw one and laughed, looking for the friend who was teasing him. But Roger had whipped behind the palm again, was leaning against it breathing quickly, his eyelids fluttering. Then Henry lost interest in stones and wandered off.

"Roger."

Jack was standing under a tree about ten yards away. When Roger opened his eyes and saw him, a darker shadow crept beneath the swarthiness of his skin; but Jack noticed nothing. He was eager, impatient, beckoning, so that Roger went to him.

There was a small pool at the end of the river, dammed back by the sand and full of white water-lilies and needle-like reeds. Here Sam and Eric were waiting, and Bill. Jack, concealed from the sun, knelt by the pool and opened the two large leaves that he carried. One of them contained white clay, and the other red. By them lay a stick of charcoal brought down from the fire.

Jack explained to Roger as he worked.

"They don't smell me. They see me, I think. Something pink, under the trees."

He smeared on the clay.

"If only I'd some green!"

He turned a half-concealed face up to Roger and answered the incomprehension of his gaze.

"For hunting. Like in the war. You know—dazzle paint. Like things trying to look like something else—" He twisted in the urgency of telling. "—Like moths on a tree trunk"

Roger understood and nodded gravely. The twins moved toward Jack and began to protest timidly about something. Jack waved them away.

"Shut up."

He rubbed the charcoal stick between the patches of red and white on his face.

"No. You two come with me."

He peered at his reflection and disliked it. He bent down, took up a double handful of lukewarm water and rubbed the mess from his face. Freckles and sandy eyebrows appeared.

Roger smiled, unwillingly.

"You don't half look a mess."

Jack planned his new face. He made one cheek and one eye-socket white, then he rubbed red over the other half of his face and slashed a black bar of charcoal across from right ear to left jaw. He looked in the pool for his reflection, but his breathing troubled the mirror.

"Samneric. Get me a coconut. An empty one."

He knelt, holding the shell of water. A rounded patch of sunlight fell on his face and a brightness appeared in the depths of the water. He looked in astonishment, no longer at himself but at an awesome stranger. He spilt the water and leapt to his feet, laughing excitedly. Beside the pool his sinewy body held up a mask that drew their eyes and appalled them. He began to dance and his laughter became a bloodthirsty snarling. He capered toward Bill, and the mask was a thing on its own, behind which Jack hid, liberated from shame and self-consciousness. The face of red and white and black swung through the air and jigged toward Bill. Bill started up laughing; then suddenly he fell silent and blundered away through the bushes.

Jack rushed toward the twins.

"The rest are making a line. Come on!"

"But—"

"—we—"

"Come on! I'll creep up and stab—"

The mask compelled them.

Ralph climbed out of the bathing pool and trotted up the beach and sat in the shade beneath the palms. His fair hair was plastered over his eyebrows and he pushed it back. Simon was floating in the water and kicking with his feet, and Maurice was practicing diving. Piggy was mooning about, aimlessly picking up things and discarding them. The rock-pools which so facinated him were covered by the tide, so he was without an interest until the tide went back. Presently, seeing Ralph under the palms, he came and sat by him.

Piggy wore the remainders of a pair of shorts, his fat body was golden brown, and the glasses still flashed when he looked at anything. He was the only boy on the island whose hair never seemed to grow. The rest were shockheaded, but Piggy's hair still lay in wisps over his head as though baldness were his natural state and this imperfect covering would soon go, like the velvet on a young stag's antlers.

"I've been thinking," he said, "about a clock. We could make a sundial. We could put a stick in the sand, and then—"

The effort to express the mathematical processes involved was too great. He made a few passes instead.

"And an airplane, and a TV set," said Ralph sourly, "and a steam engine."

Piggy shook his head.

"You have to have a lot of metal things for that," he said, "and we haven't got no metal, But we got a stick."

Ralph turned and smiled involuntarily. Piggy was a bore; his fat, his ass-mar and his matter-of-fact ideas were dull, but there was always a little pleasure to be got out of pulling his leg, even if one did it by accident.

Piggy saw the smile and misinterpreted it as friendliness. There had grown up tacitly among the biguns the opinion that Piggy was an outsider, not only by accent, which did not matter, but by fat, and ass-mar, and specs, and a certain disinclination for manual labor. Now, finding that something he had said made Ralph smile, he rejoiced and pressed his average.

"We got a lot of sticks. We could have a sundial each. Then we should know what the time was."

"A fat lot of good that would be."

"You said you wanted things done. So as we could be rescued."

He leapt to his feet and trotted back to the pool, just as Maurice did a rather poor dive. Ralph was glad of a chance to change the subject. He shouted as Maurice came to the surface.

"Belly flop! Belly flop!"

Maurice flashed a smile at Ralph who slid easily into the water. Of all the boys, he was the most at home there; but today, irked by the mention of rescue, the useless, footling mention of rescue, even the green depths of water and the shattered, golden sun held no balm. Instead of remaining and playing, he swam with steady strokes under Simon and crawled out of the other side of the pool to lie there, sleek and streaming like a seal. Piggy, always clumsy, stood up and came to stand by him, so that Ralph rolled on his stomach and pretended not to see. The mirages had died away and gloomily he ran his eye along the taut blue line of the horizon.

The next moment he was on his feet and shouting.

"Smoke! Smoke!"

Simon tried to sit up in the water and got a mouthful. Maurice, who had been standing ready to dive, swayed back on his heels, made a bolt for the platform, then swerved back to the grass under the palms. There he started to pull on his tattered shorts, to be ready for anything.

Ralph stood, one hand holding back his hair, the other clenched. Simon was climbing out of the water. Piggy was rubbing his glasses on his shorts and squinting at the sea. Maurice had got both legs through one leg of his shorts. Of all the boys, only Ralph was still.

"I can't see no smoke," said Piggy incredulously. "I can't see no smoke, Ralph—where is it?"

Ralph said nothing. Now both his hands were clenched over his forehead so that the fair hair was kept out of his eyes. He was leaning forward and already the salt was whitening his body.

"Ralph—where's the ship?"

Simon stood by, looking from Ralph to the horizon. Maurice's trousers gave way with a sigh and he abandoned them as a wreck, rushed toward the forest, and then came back again.

The smoke was a tight little knot on the horizon and was uncoiling slowly. Beneath the smoke was a dot that might be a funnel. Ralph's face was pale as he spoke to himself.

"They'll see our smoke."

Piggy was looking in the right direction now.

"It don't look much."

He turned round and peered up at the mountain. Ralph continued to watch the ship, ravenously. Color was coming back into his face. Simon stood by him, silent.

"I know I can't see very much," said Piggy, "but have we got any smoke?"

Ralph moved impatiently, still watching the ship.

"The smoke on the mountain."

Maurice came running, and stared out to sea. Both Simon and Piggy were looking up at the mountain. Piggy screwed up his face but Simon cried out as though he had hurt himself.

"Ralph! Ralph!"

The quality of his speech twisted Ralph on the sand.

"You tell me," said Piggy anxiously. "Is there a signal?"

Simon put out his hand, timidly, to touch Ralph; but Ralph started to run, splashing through the shallow end of the bathing pool, across the hot, white sand and under the palms. A moment later he was battling with the complex undergrowth that was already engulfing the scar. Simon ran after him, then Maurice. Piggy shouted.

"Ralph! Please—Ralph!"

Then he too started to run, stumbling over Maurice's discarded shorts before he was across the terrace. Behind the four boys, the smoke moved gently along the horizon; and on the beach, Henry and Johnny were throwing sand at Percival who was crying quietly again; and all three were in complete ignorance of the excitement.

By the time Ralph had reached the landward end of the scar he was using precious breath to swear. He did desperate violence to his naked body among the rasping creepers so that blood was sliding over him. Just where the steep ascent of the mountain began, he stopped. Maurice was only a few yards behind him.

"Piggy's specs!" shouted Ralph. "If the fire's all out, we'll need them—"

He stopped shouting and swayed on his feet. Piggy was only just visible, bumbling up from the beach. Ralph looked at the horizon, then up to the mountain. Was it better to fetch Piggy's glasses, or would the ship have gone? Or if they climbed on, supposing the fire was all out, and they had to watch Piggy crawling nearer and the ship sinking under the horizon? Balanced on a high peak of need, agonized by indecision, Ralph cried out:

"Oh God, oh God!"

Simon, struggling with bushes, caught his breath. His face was twisted. Ralph blundered on, savaging himself, as the wisp of smoke moved on.

The fire was dead. They saw that straight away; saw what they had really known down on the beach when the smoke of home had beckoned. The fire was out, smokeless and dead; the watchers were gone. A pile of unused fuel lay ready.

Ralph turned to the sea. The horizon stretched, impersonal once more, barren of all but the faintest trace of smoke. Ralph ran stumbling along the rocks, saved himself on the edge of the pink cliff, and screamed at the ship.

"Come back! Come back!"

Simon and Maurice arrived. Ralph looked at them with unwinking eyes. Simon turned away, smearing the water from his cheeks. Ralph reached inside himself for the worst word he knew.

"They let the bloody fire go out."

He looked down the unfriendly side of the mountain. Piggy arrived, out of breath and whimpering like a littlun. Ralph clenched his fist and went very red. The intentness of his gaze, the bitterness of his voice, pointed for him.

"There they are."

A procession had appeared, far down among the pink stones that lay near the water's edge. Some of the boys wore black caps but otherwise they were almost naked. They lifted sticks in the air together whenever they came to an easy patch. They were chanting, something to do with the bundle that the errant twins carried so carefully. Ralph picked out Jack easily, even at that distance, tall, red-haired, and inevitably leading the procession.

Simon looked now, from Ralph to Jack, as he had looked from Ralph to the horizon, and what he saw seemed to make him afraid. Ralph said nothing more, but waited while the procession came nearer. The chant was audible but at that distance still wordless. Behind Jack walked the twins, carrying a great stake on their shoulders. The gutted carcass of a pig swung from the stake, swinging heavily as the twins toiled over the uneven ground. The pig's head hung down with gaping neck and seemed to search for something on the ground. At last the words of the chant floated up to them, across the bowl of blackened wood and ashes.

"Kill the pig. Cut her throat. Spill her blood."

Yet as the words became audible, the procession reached the steepest part of the mountain, and in a minute or two the chant had died away. Piggy sniveled and Simon shushed him quickly as though he had spoken too loudly in church.

Jack, his face smeared with clays, reached the top first and hailed Ralph excitedly, with lifted spear.

"Look! We've killed a pig—we stole up on them—we got in a circle—"

Voices broke in from the hunters.

"We got in a circle—"

"We crept up—"

"The pig squealed—"

The twins stood with the pig swinging between them, dropping back gouts on the rock. They seemed to share one wide, ecstatic grin. Jack had too many things to tell Ralph at once. Instead, he danced a step or two, then remembered his dignity and stood still, grinning. He noticed blood on his hands and grimaced distastefully, looked for something on which to clean them, then wiped them on his shorts and laughed.

Ralph spoke.

"You let the fire go out."

Jack checked, vaguely irritated by this irrelevance but too happy to let it worry him.

"We can light the fire again. You should have been with us, Ralph. We had a smashing time. The twins got knocked over—"

"We hit the pig—"

"—I fell on top—"

"I cut the pig's throat," said Jack, proudly, and yet twiched as he said it. "Can I borrow yours, Ralph, to make a nick in the hilt?"

The boys chattered and danced. The twins continued to grin.

"There was lashings of blood," said Jack, laughing and shuddering, "you should have seen it!"

"We'll go hunting every day—"

Ralph spoke again, hoarsely. He had not moved.

"You let the fire go out."

This repetition made Jack uneasy. He looked at the twins and then back at Ralph.

"We had to have them in the hunt," he said, "or there wouldn't have been enough for a ring."

He flushed, conscious of a fault.

"The fire's only been out an hour or two. We can light up again—"

He noticed Ralph's scarred nakedness, and the sombre silence of all four of them. He sought, charitable in his happiness, to include them in the thing that had happened. His mind was crowded with memories; memories of the knowledge that had come to them when they closed in on the struggling pig, knowledge that they had outwitted a living thing, imposed their will upon it, taken away its life like a long satisfying drink.

He spread his arms wide.

"You should have seen the blood!"

The hunters were more silent now, but at this they buzzed again. Ralph flung back his hair. One arm pointed at the empty horizon. His voice was loud and savage, and struck them into silence.

"There was a ship."

Jack, faced at once with too many awful implications, ducked away from them. He laid a hand on the pig and drew his knife. Ralph brought his arm down, fist clenched, and his voice shook.

"There was a ship. Out there. You said you'd keep the fire going and you let it out!" He took a step toward Jack, who turned and faced him.

"They might have seen us. We might have gone home—"

This was too bitter for Piggy, who forgot his timidity in the agony of his loss. He began to cry out shrilly:

"You and your blood, Jack Merridew! You and your hunting! We might have gone home—"

Ralph pushed Piggy to one side.

"I was chief, and you were going to do what I said. You talk. But you can't even build huts—then you go off hunting and let out the fire—"

He turned away, silent for a moment. Then his voice came again on a peak of feeling.

"There was a ship—"

One of the smaller hunters began to wail. The dismal truth was filtering through to everybody. Jack went very red as he hacked and pulled at the pig.

"The job was too much. We needed everyone."

Ralph turned.

"You could have had everyone when the shelters were finished. But you had to hunt—"

"We needed meat."

Jack stood up as he said this, the bloodied knife in his hand. The two boys faced each other. There was the brilliant world of hunting, tactics, fierce exhileration, skill; and there was the world of longing and baffled common-sense. Jack transferred the knife to his left hand and smudged blood over his forehead as he pushed down the plastered hair.

Piggy began again.

"You didn't ought to have let that fire out. You said you'd keep the smoke going—"

This from Piggy, and the wails of agreement from some of the hunters, drove Jack to violence. The bolting look came into his blue eyes. He took a step, and able at last to hit someone, struck his fist into Piggy's stomach. Piggy sat down with a grunt. Jack stood over him. His voice was vicious with humiliation.

"You would, would you? Fatty!"

Ralph made a step forward and Jack smacked Piggy's head. Piggy's glasses flew off and tinkled on the rocks. Piggy cried out in terror:

"My specs!"

He went crouching and feeling over the rocks but Simon, who got there first, found them for him. Passions beat about Simon on the mountain-top with awful wings.

"One side's broken."

Piggy grabbed and put on the glasses. He looked malevolently at Jack.

"I got to have them specs. Now I only got one eye. Jus' you wait—"

Jack made a move toward Piggy who scrambled away till a great rock lay between them. He thrust his head over the top and glared at Jack through his one flashing glass.

"Now I only got one eye. Just you wait—"

Jack mimicked the whine and scramble.

"Jus' you wait—yah!"

Piggy and the parody were so funny that the hunters began to laugh. Jack felt encouraged. He went on scrambling and the laughter rose to a gale of hysteria. Unwillingly Ralph felt his lips twitch; he was angry with himself for giving way.

He muttered.

"That was a dirty trick."

Jack broke out of his gyration and stood facing Ralph. His words came in a shout.

"All right, all right!"

He looked at Piggy, at the hunters, at Ralph.

"I'm sorry. About the fire, I mean. There. I—"

He drew himself up.

"—I apologize."

The buzz from the hunters was one of admiration at this handsome behavior. Clearly they were of the opinion that Jack had done the decent thing, had put himself in the right by his generous apology and Ralph, obscurely, in the wrong. They waited for an appropriately decent answer.

Yet Ralph's throat refused to pass one. He resented, as an addition to Jack's misbehavior, this verbal trick. The fire was dead, the ship was gone. Could they not see? Anger instead of decency passed his throat.

"That was a dirty trick."

They were silent on the mountain-top while the opaque look appeared in Jack's eyes and passed away.

Ralph's final word was an ungracious mutter.

"All right. Light the fire."

With some positive action before them, a little of the tension died. Ralph said no more, did nothing, stood looking down at the ashes round his feet. Jack was loud and active. He gave orders, sang, whistled, threw remarks at the silent Ralph—remarks that did not need an answer, and therefore could not invite a snub; and still Ralph was silent. No one, not even Jack, would ask him to move and in the end they had to build the fire three yards away and in a place not really as convenient. So Ralph asserted his chieftainship and could not have chosen a better way if he had thought for days. Against this weapon, so indefinable and so effective, Jack was powerless and raged without knowing why. By the time the pile was built, they were on different sides of a high barrier.

When they had dealt with the fire another crisis arose. Jack had no means of lighting it. Then to his surprise, Ralph went to Piggy and took the glasses from him. Not even Ralph knew how a link between him and Jack had been snapped and fastened elsewhere.

"I'll bring 'em back."

"I'll come too."

Piggy stood behind him, islanded in a sea of meaningless color, while Ralph knelt and focused the glossy spot. Instantly the fire was alight Piggy held out his hands and grabbed the glasses back.

Before these fantastically attractive flowers of violet and red and yellow, unkindness melted away. They became a circle of boys round a camp fire and even Piggy and Ralph were half-drawn in. Soon some of the boys were rushing down the slope for more wood while Jack hacked the pig. They tried holding the whole carcass on a stake over the fire, but the stake burnt more quickly than the pig roasted. In the end they skewered bits of meat on branches and held them in the flames: and even then almost as much boy was roasted as meat.

Ralph's mouth watered. He meant to refuse meat but his past diet of fruit and nuts, with an odd crab or fish, gave him too little resistance. He accepted a piece of half-raw meat and gnawed it like a wolf.

Piggy spoke, also dribbling.

"Aren't I having none?"

Jack had meant to leave him in doubt, as an assertion of power; but Piggy by advertising his omission made more cruelty necessary.

"You didn't hunt."

"No more did Ralph," said Piggy wetly, "nor Simon." He amplified. "There isn't more than a ha'porth of meat in a crab."

Ralph stirred uneasily. Simon, sitting between the twins and Piggy, wiped his mouth and shoved his piece of meat over the rocks to Piggy, who grabbed it. The twins giggled and Simon lowered his face in shame.

Then Jack leapt to his feet, slashed off a great hunk of meat, and flung it down at Simon's feet.

"Eat! Damn you!"

He glared at Simon.

"Take it!"

He spun on his heel, center of a bewildered circle of boys.

"I got you meat!"

Numberless and inexpressible frustrations combined to make his rage elemental and awe-inspiring.

"I painted my face—I stole up. Now you eat—all of you—and I—"

Slowly the silence on the mountain-top deepened till the click of the fire and the soft hiss of roasting meat could be heard clearly. Jack looked round for understanding but found only respect. Ralph stood among the ashes of the signal fire, his hands full of meat, saying nothing.

Then at last Maurice broke the silence. He changed the subject to the only one that could bring the majority of them together.

"Where did you find the pig?"

Roger pointed down the unfriendly side. "They were there—by the sea."

Jack, recovering, could not bear to have his story told. He broke in quickly.

"We spread round. I crept, on hands and knees. The spears fell out because they hadn't barbs on. The pig ran away and made an awful noise—"

"It turned back and ran into the circle, bleeding—"

All the boys were talking at once. relieved and excited.

"We closed in—"

The first blow had paralyzed its hind quarters, so then the circle could close in and beat and beat—

"I cut the pig's throat—"

The twins, still sharing their identical grin, jumped up and ran round each other. Then the rest joined in, making pig-dying noises and shouting.

"One for his nob!"

"Give him a fourpenny one!"

Then Maurice pretended to be the pig and ran squealing into the center, and the hunters, circling still, pretended to beat him. As they danced, they sang.

"Kill the pig. Cut her throat. Bash her in."

Ralph watched them, envious and resentful. Not till they flagged and the chant died away, did he speak.

"I'm calling an assembly."

One by one, they halted, and stood watching him.

"With the conch. I'm calling a meeting even if we have to go on into the dark. Down on the platform. When I blow it. Now."

He turned away and walked off, down the mountain.

QUESTION

What function does conflict perform in society, and do you see any example of this in your own life and society?

Chapter 2

Culture

Culture is one of the most complex concepts in sociology, and there is no one definition of it that satisfies every sociologist. One current concept of culture puts forth the thesis that culture is similar to a cognitive map. This map consists of a series of learned plans, categories, and rules which an individual uses to interpret behavior and its meaning and to adapt to the society in which he or she exists.

To support these series of plans, categories, and rules, the society creates a system of values or "abstract ideas about what is good or desirable." These values then become the basis for social norms or "rules and standards of the proper conduct in a given situation." The importance of these values and norms is significant because they aid in the society's desire for self-preservation. In *A Man for All Seasons* the strength of values and norms is shown when Sir Thomas More refuses to go against his values and norms, even at the risk of his own life.

As an individual grows up, he or she can become steeped in norms and values to the point where any other norms and values are deemed inferior.

This is the problem of ethnocentricity, which the selection from *Hawaii* illustrates quite well.

A Man for All Seasons

Robert Bolt

Every culture has certain values and norms that it wants to pass on to the next generation for what it believes is necessary for the existence of that culture. As such, the values and norms are taught in such a manner that they will be accepted by the individual member without a great deal of question.

In *A Man for All Seasons,* Sir Thomas More, a devout Catholic and former adviser to Henry VIII of England, has been taught that marriage is a sacred institution and divorce under any circumstance is wrong. Thus, he has refused to sign a document that would legitimize the king's divorce from Catherine of Aragon, thereby legalizing the king's marriage to Anne Boleyn. A contingent of the king's men has come to More's prison cell to try to persuade him to sign the document. More's values and norms are so strong though that he cannot sign, even though it might and does cost him his life.

Norfolk: Wake up, Sir Thomas.

More: What, again?

Jailer: Sorry, sir.

More: What time is it?

Jailer: One o'clock, sir.

More: Oh, this is iniquitous!

Jailer: Sir.

More: All right. Who's there?

Jailer: The Secretary, the Duke, and the Archbishop.

More: I'm flattered.

Norfolk: A seat for the prisoner. This is the Seventh Commission to inquire into the case of Sir Thomas More, appointed by His Majesty's Council. Have you anything to say?

More: No. Thank you.

Norfolk: Master Secretary.

Cromwell: Sir Thomas— Do the witnesses attend?

Rich: Secretary.

Jailer: Sir.

Cromwell: Nearer! Come where you can hear! Sir Thomas, you have seen this document before?

More: Many times.

Cromwell: It is the Act of Succession. These are the names of those who have sworn to it.

More: I have, as you say, seen it before.

Cromwell: Will you swear to it?

More: No.

Norfolk: Thomas, we must know plainly—

Cromwell: Your Grace, please!

Norfolk: Master Cromwell!

Cromwell: I beg Your Grace's pardon.

Norfolk: Thomas, we must know plainly whether you recognize the offspring of Queen Anne as heirs to His Majesty.

More: The King in Parliament tells me that they are. Of course I recognize them.

Norfolk: Will you swear that you do?

More: Yes.

Norfolk: Then why won't you swear to the Act?

Cromwell: Because there is more than that in the Act.

Norfolk: Is that it?

More: Yes.

Norfolk: Then we must find out what it is in the Act that he objects to!

Cromwell: Brilliant.

Cranmer: Your Grace—May I try?

Norfolk: Certainly. I've no pretension to be an expert in police work.

Cranmer: Sir Thomas, it states in the preamble that the King's former marriage, to the Lady Catherine, was unlawful, she being previously his brother's wife and the—er—"Pope" having no authority to sanction it. Is that what you deny? Is that what you dispute? Is that what you are not sure of?

Norfolk: Thomas, you insult the King and His Council in the person of the Lord Archbishop!

More: I insult no one. I will not take the oath. I will not tell you why I will not.

Norfolk: Then your reasons must be treasonable!

More: Not "must be"; may be.

Norfolk: It's a fair assumption!

More: The law requires more than an assumption; the law requires a fact.

Cranmer: I cannot judge your legal standing in the case; but until I know the ground of your objections, I can only guess your spiritual standing too.

More: If you're willing to guess at that, Your Grace, it should be a small matter to guess my objections.

Cromwell: You do have objections to the Act?

Norfolk: Well, we know that, Cromwell!

More: You don't, my lord. You may suppose I have objections. All you know is that I will not swear to it. From sheer delight to give you trouble it might be.

Norfolk: Is it material why you won't?

More: It's most material. For refusing to swear, my goods are forfeit and I am condemned to life imprisonment. You cannot lawfully harm me further. But if you were right in supposing I had reasons for refusing and right again in supposing my reasons to be treasonable, the law would let you cut my head off.

Norfolk: Oh yes.

Cromwell: Oh, well done, Sir Thomas. I've been trying to make that clear to His Grace for some time.

Norfolk: Oh, confound all this . . . I'm not a scholar, as Master Cromwell never tires of pointing out, and frankly I don't know whether the marriage was lawful or not. But damn it, Thomas, look at those names. . . . You know those men! Can't you do what I did, and come with us, for fellowship?

More: And when we stand before God, and you are sent to Paradise for doing according to your conscience, and I am damned for not doing according to mine, will you come with me, for fellowship?

Cranmer: So those of us whose names are there are damned, Sir Thomas?

More: I don't know, Your Grace. I have no window to look into another man's conscience. I condemn no one.

Cranmer: Then the matter is capable of question?

More: Certainly.

Cranmer: But that you owe obedience to your King is not capable of question. So weigh a doubt against a certainty—and sign.

More: Some men think the Earth is round, others think it flat; it is a matter capable of question. But if it is flat, will the King's command make it round? And if it is round, will the King's command flatten it? No, I will not sign.

Cromwell: Then you have more regard to your own doubt than you have to his command!

More: For myself, I have no doubt.

Cromwell: No doubt of what?

More: No doubt of my grounds for refusing this oath. Grounds I will tell to the King alone, and which you, Master Secretary will not trick out of me.

Norfolk: Thomas—

More: Oh, gentlemen, can't I go to bed?

Cromwell: You don't seem to appreciate the seriousness of your position.

More: I deny anyone to live in that cell for a year and not appreciate the seriousness of his position.

Cromwell: Yet the State has harsher punishment.

More: You threaten like a dockside bully.

Cromwell: How should I threaten?

More: Like a Minister of State, with justice.

Cromwell: Oh, justice is what you're threatened with.

More: Then I'm not threatened.

Norfolk: Master Secretary, I think the prisoner may retire as he requests. Unless you, my lord—

Cranmer: No, I see no purpose in prolonging the interview.

Norfolk: Then good night, Thomas.

QUESTION

What are your strongly held values, and how does the effect of norms govern your behavior?

Hawaii

James Michener

The concept of ethnocentricity is shown quite well in the following selection from James Michener's novel. There is a misunderstanding between two groups of people, one represented by Reverend Hale and the other by Queen Malama. Reverend Hale is trying to convert the heathens of Hawaii to Christianity, which he feels is the only way to live. On the other hand, the Hawaiians see their life-style as natural and find Christianity strange and, in many ways, undesirable. In this part of the book, Reverend Hale is trying to impose his ethnocentric views of right and wrong

concerning the royal practice of incest between Queen Malama and her
brother Kelolo.

But if Abner thus found spiritual triumph in his missionary home, he
encountered a fairly solid defeat at Malama's grass palace, for when he
went to give the Alii Nui her day's lesson, he found that Kelolo had not
moved to the new house built for him, but lived as usual with his wife. "This
is an abomination!" Abner thundered.

The two huge lovers, well into their forties, listened in embarrassment
as he explained again why God abhorred incest, but when he was finished,
big Malama explained quietly, "I built the house for Kelolo outside the
walls, and it is a good house, but he doesn't want to stay there alone." She
began to cry and added, "He tried it for two nights while you were away,
but when I thought of him sleeping alone, I didn't like it either, so on the
third night I walked out to the gate and called, 'Kelolo, come inside where
you belong.' And he came and it was all my fault. I am to blame, Makua
Hale."

"You will never be a member of the church, Malama," Abner warned.
"And when you die, you will suffer hellfire forever."

"Tell me about hellfire again, Makua Hale," Malama begged, for she
desired to know exactly how much risk she was taking, and when Abner
repeated his awful description of souls in eternal torment, Malama shivered
and began asking specific questions while tears crept into her big eyes.

"You are sure that Kamehameha the king is in such fire."

"I am positive."

"Makua Hale, once a Catholic ship kapena came to Lahaina and spoke
to me about God. Are Catholics in the fire too?"

"They are in the fire forever," Abner said with absolute conviction.

"And the same ship kapena told me about the people in India who
have not heard of your god."

"Malama, don't speak of him as my God. He is God. He is the only
God."

"But when the people of India die, do they go into the fire, too?"

"Yes."

"So that the only people who escape are those who join your church?"

"Yes."

Triumphantly, she turned to Kelolo and said, "You see how terrible
the fire is. If you keep that platform out there, hanging onto old gods the
way you do, you will live in everlasting fire."

"Ah, no!" Kelolo resisted stubbornly. "My gods will care for me. They will never let me burn, for they will take me to their heaven, where I will live beside Kane's water of life."

"He is a foolish man!" Malama reflected sadly. "He's going to burn and he doesn't know it."

"But, Malama," Abner pointed out, "if you continue to live with Kelolo in such horrible sin, you also will live in everlasting fire."

"Oh, no!" the big woman corrected. "I believe in God. I love Jesus Christ. I am not going to live in fire at all. I will keep Kelolo with me only until I begin to feel sick. We have agreed that before I die I will send him far away, and then I shall be saved."

Then Abner played his trump card. Pointing his finger at her, he boldly faced her and warned: "But it is your minister alone who can let you enter the church. Have you thought of that?"

Malama pondered this unexpected news and studied her tormentor. He was a foot shorter than she, less than half her age, and weighed about a third as much. Cautiously she probed: "And it will be you who judges whether I have been a good woman or not."

"I will be the judge," Abner assured her.

"And if I haven't been . . ."

"You will not be accepted into the church."

Malama reviewed this impasse for some time, looking first at Abner and then at Kelolo, until finally she asked briskly, "But maybe you won't be here at the time, Makua Hale. Maybe there will be some other minister."

"I will be here," Abner said firmly.

Malama studied this gloomy prospect, sighed in resignation, and then changed the subject abruptly. "Tell me, Makua Hale, what things must I do if I am to be a good Alii Nui for my people?"

And Abner lauched into the work which would have great political consequence in Hawaii. At first only Malama and Kelolo attended his daily instruction, but gradually the lesser alii reported, and when King Liholiho or his regent-mother Kaahumanu were in residence, they too appeared, questioning, rejecting, pondering.

Constantly, Abner reiterated a few simple ideas. "There must be no slaves," he said.

"There are slaves in America," the alii countered.

"It is wrong in America, and it is wrong here. There must be no slaves."

"There are slaves in England," his listeners insisted.

"And in both America and England good men fight against slavery.

Good men should do the same here." When his moral arguments bore no fruit, he resorted to exhortation, crying, "I was afloat on the ocean on my way to Hawaii, and we passed a ship at sundown, and it was a slave ship, and we could hear the chains clashing in the dismal holds. How would you like it. King Liholiho, if your hands were chained to a beam, and your back was cut with lashes, and the sweat poured down your face and blinded your eyes? How would you like that, King Liholiho?"

"I would not like it," the king replied.

"And the alii should see to it that no more babies are killed," Abner thundered.

Malama interrupted. "How should we greet captains from foreign warships when they come ashore at Lahaina?"

"All civilized nations," Abner explained, using a phrase that was especially cherished by the missionaries, "conduct formal relations with other civilized nations. The captain of a warship is the personal representative of the king of the nation whose flag he flies. When he comes ashore, you should fire a small cannon, and you should have four alii dressed in fine robes, wearing pants and shoes, and they should present themselves to the captain and say . . ."

There was no problem on which Abner was unprepared to give specific advice. This puny boy from the bleak farm at Marlboro, Massachusetts, had not in his youth foreseen that every book he read would one day be of value to him. He could recall whole passages about medical care in London, or the banking system in Antwerp. But most of all he remembered the studies he had conducted regarding the manner in which Calvin and Beza had governed Geneva, and it often seemed prophetic to him that each problem encountered by John Calvin in Switzerland now had to be faced by Abner Hale in Lahaina.

On money: "You should coin your own island money, and protect it against counterfeiters."

On wealth: "Money is not wealth, but the things you make and grow are. It is supreme folly for you to allow individual chiefs to trade away your precious sandalwood. And for any man to grub up the very roots of young trees is insane. The greatest wealth you have is your ability to service the whaling ships as they come into Lahaina and Honolulu. If the alii were wise, they would establish port dues for such ships and also tax each merchant who supplies the whalers."

On education: "The surest way to improve the people is to teach them to read."

On an army: "Every government needs a police force of some kind. I grant that if you had had a respectable army in Lahaina the whaling sailors would not have dared to riot. But I am afraid a large army such as you propose is ridiculous. You cannot fight France or Russia or America. You are too small. Do not waste your money on an army. But get a good police force. Build a jail."

On the good alii: "He is courageous. He protects the weak. He is honest with government money. He listens to advice. He dresses neatly and wears pants. He has only one wife. He does not get drunk. He helps his people as well as himself. He believes in God."

On Hawaii's greatest need: "Teach the people to read."

But often when he returned to the mission he would cry dejectedly, "Jerusha, I truly believe they didn't understand a word I said. We work and work and there is no improvement." Jerusha did not share his apprehensions, for in her school it was obvious that she was accomplishing miracles. She taught her women to sew, to cook better and to raise their own babies. "You must not give your children away!" she insisted. "It is against God's law." She was pleased when they nodded, but her greatest joy was young Iliki, who had once run off to the whalers but who could now recite the Psalms.

In teaching boys and men Keoki was indefatigable. He was both a devout Christian and a skilled instructor, so that his school was one of the best in the island group, but where he excelled was in his daily sermons, for he had the innate oratorical gift of the Hawaiian and exercised it in robust imagery and appropriate incident. So realistic was his description of the Flood that his listeners watched the sea out of the corners of their eyes, expecting engulfing waves to sweep in from Lahaina Roads.

But in long-range importance the most effective school was Abner's, where the alii studied, and his choice pupil was Malama's daughter, Noelani, whom he had rescued from the sailors. The girl was, by birth, entitled to be the next alii nui, for her blood strain was impeccable. Her parents were full brother and sister, each noble in his own right, so that she inherited the glory of numberless generations of Hawaiian greatness. She was clever and industrious, an ornament in any society. In a report to Honolulu, Abner said of her, "She is almost as good a student as her mother. She can read and write, speak English and do the easier sums. And I feel certain that she is dedicated to the way of God and will be one of our first full members of the church." When he told the girl this, she was radiant.

QUESTION

How would ethnocentric attitudes affect the understanding of a different society?

Chapter 3

Socialization

In the previous chapter, the concept of culture was examined and the point was made that culture is not inherited but learned. The process of learning or internalizing a culture is socialization, a process that begins at birth and continues for the rest of the individual's life. Socialization is a never-ending process that gives a person the physical, mental, and social skills necessary to function within a society.

One of the paramount features of becoming socialized is the interpretation of symbols. Most human interactions involve symbols, and so an individual must learn how to interpret them in order to exist as a member of that society. Language is an important symbol system because it is a primary mode of communication in socialization. But language is often unclear and imprecise, thus causing problems as shown by the excerpt from *Through the Looking Glass* in which Alice is confused by the poem "Jabberwocky."

To a great extent, an individual is the product of the agents of socialization, and the primary agent is the family. It is the family who has the responsibility to teach the offspring the necessary and proper values and norms so that he can become a functioning member of the society. The song "Carefully Taught" reveals the importance of the family in the socialization process.

Another concept of the socialization process is that of the "looking-glass" theory. Proposed by Charles H. Cooley, the basic idea is that an individual will see himself as others see him or how he perceives that they see him. This principle is illustrated in "Baa, Baa, Black Sheep," in which a boy finds difficulty and confusion in trying to form his self-image as he moves from one social group to another.

Through the Looking Glass
Lewis Carroll

Of all of the symbol systems that man has devised to interpret human interactions, one of the most important is language, because it is the mode of communication between the members of a society. Because of its importance and its complexity, the correct interpretation of language is very necessary for the survival of the individual in the society.

In *Through the Looking Glass,* a little girl, Alice, is confronted by a poem, "Jabberwocky," and because it can mean almost anything, Alice is quite confused, a situation which is not unusual for many people.

There was a book lying near Alice on the table, and while she sat watching the White King (for she was still a little anxious about him, and had the ink all ready to throw over him, in case he fainted again), she turned over the leaves, to find some part that she could read, "—for it's all in some language I don't know," she said to herself.

It was like this.

JABBERWOCKY.

'Twas brillig, and the slithy toves
Did gyre and gimble in the wabe:
All mimsy were the borogoves,
And the mome raths outgrabe.

She puzzled over this for some time, but at last a bright thought struck her. "Why, it's a Looking-Glass book, of course! And, if I hold it up to a glass, the words will all go the right way again."

This was the poem that Alice read.

JABBERWOCKY.

'Twas brillig, and the slithy toves

Lewis Carroll, *Through the Looking Glass,* 1872.

Did gyre and gimble in the wabe:
All mimsy were the borogoves,
And the mome raths outgrabe.

"Beware the Jabberwock, my son!
The jaws that bite, the claws that catch!
Beware the Jubjub bird, and shun
The frumious Bandersnatch!"

He took his vorpal sword in hand:
Long time the manxome foe he sought—
So rested he by the Tumtum tree,
And stood awhile in thought.

And, as in uffish thought he stood,
The Jabberwock, with eyes of flame,
Came whiffing through the tulgey wood,
And burbled as it came!

One, two! One, two! And through and through
The vorpal blade went snicker-snack!
He left it dead, and with its head
He went galumphing back.

"And hast thou slain the Jabberwock?
Come to my arms, my beamish boy!
O frabjous day! Callooh! Callay!"
He chortled in his joy.

'Twas brillig, and the slithy toves
Did gyre and gimble in the wabe:
All mimsy were the borogoves,
And the mome raths outgrabe.

"It seems very pretty," she said when she had finished it, "but it's *rather* hard to understand!" (You see she didn't like to confess, even to herself, that she couldn't make it out at all.) "Somehow it seems to fill my head with ideas—only I don't exactly know what they are! However, *some-body* killed *something:* that's clear, at any rate—"

But oh!" thought Alice, suddenly jumping up, "if I don't make haste, I shall have to go back through the Looking-Glass, before I've seen what the rest of the house is like! Let's have a look at the garden first!" She was out of the room in a moment, and ran down stairs—or, at least, it wasn't exactly running, but a new invention for getting down stairs quickly and easily, as Alice said to herself. She just kept the tips of her fingers on the hand-rail, and floated gently down without even touching the stairs with her feet: then she floated on through the hall, and would have gone straight out at the door in the same way, if she hadn't cought hold of the door-post. She was getting a little giddy with so much floating in the air, and was rather glad to find herself walking again in the natural way.

QUESTION

How does one feel when unfamiliar terminology is used in a conversation, and why?

Carefully Taught

Richard Rodgers and Oscar Hammerstein II

To a great extent, an individual is a product of his or her environment. Physical surroundings, both animate and inanimate, help shape and mold the individual into a functioning member of the society, and the primary souce of this process is the family. In "Carefully Taught," a song from the musical *South Pacific,* the point is made that children must be taught the proper cultural values so that they can continue to exist within the society.

You've got to be taught to hate and fear,
You've got to be taught from year to year,
It's got to be drummed in your dear little ear—
You've got to be carefully taught!

You've got to be taught to be afraid
Of people whose eyes are oddly made,
And people whose skin is a different shade—
You've got to be carefully taught.

You've got to be taught before it's too late,
Before you are six or seven or eight,
To hate all the people your relatives hate—
You've got to be carefully taught!
You've got to be carefully taught!

QUESTION

Can you reflect upon at least three attitudes about other people you have been taught that you thought were "natural"?

Baa, Baa, Black Sheep
Rudyard Kipling

In this short story, the concept of the "looking-glass" theory of socialization is exhibited. The young boy undergoes numerous trials and tribulations as his parents send him to another land to live with some relatives. As the story unfolds, it becomes clear that the young boy is having a difficult time in trying to find his self-image.

Baa Baa, Black Sheep,
Have you any wool?
Yes, Sir, yes, Sir, three bags full.
One for the Master, one for the Dame—
None for the Little Boy that cries down the lane.

NURSERY RHYME

The First Bag

When I was in my father's house, I was in a better place.

They were putting Punch to bed—the *ayah* and the *hamal* and Meeta, the big *Surti* boy, with the red and gold turban. Judy, already tucked inside her mosquito-curtains, was nearly asleep. Punch had been allowed to stay up for dinner. Many privileges had been accorded to Punch within the last ten days, and a greater kindness from the people of his world had encompassed

Rudyard Kipling, "Baa, Baa, Black Sheep," from *Wee Willie Winkie*, 1888.

his ways and works, which were mostly obstreperous. He sat on the edge of his bed and swung his bare legs defiantly.

"Punch-*baba* going to bye-lo?" said the *ayah* suggestively.

"No," said Punch. "Punch-*baba* wants the story about the Ranee that was turned into a tiger. Meeta must tell it, and the *hamal* shall hide behind the door and make tiger-noises at the proper time."

"But Judy-*baba* will wake up," said the *ayah*.

"Judy-*baba* is waked," piped a small voice from the mosquito-curtains. "There was a Ranee that lived at Delhi. Go on, Meeta," and she fell fast asleep again while Meeta began the story.

Never had Punch secured the telling of that tale with so little opposition. He reflected for a long time. The *hamal* made the tiger-noises in twenty different keys.

"'Top!" said Punch authoritatively. "Why doesn't Papa come in and say he is going to give me *put-put?*"

"Punch-*baba* is going away," said the *ayah*. "In another week there will be no Punch-*baba* to pull my hair any more." She sighed softly, for the boy of the household was very dear to her heart.

"Up the Ghauts in a train?" said Punch, standing on his bed. "All the way to Nassick where the Ranee-Tiger lives?"

"Not to Nassick this year, little Sahib," said Meeta, lifting him on his shoulder. "Down to the sea where the cocoanuts are thrown, and across the sea in a big ship. Will you take Meeta with you to *Belait?*"

"You shall all come," said Punch, from the height of Meeta's strong arms. "Meeta and the *ayah* and the *hamal* and Bhini-in-the-Garden, and the salaam-Captain-Sahib-snake-man."

There was no mockery in Meeta's voice when he replied—"Great is the Sahib's favour," and laid the little man down in the bed, while the *ayah,* sitting in the moonlight at the doorway, lulled him to sleep with an interminable canticle such as they sing in the Roman Catholic Church at Parel. Punch curled himself into a ball and slept.

Next morning Judy shouted that there was a rat in the nursery, and thus he forgot to tell her the wonderful news. It did not much matter, for Judy was only three and she would not have understood. But Punch was five; and he knew that going to England would be much nicer than a trip to Nassick.

Papa and Mamma sold the brougham and the piano, and stripped the house, and curtailed the allowance of crockery for the daily meals, and took long council together over a bundle of letters bearing the Rocklington postmark.

"The worst of it is that one can't be certain of anything," said Papa, pulling his moustache. "The letters in themselves are excellent, and the terms are moderate enough."

"The worst of it is that the children will grow up away from me," thought Mamma: but she did not say it aloud.

"We are only one case among hundreds," said Papa bitterly. "You shall go Home again in five years, dear."

"Punch will be ten then—and Judy eight. Oh, how long and long and long the time will be! And we have to leave them among strangers."

"Punch is a cheery little chap. He's sure to make friends wherever he goes."

"And who could help loving my Ju?"

They were standing over the cots in the nursery late at night, and I think that Mamma was crying softly. After Papa had gone away, she knelt down by the side of Judy's cot. The *ayah* saw her and put up a prayer that the *memsahib* might never find the love of her children taken away from her and given to a stranger.

Mamma's own prayer was a slightly illogical one. Summarised it ran: "Let strangers love my children and be as good to them as I should be, but let *me* preserve their love and their confidence for ever and ever. Amen." Punch scratched himself in his sleep, and Judy moaned a little.

Next day, they all went down to the sea, and there was a scene at the Apollo Bunder when Punch discovered that Meeta could not come too, and Judy learned that the *ayah* must be left behind. But Punch found a thousand facinating things in the rope, block, and steam-pipe line on the big P. and O. Steamer long before Meeta and the *ayah* had dried their tears.

"Come back, Punch-*baba*," said the *ayah*.

"Come back," said Meeta, "and be a *Burra-Sahib*" (a big man).

"Yes," said Punch, lifted up in his father's arms to wave good-bye. "Yes, I will come back, and I will be a *Burra Sahib Bahadur!*" (a very big man indeed).

At the end of the first day Punch demanded to be set down in England, which he was certain must be close at hand. Next day there was a merry breeze, and Punch was very sick. "When I come back to Bombay," said Punch on his recovery, "I will come by the road—in a broom *gharri*. This is a very naughty ship."

The Swedish boatswain consoled him, and he modified his opinions as the voyage went on. There was so much to see and to handle and ask questions about that Punch nearly forgot the *ayah* and Meeta and the *hamal,* and with difficulty remembered a few words of the Hindustani, once his second-speech.

But Judy was much worse. The day before the steamer reached South-ampton, Mamma asked her if she would not like to see the *ayah* again. Judy's blue eyes turned to the stretch of sea that had swallowed all her tiny past, and said: *"Ayah!* What *ayah?"*

Mamma cried over her and Punch marvelled. It was then that he heard for the first time Mamma's passionate appeal to him never to let Judy forget Mamma. Seeing that Judy was young, ridiculously young, and that Mamma, every evening for four weeks past, had come into the cabin to sing her and Punch to sleep with a mysterious rune that he called "Sonny, my soul," Punch could not understand what Mamma meant. But he strove to do his duty; for, the moment Mamma left the cabin, he said to Judy: "Ju, you bemember Mamma?"

" 'Torse I do," said Judy.

"Then *always* bemember Mamma, 'r else I won't give you the paper ducks that the red-haired Captain Sahib cut out for me."

So Judy promised always to "bemember Mamma."

Many and many a time was Mamma's command laid upon Punch, and Papa would say the same thing with an insistence that awed the child.

"You must make haste and learn to write, Punch," said Papa, "and then you'll be able to write letters to us in Bombay."

"I'll come into your room," said Punch, and Papa choked.

Papa and Mamma were always choking in those days. If Punch took Judy to task for not "bemembering," they choked. If Punch sprawled on the sofa in the Southampton lodging-house and sketched his future in purple and gold, they choked; and so they did if Judy put her mouth for a kiss.

Through many days all four were vagabonds on the face of the earth— Punch with no one to give orders to, Judy too young for anything, and Papa and Mamma grave, distracted, and choking.

"Where," demanded Punch, wearied of a loathsome contrivance on four wheels with a mound of luggage atop—*"where* is our broom-*gharri?* This thing talks so much that *I* can't talk. Where is our *own* broom-*gharri?* When I was at Bandstand before we comed away, I asked Inverarity Sahib why he was sitting in it, and he said it was his own. And I said, "I will *give* it you"—I like Inverarity Sahib—and I said, "Can you put your legs through the pully-wag loops by the windows?" And Inverarity Sahib said No, and laughed. *I* can put my legs through the pully-wag loops. I can put my legs through *these* pully-wag loops. Look! Oh, Mamma's crying again! I didn't know I wasn't to do *so."*

Punch drew his legs out of the loops of the fourwheeler: the door opened and he slid to the earth, in a cascade of parcels, at the door of an austere little villa whose gates bore the legend "Downe Lodge." Punch gathered himself together and eyed the house with disfavour. It stood on a sandy road, and a cold wind tickled his knickerbockered legs.

"Let us go away," said Punch. "This is not a pretty place."

But Mamma and Papa and Judy had left the cab, and all the luggage was being taken into the house. At the doorstep stood a woman in black, and she smiled largely, with dry chapped lips. Behind here was a man, big, bony, gray, and lame as to one leg—behind him a boy of twelve, black-haired and oily in appearance. Punch surveyed the trio, and advanced without fear, as he had been accustomed to do in Bombay when callers came and he happened to be playing in the veranda.

"How do you do?" said he. "I am Punch." But they were all looking at the luggage—all except the gray man, who shook hands with Punch, and said he was "a smart little fellow." There was much running about and banging of boxes, and Punch curled himself up on the sofa in the dining-room and considered things.

"I don't like these people," said Punch. "But never mind. We'll go away soon. We have always went away soon from everywhere. I wish we was gone back to Bombay *soon.*"

The wish bore no fruit. For six days Mamma wept at intervals, and showed the woman in black all Punch's clothes—a liberty which Punch resented. "But p'raps she's a new white *ayah,*" he thought. "I'm to call her Antirosa, but she doesn't call *me* Sahib. She says just Punch," he confided to Judy. "What is Antirosa?"

Judy didn't know. Neither she nor Punch had heard anything of an animal called an aunt. Their world had been Papa and Mamma, who knew everything, permitted everything, and loved everybody—even Punch when he used to go into the garden at Bombay and fill his nails with mould after the weekly nail-cutting, because, as he explained between two strokes of the slipper to his sorely tried Father, his fingers "felt so new at the ends."

In an undefined way Punch judged it advisable to keep both parents between himself and the woman in black and the boy in black hair. He did not approve of them. He liked the gray man, who had expressed a wish to be called "Uncleharri." They nodded at each other when they met, and the gray man showed him a little ship with rigging that took up and down.

"She is a model of the *Brisk*—the little *Brisk* that was sore exposed that day at Navarino." The gray man hummed the last words and fell into a reverie. "I'll tell you about Navarino, Punch, when we go for walks together; and you mustn't touch the ship, because she's the *Brisk.*"

Long before that walk, the first of many, was taken, they roused Punch and Judy in the chill dawn of a February morning to say Good-bye; and of all people in the wide earth to Papa and Mamma—both crying this time.

Punch was very sleepy and Judy was cross.

"Don't forget us," pleaded Mamma. "Oh, my little son, don't forget us, and see that Judy remembers too."

"I've told Judy to bemember," said Punch, wriggling, for his father's beard tickled his neck. "I've told Judy—ten—forty—'leven thousand times. But Ju's so young—quite a baby—isn't she?"

Punch was back in his bed again. Judy was fast asleep, and there was the rattle of a cab below. Papa and Mamma had gone away. Not to Nassick; that was across the sea. To some place much nearer, of course, and equally of course they would return. They came back after dinner-parties, and Papa had come back after he had been to a place called "The Snows," and Mamma with him, to Punch and Judy at Mrs. Inverarity's house in Marine Lines. Assuredly they would come back again. So Punch fell asleep till the true morning, when the black-haired boy met him with the information that Papa and Mamma had gone to Bombay, and that he and Judy were to stay at Downe Lodge "for ever." Antirosa, tearfully appealed to for a contradiction, said that Harry had spoken the truth, and that it behooved Punch to fold up his clothes neatly on going to bed. Punch went out and wept bitterly with Judy, into whose fair head he had driven some ideas of the meaning of separation.

When a matured man discovers that he has been deserted by Providence, deprived of his God, and cast, without help, comfort, or sympathy, upon a world which is new and strange to him, his despair, which may find expression in evil-living, the writing of his experiences, or the more satisfactory diversion of suicide, is generally supposed to be impressive. A child, under exactly similar circumstances as far as its knowledge goes, cannot very well curse God and die. It howls till its nose is red, its eyes are sore, and its head aches. Punch and Judy, through no fault of their own, had lost all their world. They sat in the hall and cried; the black-haired boy looking on from afar.

The model of the ship availed nothing, though the gray man assured Punch that he might pull the rigging up and down as much as he pleased; and Judy was promised free entry into the kitchen. They wanted Papa and Mamma gone to Bombay beyond the seas, and their grief while it lasted was without remedy.

When the tears ceased the house was very still. Antirosa had decided that it was better to let the children "have their cry out," and the boy had gone to school. Punch raised his head from the floor and sniffed mournfully. Judy was nearly asleep. Three short years had not taught her how to bear sorrow with full knowledge. There was a distant, dull boom in the air—a repeated heavy thud. Punch knew that sound in Bombay in the

Monsoon. It was the sea—the sea that must be traversed before any one could get to Bombay.

"Quick, Ju!" he cried, "we're close to the sea. I can hear it! Listen! That's where they've went. P'raps we can catch them if we was in time. They didn't mean to go without us. They've only forgot."

"Iss," said Judy. "They've only forgotten. Less go to the sea."

The hall-door was open and so was the garden-gate.

"It's very, very big, this place," he said, looking cautiously down the road, "and we will get lost; but *I* will find a man and order him to take me back to my house—like I did in Bombay."

He took Judy by the hand, and the two ran hatless in the direction of the sound of the sea. Downe Villa was almost the last of a range of newly-built houses running out, through a field of brick-mounds, to a heath where gypsies occasionally camped and where the Garrison Artillery of Rockling-ton practised. There were few people to be seen, and the children might have been taken for those of the soldiery who ranged far. Half an hour the wearied little legs tramped across heath, potato-patch, and sand-dune.

"I'se so tired," said Judy, "and Mamma will be angry."

"Mamma's *never* angry. I suppose she is waiting at the sea now while Papa gets tickets. We'll find them and go along with. Ju, you mustn't sit down. Only a little more and we'll come to the sea. Ju, if you sit down I'll *thmack* you!" said Punch.

They climbed another dune, and came upon the great gray sea at low tide. Hundreds of crabs were scuttling about the beach, but there was no trace of Papa and Mamma, not even of a ship upon the waters—nothing but sand and mud for miles and miles.

And "Uncleharri" found them by chance—very muddy and very forlorn—Punch dissolved in tears, but trying to divert Judy with an "ickle trab," and Judy wailing to the pitiless horizon for "Mamma, Mamma!"—and again "Mamma!"

The Second Bag

Ah, well-a-day, for we are souls bereaved!
Of all the creatures under Heaven's wide scope

We are most hopeless, who had once most hope,
And most beliefless, who had most believed.

THE CITY OF DREADFUL NIGHT

All this time not a word about Black Sheep. He came later, and Harry the black-haired boy was mainly responsible for his coming.

Judy—who could help loving little Judy?—passed, by special permit, into the kitchen and thence straight to Aunty Rosa's heart. Harry was Aunty Rosa's one child, and Punch was the extra boy about the house. There was no special place for him or his little affairs, and he was forbidden to sprawl on sofas and explain his ideas about the manufacture of this world and his hopes for his future. Sprawling was lazy and wore out sofas, and little boys were not expected to talk. They were talked to, and the talking to was intended for the benefit of their morals. As the unquestioned despot of the house at Bombay, Punch could not quite understand how he came to be of no account in this his new life.

Harry might reach across the table and take what he wanted; Judy might point and get what she wanted. Punch was forbidden to do either. The gray man was his great hope and stand-by for many months after Mamma and Papa left, and he had forgotten to tell Judy to "bemember Mamma."

This lapse was excusable, because in the interval he had been introduced by Aunty Rosa to two very impressive things—an abstraction called God, the intimate friend and ally of Aunty Rosa, generally believed to live behind the kitchen-range because it was hot there—and a dirty brown book filled with unintelligible dots and marks. Punch was always anxious to oblige everybody. He therefore welded the story of the Creation on to what he could recollect of his Indian fairy tales, and scandalised Aunty Rosa by repeating the result to Judy. It was a sin, a grievous sin, and Punch was talked to for a quarter of an hour. He could not understand where the iniquity came in, but was careful not to repeat the offence. because Aunty Rosa told him that God had heard every word he had said and was very angry. If this were true, why didn't God come and say so, thought Punch, and dismissed the matter from his mind. Afterwards he learned to know the Lord as the only thing in the world more awful than Aunty Rosa—as a Creature that stood in the background and counted the strokes of the cane.

But the reading was, just then, a much more serious matter than any creed. Aunty Rosa sat him upon a table and told him that A B meant ab.

"Why?" said Punch. "A is a and B is bee. *Why* does A B mean ab?"

"Because I tell you it does," said Aunty Rosa, "and you've got to say it."

Punch said it accordingly, and for a month, hugely against his will, stumbled through the brown book, not in the least comprehending what it meant. But Uncle Harry, who walked much and generally alone, was wont to come into the nursery and suggest to Aunty Rosa that Punch should walk with him. He seldom spoke, but he showed Punch all Rocklington, from the mudbanks and the sand of the back-bay to the great harbours where ships lay at anchor, and the dockyards where the hammers were never still, and the marinestore shops, and the shiny brass counters in the Offices where Uncle Harry went once every three months with a slip of blue paper and received sovereigns in exchange; for he held a wound-pension. Punch heard, too, from his lips the story of the battle of Navarino, where the sailors of the Fleet, for three days afterwards, were deaf as posts and could only sign to each other. "That was because of the noise of the guns," said Uncle Harry, "and I have got the wadding of a bullet somewhere inside me now."

Punch regarded him with curiosity. He had not the least idea what wadding was, and his notion of a bullet was a dockyard cannon-ball bigger than his own head. How could Uncle Harry keep a cannon-ball inside him? He was ashamed to ask, for fear Uncle Harry might be angry.

Punch had never known what anger—real anger—meant until one terrible day when Harry had taken his paint-box to paint a boat with, and Punch had protested. Then Uncle Harry had appeared on the scene and, muttering something about "strangers' children," had with a stick smitten the black-haired boy across the shoulders till he wept and yelled, and Aunty Rosa came in and abused Uncle Harry for cruelty to his own flesh and blood, and Punch shuddered to the tips of his shoes. "It wasn't my fault," he explained to the boy, but both Harry and Aunty Rosa said that it was, and that Punch had told tales, and for a week there were no more walks with Uncle Harry.

But that week brought a great joy to Punch.

He had repeated till he was thrice weary the statement that "the Cat lay on the Mat and the Rat came in."

"Now I can truly read," said Punch, "and now I will never read anything in the world."

He put the brown book in the cupboard where his school-books lived and accidentally tumbled out a venerable volume, without covers, labelled *Sharpe's Magazine.* There was the most portentous picture of a Griffin on the first page, with verses below. The Griffin carried off one sheep a day from a German village, till a man came with a "falchion" and split the Griffin open. Goodness only knew what a falchion was, but there was the Griffin, and his history was an improvement upon the eternal Cat.

"This," said Punch, "means things, and now I will know all about everything in all the world." He read till the light failed, not understanding a tithe of the meaning, but tantalised by glimpses of new worlds hereafter to be revealed.

"What is a 'falchion'? What is a 'e-wee lamb'? What is a 'base *ussur-per*'? What is a 'verdant me-ad'?" he demanded with flushed cheeks, at bedtime, of the astonished Aunty Rosa.

"Say your prayers and go to sleep," she replied, and that was all the help Punch then or afterwards found at her hands in the new and delightful exercise of reading.

"Aunty Rosa only knows about God and things like that," argued Punch. "Uncle Harry will tell me."

The next walk proved that Uncle Harry could not help either; but he allowed Punch to talk, and even sat down on a bench to hear about the Griffin. Other walks brought other stories as Punch ranged further afield, for the house held large store of old books that no one ever opened—from *Frank Fairlegh* in serial numbers, and the earlier poems of Tennyson, contributed anonymously to *Sharpe's Magazine,* to '62 Exhibition Catalogues, gay with colours and delightfully incomprehensible, and odd leaves of *Gulliver's Travels.*

As soon as Punch could string a few pot-hooks together, he wrote to Bombay, demanding by return of post "all the books in all the world." Papa could not comply with this modest indent, but sent *Grimm's Fairy Tales* and a Hans Andersen. That was enough. If he were only left alone Punch could pass, at any hour he chose, into a land of his own, beyond reach of Aunty Rosa and her God, Harry and his teasements, and Judy's claims to be played with.

"Don't disturve me, I'm reading. Go and play in the kitchen," grunted Punch. "Aunty Rosa lets *you* go there." Judy was cutting her second teeth and was fretful. She appealed to Aunty Rosa, who descended on Punch.

"I was reading," he explained, "reading a book. I *want* to read."

"You're only doing that to show off," said Aunty Rosa. "But we'll see. Play with Judy now, and don't open a book for a week."

Judy did not pass a very enjoyable playtime with Punch, who was consumed with indignation. There was a pettiness at the bottom of the prohibition which puzzled him.

"It's what I like to do," he said, "and she's found out that and stopped me. Don't cry, Ju—it wasn't your fault—*please* don't cry, or she'll say I made you."

Ju loyally mopped up her tears, and the two played in their nursery, a room in the basement and half underground, to which they were regularly sent after the midday dinner while Aunty Rosa slept. She drank wine—that is to say, something from a bottle in the cellaret—for her stomach's sake, but if she did not fall asleep she would sometimes come into the nursery to see that the children were really playing. Now bricks, wooden hoops, ninepins, and chinaware cannot amuse for ever, especially when all Fairyland is to be won by the mere opening of a book, and, as often as not, Punch would be discovered reading to Judy or telling her interminable tales. That was an offence in the eyes of the law, and Judy would be whisked off by Aunty Rosa, while Punch was left to play alone, "and be sure that I hear you doing it."

It was not a cheering employ, for he had to make a playful noise. At last, with infinite craft, he devised an arrangement whereby the table could be supported as to three legs on toy bricks, leaving the fourth clear to bring down on the floor. He could work the table with one hand and hold a book with the other. This he did till an evil day when Aunty Rosa pounced upon him unawares and told him that he was "acting a lie."

"If you're old enough to do that," she said—her temper was always worst after dinner—"you're old enough to be beaten."

"But—I'm—I'm not an animal!" said Punch aghast. He remembered Uncle Harry and the stick, and turned white. Aunty Rosa had hidden a light cane behind her, and Punch was beaten then and there over the shoulders. It was a revelation to him. The room-door was shut, and he was left to weep himself into repentance and work out his own gospel of life.

Aunty Rosa, he argued, had the power to beat him with many stripes. It was unjust and cruel, and Mamma and Papa would never have allowed it. Unless perhaps, as Aunty Rosa seemed to imply, they had sent secret orders. In which case he was abandoned indeed. It would be discreet in the future to propitiate Aunty Rosa, but, then, again, even in matters in which he was innocent, he had been accused of wishing to "show off." He had "shown off" before visitors when he had attacked a strange gentleman—Harry's uncle, not his own—with requests for information about the Griffin and the falchion, and the precise nature of the Tilbury in which Frank Fairlegh rode—all points of paramount interest which he was bursting to understand. Clearly it would not do to pretend to care for Aunty Rosa.

At this point Harry entered and stood afar off, eying Punch, a dishevelled heap in the corner of the room, with disgust.

"You're a liar—a young liar," said Harry, with great unction, "and you're to have tea down here because you're not fit to speak to us. And you're not to speak to Judy again till Mother gives you leave. You'll corrupt her. You're only fit to associate with the servant. Mother says so."

Having reduced Punch to a second agony of tears, Harry departed upstairs with the news that Punch was still rebellious.

Uncle Harry sat uneasily in the dining-room. "Damn it all, Rosa," said he at last, "can't you leave the child alone? He's a good enough little chap when I meet him."

"He puts on his best manners with you, Henry," said Aunty Rosa, "but I'm afraid, I'm very much afraid, that he is the Black Sheep of the family."

Harry heard and stored up the name for future use. Judy cried till she was bidden to stop, her brother not being worth tears; and the evening concluded with the return of Punch to the upper regions and a private sitting at which all the blinding horrors of Hell were revealed to Punch with such store of imagery as Aunty Rosa's narrow mind possessed.

Most grievous of all was Judy's round-eyed reproach, and Punch went to bed in the depths of the Valley of Humiliation. He shared his room with Harry and knew the torture in store. For an hour and a half he had to answer that young gentleman's question as to his motives for telling a lie, and a grievous lie, the precise quantity of punishment inflicted by Aunty Rosa, and had also to profess his deep gratitude for such religious instruction as Harry thought fit to impart.

From that day began the downfall of Punch, now Black Sheep.

"Untrustworthy in one thing, untrustworthy in all," said Aunty Rosa, and Harry felt that Black Sheep was delivered into his hands. He would wake him up in the night to ask him why he was such a liar.

"I don't know," Punch would reply.

"Then don't you think you ought to get up and pray to God for a new heart?"

"Y-yess."

"Get out and pray, then!" And Punch would get out of bed with raging hate in his heart against all the world, seen and unseen. He was always tumbling into trouble. Harry had a knack of cross-examining him as to his day's doings, which seldom failed to lead him, sleepy and savage, into a half a dozen contradictions—all duly reported to Aunty Rosa next morning.

"But it *wasn't* a lie," Punch would begin, charging into a laboured explanation that landed him more hopelessly in the mire. "I said that I didn't say my prayers *twice* over in the day, and *that* was on Tuesday. *Once*

I did. I *know* I did, but Harry said I didn't," and so forth, till the tension brought tears, and he was dismissed from the table in disgrace.

"You usen't to be as bad as this." said Judy, awe-stricken at the catalogue of Black Sheep's crimes. "Why are you so bad now?"

"I don't know," Black Sheep would reply. "I'm not, if I only wasn't bothered upside down. I knew what I *did,* and I want to say so; but Harry always makes it out different somehow, and Aunty Rosa doesn't believe a word I say. Oh, Ju! don't *you* say I'm bad too."

"Aunty Rosa says you are," said Judy. "She told the Vicar so when he came yesterday."

"Why does she tell all the people outside the house about me? It isn't fair," said Black Sheep. "When I was in Bombay, and was bad—*doing* bad, not made-up bad like this—Mamma told Papa, and Papa told me he knew, and that was all. *Outside* people didn't know too—even Meeta didn't know."

"I don't remember," said Judy wistfully. "I was all little then. Mamma was just as fond of you as she was of me, wasn't she?"

" 'Course she was. So was Papa. So was everybody."

"Aunty Rosa likes me more than she does you. She says that you are a Trial and a Black Sheep, and I'm not to speak to you more than I can help."

"Always? Not outside of the times when you mustn't speak to me at all?"

Judy nodded her head mournfully. Black Sheep turned away in despair, but Judy's arms were round his neck.

"Never mind, Punch," she whispered. "I *will* speak to you just the same as ever and ever. You're my own own brother though you are—though Aunty Rosa says you're Bad, and Harry says you're a little coward. He says that if I pulled your hair hard, you'd cry."

"Pull, then," said Punch.

Judy pulled gingerly.

"Pull harder—as hard as you can! There! I don't mind how much you pull it *now*. If you'll speak to me same as ever I'll let you pull it as much as you like—pull it out if you like. But I know if Harry came and stood by and made you do it I'd cry."

So the two children sealed the compact with a kiss, and Black Sheep's heart was cheered within him, and by extreme caution and careful avoidance of Harry he acquired virtue, and was allowed to read undisturbed for a week. Uncle Harry took him for walks, and consoled him with rough tenderness, never calling him Black Sheep. "It's good for you, I suppose, Punch," he used to say. "Let us sit down. I'm getting tired." His steps led him now not to the beach, but to the Cemetery of Rocklington, amid the potato-fields. For hours the gray man would sit on a tombstone, while Black Sheep read epitaphs, and then with a sigh would stump home again.

"I shall lie there soon," said he to Black Sheep, one winter evening, when his face showed white as a worn coin under the light of the lych-gate. "You needn't tell Aunty Rosa."

A month later, he turned sharp round, ere half a morning walk was completed, and stumped back to the house. "Put me to bed, Rosa," he muttered. "I've walked my last. The wadding has found me out."

They put him to bed, and for a fortnight the shadow of his sickness lay upon the house, and Black Sheep went to and fro unobserved. Papa had sent him some new books, and he was told to keep quiet. He retired into his own world, and was perfectly happy. Even at night his felicity was unbroken. He could lie in bed and string himself tales of travel and adventure while Harry was downstairs.

"Uncle Harry's going to die," said Judy, who now lived almost entirely with Aunty Rosa.

"I'm very sorry," said Black Sheep soberly. "He told me that a long time ago."

Aunty Rosa heard the conversation. "Will nothing check your wicked tongue?" she said angrily. There were blue circles round her eyes.

Black Sheep retreated to the nursery and read *Cometh up as a Flower* with deep and uncomprehending interest. He had been forbidden to open it on account of its "sinfulness," but the bonds of the Universe were crumbling, and Aunty Rosa was in great grief.

"I'm glad," said Black Sheep. "She's unhappy now. It wasn't a lie, though. *I* knew. He told me not to tell."

That night Black Sheep woke with a start. Harry was not in the room, and there was a sound of sobbing on the next floor. Then the voice of Uncle Harry, singing the song of the Battle of Navarino, came through the darkness:—

"Our vanship was the Asia—
The Albion and Genoa!"

"He's getting well," thought Black Sheep, who knew the song through all its seventeen verses. But the blood froze at his little heart as he thought. The voice leapt an octave, and rang shrill as a boatswain's pipe:—

"And next came on the lively Rose,
The Philomel, her fire-ship, closed,
And the little Brisk was sore exposed
That day at Navarino."

"That day at Navarino, Uncle Harry!" shouted Black Sheep, half wild
with excitement and fear of he knew not what.

A door opened and Aunty Rosa screamed up the staircase: "Hush!
For God's sake hush, you little devil. Uncle Harry is *dead!*"

The Third Bag

Journeys end in lovers' meeting,
Every wise man's son doth know.

"I wonder what will happen to me now," thought Black Sheep, when semi-
pagan rites peculiar to the burial of the Dead in middle-class houses had
been accomplished, and Aunty Rosa, awful in black crape, had returned to
this life. "I don't think I've done anything bad that she knows of. I suppose
I will soon. She will be very cross after Uncle Harry's dying, and Harry will
be cross too. I'll keep in the nursery."

Unfortunately for Punch's plans, it was decided that he should be sent
to a day-school which Harry attended. This meant a morning walk with
Harry, and perhaps an evening one; but the prospect of freedom in the
interval was refreshing. "Harry'll tell everything I do, but I won't do anything," said Black Sheep. Fortified with this virtuous resolution, he went to
school only to find that Harry's version of his character had preceded him,
and that life was a burden in consequence. He took stock of his associates.
Some of them were unclean, some of them talked in dialect, many dropped
their h's, and there were two Jews and a negro, or some one quite as dark,
in the assembly. "That's a *hubshi*," said Black Sheep to himself. "Even
Meeta used to laugh at a *hubshi*. I don't think this is a proper place." He
was indignant for at least an hour, till he reflected that any expostulation on
his part would be by Aunty Rosa construed into "showing off," and that
Harry would tell the boys.

"How do you like school?" said Aunty Rosa at the end of the day.

"I think it is a very nice place," said Punch quietly.

"I suppose you warned the boys of Black Sheep's character?" said Aunty Rosa to Harry.

"Oh, yes," said the censor of Black Sheep's morals. "They know all about him."

"If I was with my father," said Black Sheep, stung to the quick, "I shouldn't *speak* to those boys. He wouldn't let me. They live in shops. I saw them go into shops—where their fathers live and sell things."

"You're too good for that school, are you?" said Aunty Rosa, with a bitter smile. "You ought to be grateful, Black Sheep, that those boys speak to you at all. It isn't every school that takes little liars."

Harry did not fail to make much capital out of Black Sheep's ill-considered remark; with the result that several boys, including the *hubshi*, demonstrated to Black Sheep the eternal equality of the human race by smacking his head, and his consolation from Aunty Rosa was that it "served him right for being vain." He learned, however, to keep his opinions to himself, and by propitating Harry in carrying books and the like to get a little peace. His existence was not too joyful. From nine till twelve he was at school, and from two to four, except on Saturdays. In the evenings he was sent down into the nursery to prepare his lessons for the next day, and every night came the dreaded cross-questionings at Harry's hand. Of Judy he saw but little. She was deeply religious—at six years of age Religion is easy to come by—and sorely divided between her natural love for Black Sheep and her love for Aunty Rosa, who could do no wrong.

The lean woman returned that love with interest, and Judy, when she dared, took advantage of this for the remission of Black Sheep's penalties. Failures in lessons at school were punished at home by a week without reading other than schoolbooks, and Harry brought the news of such a failure with glee. Further, Black Sheep was then bound to repeat his lessons at bedtime to Harry, who generally succeeded in making him break down, and consoled him by gloomiest forebodings for the morrow. Harry was at once spy, practical joker, inquisitor, and Aunty Rosa's deputy executioner. He filled his many posts to admiration. From his actions, now that Uncle Harry was dead, there was no appeal. Black Sheep had not been permitted to keep any self-respect at school: at home he was of course utterly discredited, and grateful for any pity that the servant-girls—they changed frequently at Downe Lodge because they, too, were liars—might show. "You're just fit to row in the same boat with Black Sheep," was a sentiment that each new Jane or Eliza might expect to hear, before a month was over, from Aunty Rosa's lips; and Black Sheep was used to ask new girls whether they had yet been compared to him. Harry was "Master Harry" in their mouths; Judy was officially "Miss Judy"; but Black Sheep was never anything more than Black Sheep *tout court*.

As time went on and the memory of Papa and Mamma became wholly overlaid by the unpleasant task of writing them letters, under Aunty Rosa's eye, each Sunday, Black Sheep forgot what manner of life he had led in the beginning of things. Even Judy's appeals to "try and remember about Bombay" failed to quicken him.

"I can't remember," he said. "I know I used to give orders and Mamma kissed me."

"Aunty Rosa will kiss you if you are good," pleaded Judy.

"Ugh! I don't want to be kissed by Aunty Rosa. She'd say I was doing it to get something more to eat."

The weeks lengthened into months, and the holidays came; but just before the holidays Black Sheep fell into deadly sin.

Among the many boys whom Harry had incited to "punch Black Sheep's head because he daren't hit back," was one more aggravating than the rest, who, in an unlucky moment, fell upon Black Sheep when Harry was not near. The blows stung, and Black Sheep struck back at random with all the power at his command. The boy dropped and whimpered. Black Sheep was astounded at his own act, but, feeling the unresisting body under him, shook it with both his hands in blind fury and then began to throttle his enemy; meaning honestly to slay him. There was a scuffle, and Black Sheep was torn off the body by Harry and some colleagues, and cuffed home tingling but exultant. Aunty Rosa was out: pending her arrival, Harry sent himself to lecture Black Sheep on the sin of murder—which he described as the offence of Cain.

"Why didn't you fight him fair? What did you hit him when he was down for, you little cur?"

Black Sheep looked up at Harry's throat and then at a knife on the dinner-table.

"I don't understand," he said wearily. "You always set him on me and told me I was a coward when I blubbed. Will you leave me alone until Aunty Rosa comes in? She'll beat me if you tell her I ought to be beaten; so it's all right."

"It's all wrong," said Harry magisterially. "You nearly killed him, and I shouldn't wonder if he dies."

"Will he die?" said Black Sheep.

"I dare say," said Harry, "and then you'll be hanged, and go to Hell."

"All right," said Black Sheep, picking up the tableknife. "Then I'll kill *you* now. You say things and do things and—and *I* don't know how things happen, and you never leave me alone—and I don't care *what* happens!"

He ran at the boy with the knife, and Harry fled upstairs to his room, promising Black Sheep the finest thrashing in the world when Aunty Rosa returned. Black Sheep sat at the bottom of the stairs, the tableknife in his hand, and wept for that he had not killed Harry. The servant-girl came up from the kitchen, took the knife away, and consoled him. But Black Sheep was beyond consolation. He would be badly beaten by Aunty Rosa; then there would be another beating at Harry's hands; then Judy would not be allowed to speak to him; then the tale would be told at school and then—

There was no one to help and no one to care, and the best way out of the business was by death. A knife would hurt, but Aunty Rosa had told him, a year ago, that if he sucked paint he would die. He went into the nursery, unearthed the disused Noah's Ark, and sucked the paint off as many animals as remained. It tasted abominable, but he had licked Noah's Dove clean by the time Aunty Rosa and Judy returned. He went upstairs and greeted them with: "Please, Aunty Rosa, I believe I've nearly killed a boy at school, and I've tried to kill Harry, and when you've done all about God and Hell, will you beat me and get it over?"

The tale of the assault as told by Harry could only be explained on the ground of possession by the Devil. Wherefore Black Sheep was not only most excellently beaten, once by Aunty Rosa and once, when thoroughly cowed down, by Harry, but he was further prayed for at family prayers, together with Jane who had stolen a cold rissole from the pantry and snuffled audibly as her sin was brought before the Throne of Grace. Black Sheep was sore and stiff but triumphant. He would die that very night and be rid of them all. No, he would ask for no forgiveness from Harry, and at bedtime would stand no questioning at Harry's hands, even though addressed as "Young Cain."

"I've been beaten," said he, "and I've done other things. I don't care what I do. If you speak to me to-night, Harry, I'll get out and try to kill you. Now you can kill me if you like."

Harry took his bed into the spare room, and Black Sheep lay down to die.

It may be that the makers of Noah's Arks know that their animals are likely to find their way into young mouths, and paint them accordingly. Certain it is that the common, weary next morning broke through the windows and found Black Sheep quite well and a good deal ashamed of himself, but richer by the knowledge that he could, in extremity, secure himself against Harry for the future.

When he decended to breakfast on the first day of the holidays, he was greeted with the news that Harry, Aunty Rosa, and Judy were going away to Brighton, while Black Sheep was to stay in the house with the servant. His latest outbreak suited Aunty Rosa's plans admirably. It gave her good excuse for leaving the extra boy behind. Papa in Bombay, who really seemed to know a young sinner's wants to the hour, sent, that week, a package of new books. And with these, and the society of Jane on board-wages, Black Sheep was left alone for a month.

The books lasted for ten days. They were eaten too quickly, in long

gulps of four and twenty hours at a time. Then came days of doing absolutely nothing, of dreaming dreams and marching imaginary armies up and
downstairs, of counting the number of banisters, and of measuring the
length and breadth of every room in handspans—fifty down the side, thirty
across, and fifty back again. Jane made many friends, and, after receiving
Black Sheep's assurance that he would not tell of her absences, went out
daily for long hours. Black Sheep would follow the rays of the sinking sun
from the kitchen to the dining-room and thence upward to his own bedroom until all was grey dark, and he ran down to the kitchen fire and read
by its light. He was happy in that he was left alone and could read as much
as he pleased. But, later, he grew afraid of the shadows of window-curtains
and the flapping of doors and the creaking of shutters. He went out into the
garden, and the rustling of the laurel-bushes frightened him.

He was glad when they all returned—Aunty Rosa, Harry, and Judy—
full of news, and Judy laden with gifts. Who could help loving loyal little
Judy? In return for all her merry babblement, Black Sheep confided to her
that the distance from the hall-door to the top of the first landing was
exactly one hundred and eighty-four handspans. He had found it out himself.

Then the old life recommenced; but with a difference, and a new sin.
To his other iniquities Black Sheep had now added a phenomenal clumsi-
ness—was as unfit to trust in action as he was in word. He himself could
not account for spilling everything he touched, upsetting glasses as he put
his hand out, and bumping his head against doors that were manifestly
shut. There was a grey haze upon all his world, and it narrowed month by
month, until at last it left Black Sheep almost alone with the flapping cur-
tains that were so like ghosts, and the nameless terrors of broad daylight
that were only coats on pegs after all.

Holidays came and holidays went and Black Sheep was taken to see
many people whose faces were all exactly alike; was beaten when occasion
demanded, and tortured by Harry on all possible occasions; but defended
by Judy through good and evil report, though she hereby drew upon herself
the wrath of Aunty Rosa.

The weeks were interminable and Papa and Mamma were clean forgotten. Harry had left school and was a clerk in a Banking-Office. Freed
from his presence, Black Sheep resolved that he should no longer be deprived of his allowance of pleasure-reading. Consequently when he failed at
school he reported that all was well, and conceived a large contempt for
Aunty Rosa as he say how easy it was to deceive her. "She says I'm a little
liar when I don't tell lies, and now I do, she doesn't know," thought Black
Sheep. Aunty Rosa had credited him in the past with petty cunning and
strategem that had never entered into his head. By the light of the sordid

knowledge that she had revealed to him he paid her back full tale. In a household where the most innocent of his motives, his natural yearning for a little affection, had been interpreted into a desire for more bread and jam or to ingratiate himself with strangers and so put Harry into the background, his work was easy. Aunty Rosa could penetrate certain kinds of hypocrisy, but not all. He set his child's wits against hers and was no more beaten. It grew monthly more and more of a trouble to read the schoolbooks, and even the pages of the open-print story-books danced and were dim. So Black Sheep brooded in the shadows that fell about him and cut him off from the world, inventing horrible punishments for "dear Harry," or plotting another line of the tangled web of deception that he wrapped round Aunty Rosa.

Then the crash came and the cobwebs were broken. It was impossible to foresee everything. Aunty Rosa made personal enquiries as to Black Sheep's progress and received information that startled her. Step by step, with a delight as keen as when she convicted an underfed housemaid of the theft of cold meats, she followed the trail of Black Sheep's delinquencies. For weeks and weeks, in order to escape banishment from the book-shelves, he had made a fool of Aunty Rosa, of Harry, of God, of all the world! Horrible, most horrible, and evidence of an utterly depraved mind.

Black Sheep counted the cost. "It will only be one big beating and then she'll put a card with 'Liar' on my back, same as she did before. Harry will whack me and pray for me, and she will pray for me at prayers and tell me I'm a Child of the Devil and give me hymns to learn. But I've done all my reading and she never knew. She'll say she knew all along. She's an old liar too," said he.

For three days Black Sheep was shut in his own bedroom—to prepare his heart. "That means two beatings. One at school and one here. *That* one will hurt most." And if fell even as he thought. He was thrashed at school before Jews and the *hubshi,* for the heinous crime of bringing home false reports of progress. He was thrashed at home by Aunty Rosa on the same count, and then the placard was produced. Aunty Rosa stiched it between his shoulders and bade him go for a walk with it upon him.

"If you make me do that," said Black Sheep very quietly, "I shall burn this house down, and perhaps I'll kill you. I don't know whether I *can* kill you—you're so bony—but I'll try."

No punishment followed this blasphemy, though Black Sheep held himself ready to work his way to Aunty Rosa's withered throat, and grip there till he was beaten off. Perhaps Aunty Rosa was afraid, for Black Sheep, having reached the Nadir of Sin, bore himself with a new recklessness.

In the midst of all the trouble there came a visitor from over the seas to

Downe Lodge, who knew Papa and Mamma, and was commissioned to see Punch and Judy. Black Sheep was sent to the drawing-room and charged into a solid tea-table laden with china.

"Gently, gently, little man," said the visitor, turning Black Sheep's face to the light slowly. "What's that big bird on the palings?"

"What bird?" asked Black Sheep.

The visitor looked deep down into Black Sheep's eyes for half a minute, and then said suddenly: "Good God, the little chap's nearly blind!"

It was a most business-like visitor. He gave orders, on his own responsibility, that Black Sheep was not to go to school or open a book until Mamma came home. "She'll be here in three weeks, as you know of course," said he, "and I'm Inverarity Sahib. I ushered you into this wicked world, young man, and a nice use you seem to have made of your time. You must do nothing whatever. Can you do that?"

"Yes," said Punch in a dazed way. He had known that Mamma was coming. There was a chance, then, of another beating. Thank Heaven, Papa wasn't coming too. Aunty Rosa had said of late that he ought to be beaten by a man.

For the next three weeks Black Sheep was strictly allowed to do nothing. He spent his time in the old nursery looking at the broken toys, for all of which account must be rendered to Mamma. Aunty Rosa hit him over the hands if even a wooden boat were broken. But that sin was of small importance compared to the other revelations, so darkly hinted at by Aunty Rosa.

"When your Mother comes, and hears what I have to tell her, she may appreciate you properly," she said grimly, and mounted guard over Judy lest that small maiden should attempt to comfort her brother, to the peril of her soul.

And Mamma came—in a four-wheeler—fluttered with tender excitement. Such a Mamma! She was young, frivolously young, and beautiful, with delicately flushed cheeks, eyes that shone like stars, and a voice that needed no appeal of outstretched arms to draw little ones to her heart. Judy ran straight to her, but Black Sheep hesitated. Could this wonder be "showing off"? She would not put out her arms when she knew of his crimes. Meantime was it possible that by fondling she wanted to get anything out of Black Sheep? Only all his love and all his confidence; but that Black Sheep did not know. Aunty Rosa withdrew and left Mamma, kneeling between her children, half laughing, half crying, in the very hall where Punch and Judy had wept five years before.

"Well, chicks, do you remember me?"

"No," said Judy frankly, "but I said, 'God bless Papa and Mamma,' ev'vy night."

"A little," said Black Sheep. "Remember I wrote to you every week, anyhow. That isn't to show off, but 'cause of what comes afterwards."

"What comes after? What should come after, my darling boy?" And she drew him to her again. He came awkwardly, with many angles. "Not used to petting," said the quick Mother-soul. "The girl is."

"She's too little to hurt any one," thought Black Sheep, "and if I said I'd kill her, she'd be afraid. I wonder what Aunty Rosa will tell."

There was a constrained late dinner, at the end of which Mamma picked up Judy and put her to bed with endearments manifold. Faithless little Judy had shown her defection from Aunty Rosa already. And that lady resented it bitterly. Black Sheep rose to leave the room.

"Come and say good-night," said Aunty Rosa, offering a withered cheek.

"Huh!" said Black Sheep. "I never kiss you, and I'm not going to show off. Tell that woman what I've done, and see what she says."

Black Sheep climbed into bed feeling that he had lost Heaven after a glimpse through the gates. In half an hour "that woman" was bending over him. Black Sheep flung up his right arm. It wasn't fair to come and hit him in the dark. Even Aunty Rosa never tried that. But no blow followed.

"Are you showing off? I won't tell you anything more than Aunty Rosa has, and *she* doesn't know everything," said Black Sheep as clearly as he could for the arms round his neck.

"Oh my son—my little, little son! It was my fault—*my* fault, darling—and yet how could we help it? Forgive me, Punch." The voice died out in a broken whisper, and two hot tears fell on Black Sheep's forehead.

"Has she been making you cry too?" he asked. "You should see Jane cry. But you're nice, and Jane is a Born Liar—Aunty Rosa says so."

"Hush, Punch, hush! My boy, don't talk like that. Try to love me a little bit—a little bit. You don't know how I want it. Punch-*baba*, come back to me! I am your Mother—your own Mother—and never mind the rest. I know—yes, I know, dear. It doesn't matter now. Punch, won't you care for me a little?"

It is astonishing how much petting a big boy of ten can endure when he is quite sure that there is no one to laugh at him. Black Sheep had never been made much of before, and here was this beautiful woman treating him—Black Sheep, the Child of the Devil and the inheritor of undying flame—as though he were a small God.

"I care for you a great deal, Mother dear," he whispered at last, "and I'm glad you've come back; but are you sure Aunty Rosa told you everything?"

"Everything. What *does* it matter? But"—the voice broke with a sob that was also laughter—"Punch, my poor, dear, half-blind darling, don't you think it was a little foolish of you?"

"*No.* It saved a lickin'."

Mamma shuddered and slipped away in the darkness to write a long letter to Papa. Here is an extract:—

. . . Judy is a dear, plump little prig who adores the woman, and wears with as much gravity as her religious opinions—only eight, Jack!—a venerable horse-hair atrocity which she calls her Bustle! I have just burnt it, and the child is asleep in my bed as I write. She will come to me at once. Punch I cannot quite understand. He is well nourished, but seems to have been worried into a system of small deceptions which the woman magnifies into deadly sins. Don't you recollect our own upbringing, dear, when the Fear of the Lord was so often the beginning of falsehood? I shall win Punch to me before long. I am taking the children away into the country to get them to know me, and, on the whole, I am content, or shall be when you come home, dear boy, and then, thank God, we shall be all under one roof again at last!

Three months later, Punch, no longer Black Sheep, has discovered that he is the veritable owner of a real, live, lovely Mamma, who is also a sister, comforter, and friend, and that he must protect her till the Father comes home. Deception does not suit the part of a protector, and, when one can do anything without question, where is the use of deception?

"Mother would be awfully cross if you walked through that ditch," says Judy, continuing a conversation.

"Mother's never angry," says Punch. "She'd just say, 'You're a little *pagal*'; and that's not nice, but I'll show."

Punch walks through the ditch and mires himself to the knees. "Mother, dear," he shouts, "I'm just as dirty as I can pos-*sib*-ly be!"

"Then change your clothes as quickly as you pos-*sib*-ly can!" Mother's clear voice rings out from the house. "And don't be a little *pagal!*"

"There! 'Told you so," says Punch. "It's all different now, and we are just as much Mother's as if she had never gone."

Not altogether, O Punch, for when young lips have drunk deep of the bitter waters of Hate, Suspicion, and Despair, all the Love in the world will not wholly take away that knowledge; though it may turn darkened eyes for a while to the light, and teach Faith where no Faith was.

QUESTION

In what ways are you affected by the way others see you, and how important is this feeling?

Chapter 4

Social Organization

Any attempt to understand the nature of society must eventually focus on groups, because, ultimately, human survival depends upon group life. Unfortunately, groups are quite dissimilar; they vary in size and durability. As a result they establish their own identity and boundaries which go beyond the individuals' identity. It is the group that ties an individual to society and makes him a viable entity.

To distinguish between the various types of groups, sociologists have created the concept of the primary group. Primary groups are usually small and relatively durable and are characterized by face-to-face interactions on a very personal and intimate level. Consequently, primary groups instill a strong sense of group identity, and communication within the group is open and laden with emotion. The band of early man in William Golding's *The Inheritors* is an excellent example of a primary group.

However, primary groups vary within different societies and consequently influence the form of that society. One such society that results from a special type of primary group is the folk society in which relationships are close, stable, and overlapping. The Amish society in *Centennial* exemplifies a typical primary group within a folk society.

On the other hand, another society has arisen because of urbanization and technology, and with the new society came another type of primary group: the bureaucracy. In his classic study of the bureaucracy, Max Weber identified several key features of a bureaucracy: well-defined rules and regulations, a hierarchical organization, specialization, efficiency, and impersonal relationships. This primary group is illustrated by the Central Intelligence Agency in the selection from Fletcher Knebel, *Vanished.*

The Inheritors

William Golding

One of the main characteristics of a primary group is the close, intimate relationships among the group members. The small band of primitive people in *The Inheritors* demonstrates this trait when it faces a traumatic situation with the death of the leading male of the group. Even the new of Lok and Fa, a young male and female, fails to take away from the solemnity of their situation and the need for the primary group to rally and unite themselves.

But Mal was not the new man they expected. He lay collapsed and his breathing was so shallow that his chest hardly moved. They could see that his face was olive dark and shone with sweat. The old woman had kept the fire blazing and Liku had moved outside it. She was eating more liver, slowly and gravely, and watching Mal. The two women were crouched, one on either side of him, Nil bent and brushing the sweat off his forehead with her hair. There seemed no place in the underhang for Lok's news of the other. When she heard them, Nil looked up, saw no Ha and bent to dry the old man's forehead again. The old woman patted his shoulder.

"Be well and strong, old man. Fa has taken an offering to Oa for you."

At that, Lok remembered his terror beneath the ice women. He opened his mouth to chatter but Fa had shared his picture and she clapped her hand across his lips. The old woman did not notice. She took another morsel from the steaming bag.

"Sit up now and eat."

Lok spoke to him.

"Ha is gone. There are other people in the world."

Nil stood up and Lok knew that she was going to mourn but the old woman spoke as Fa had done.

"Be silent!"

She and Fa lifted Mal carefully until he was sitting, leaning back in their arms, his head rolling on Fa's breast. The old woman placed the morsel between his lips but they mumbled it out again. He was speaking.

"Do not open my head and my bones. You would only taste weakness."

Lok glanced round at each of the women, his mouth open. An involuntary laugh came from it. Then he chattered at Mal.

"But there is other. And Ha has gone."

The old woman looked up.

"Fetch water."

Lok ran down to the river and brought back two handfuls. He dripped it slowly over Mal's face. The new one appeared, yawning on Nil's shoulder, clambered over and began to suck. They could see that Mal was trying to speak again.

"Put me in the warm earth by the fire."

In the noise of the waterfall there came a great silence. Even Liku ceased to eat and stood staring. The women did not move, but kept their eyes on Mal's face. The silence filled Lok, turned to water that stood suddenly in his eyes. Then Fa and the old woman laid Mal gently on his side. They pushed the great gaunt bones of his knees against his chest, tucked in his feet, lifted his head off the earth and put his two hands under it. Mal was very close to the fire and his eyes looked into the flames. The hair on his brows began to crinkle but he did not seem to notice. The old woman took a splinter of wood and drew a line in the earth round his body. They they lifted him to one side with the same solemn quiet.

The old woman chose a flat stone and gave it to Lok.

"Dig."

The moon was through to the sunset side of the gap, but its light was hardly noticeable on the earth for the ruddy brilliance of the firelight. Liku began to eat again. She stole round behind the grown-ups and sat against the rock at the back of the overhang. The earth was hard and Lok had to lean his weight on the stone before he could shift any. The old woman gave him a sharp splinter of bone from the doe meat and he found he could break up the surface much more easily with this. Underneath it was softer. The top layer of earth came up like slate, but below it crumbled in his hands and he could scrape it out with the stone. So he continued as the moon moved. There came into his head the picture of a younger and stronger Mal doing this but on the other side of the hearth. The clay of the hearth was a bulging round on one side of the irregular shaped hole that he was digging. Soon he came to another hearth beneath it and then another. There was a little cliff of burnt clay. Each hearth seemed thinner than the one above it, until as the hole deepened the layers were stone hard and not much thicker than birch bark. The new one finished sucking, yawned, and scrambled down to the earth. He took hold of Mal's leg, hauled himself up, leaning forward and gazed unblinkingly and brightly at the fire. Then he dropped back. scuttled round Mal and investigated the hole. He overbalanced into it and scrambled mewing in the soft earth by Lok's hands. He extracted himself arse-upward and fled back to Nil and crouched in her lap.

Lok sat back with a gasp. The prespiration was running down his body. The old woman touched him on the arm.

"Dig! There is only Lok!"

Wearily he returned to the hole. He pulled out an ancient bone and flung it far into the moonlight. He heaved again on the stone, then fell forward.

"I cannot."

Then, though this was a new thing, the women took stones and dug. Liku watched them and the deepening and darkening hole and said nothing. Mal was beginning to tremble. The clay pillar of hearths narrowed as they dug. It was rooted far down in a forgotten depth of the overhang. As each clay layer appeared the earth became easier to work. They began to have difficulty in keeping the sides straight. They came on dry and scentless bones, bones so long divorced from life that they had no meaning to them and were tossed on one side, bones of the legs, rib-bones, the crushed and opened bones of a head. There were stones too, some with edges that would cut or points that would bore and these they used for a moment where they were useful but did not keep. The dug earth grew into a pyramid by the hole and little avalanches of brown grains would run back as they lifted the new earth out by the handful. There were bones scattered over the pyramid. Liku played idly with the bones of the head. Then Lok got his strength back and dug too so that the hole sank more quickly. The old woman made up the fire again and the morning was grey beyond the flames.

At last the hole was finished. The women poured more water over Mal's face. He was skin and bone now. His mouth was wide as if to bite the air he could not breathe. The people knelt in a semicircle round him. The old woman gathered them with her eyes.

"When Mal was strong he found much food."

Liku squatted against the rock at the back of the overhang, holding the little Oa to her chest. The new one slept under Nil's hair. Mal's fingers were moving aimlessly and his mouth was opening and closing. Fa and the old woman lifted the upper part of his body and held his head. The old woman spoke softly in his ear.

"Oa is warm. Sleep."

The movements of his body became spasmodic. His head rolled sideways on the old woman's breast and stayed there.

Nil began to keen. The sound filled the overhang, pulsed out across the water towards the island. The old woman lowered Mal on his side and folded his knees to his chest. She and Fa lifted him and lowered him into the hole. The old woman put his hands under his face and saw that his limbs lay low. She stood up and they saw no expression in her face. She went to a shelf of rock and chose one of the haunches of meat. She knelt and put it in the hold by his face.

"Eat, Mal, when you are hungry."

She bade them follow her with her eyes. They went down to the river, leaving Liku with the little Oa. The old woman took handfuls of water and the others dipped their hands too. She came back and poured the water over Mal's face.

"Drink when you are thirsty."

One by one the people trickled water over the grey, dead face. Each repeated the words. Lok was last, and as the water fell he was filled with a great feeling for Mal. He went back and got a second gift.

"Drink, Mal, when you are thirsty."

The old woman took handfuls of earth and cast them on his head. Last of the people came Liku, timidly, and did as the eyes bid her. Then she went back to the rock. At a sign from the old woman, Lok began to sweep the pyramid of earth into the hole. It fell with a soft swishing sound and soon Mal was blurred out of shape. Lok pressed the earth down with his hands and feet. The old woman watched the shape alter and disappear expressionlessly. The earth rose and filled the hole, rose still until where Mal had been was a little mound in the overhang. There was still some left. Lok swept it away from the mound and then trampled the mound down as firmly as he could.

The old woman squatted down by the freshly stamped earth and waited till they were all looking at her.

She spoke:

"Oa has taken Mal into her belly."

QUESTION

What are the primary characteristics of a primary group, and why are they valuable to the group?

Centennial

James Michener

In a folk society a primary group's values and traditions are so strong within the group that for any member to try to break away presents the group with a serious problem. In James Michener's *Centennial* the author writes about the Zendts, a wealthy Amish family. The mother and her five sons not only live together, but also pray, read the Bible, and look out for one another in the family as well as in the community. Of major concern to the family is the upbringing of the youngest, Levi, who the older brothers feel is getting away from their traditions and who may leave the faith and the family.

From a long distance the stately stone barn—with its red-and-yellow hex signs to ward off evil—was visible, and in the cold moonlight the young man could see the proud name worked into the masonry:

JACOB ZENDT

1713

BUTCHER

As with any self-respecting Lancaster farm, the barn was six times the size of the house, for Amish and Mennonite farmers understood priorities.

As the young man walked down the frozen lane, his heavy shoes making the snow crackle, his attention focused mainly on the trees. Because hickory and oak were so vital in his business, he could spot even a young hickory at a hundred yards, marking it in his mind against the day when it would be old enough for him to harvest.

The Zendt farm contained many fine trees: there was the perpetual woods first harvested in 1701 when Melchior Zendt arrived from Germany; then there was the line of trees along the lane, planted by his son Jacob in 1714, and best of all, there was the miniature forest set out by Lucas Zendt in 1767. It rimmed the far end of the pond and was as fine a collection of maple, ash, elm, oak and hickory as Lancaster County provided. Each tree on the Zendt farm was a masterpiece, properly placed and flourishing.

When he reached the farm buildings, the young man looked briefly at the huge barn, then at the small red building in which he worked, then at the even smaller one stained black from much smoke, then at the various snow-covered pigsties, chicken coops and corncribs. Finally, tucked in among the larger buildings, there was the house, a small clapboard affair. There was a light in the kitchen window, and pushing open the door, he saw that his mother was preparing supper while his oldest brother, Mahlon, read the Bible.

'Amos Boemer lost his bells,' he announced as he hung up his hat. 'He cursed somethin' awful.' His mother continued working and Mahlon kept to his Bible.

'I never heard cursin' like that before,' the young man continued.

'God will attend to him,' Mahlon said in a deep voice, without looking up from his Bible.

'Got into a snowdrift east of Coatesville,' the young man said. There being no response, he went to the washstand and prepared for supper.

But as he washed his face Mahlon observed, 'Amos Boemer is a blasphemous man. Little wonder God struck him down.'

'It was the left rear wheel.'

'It was the will of God,' Mahlon explained.

Now his mother lifted a heavy bell, ringing it for half a minute until the whole farm filled with sound. From the big barn came Christian, whose job it was to purchase hogs and cattle from surrounding farmers; on his ability to buy cheap at the right time depended the financial success of the family. From the pigsties came Jacob; it was his responsibility to see that there was a steady supply of pork. Levi, the youngest brother, who had watched the arrival of the Conestogas, worked in the two smallest buildings, the red and the one stained black; his job was to make sausage and scrapple, and at this he was so proficient that Zendt pork products brought the highest prices in Lancaster. There was even talk of shipping them in to Philadelphia when the railroad was completed to Lancaster.

The four younger brothers, each with the stamp of Mennonite upbringing, took their places at the two sides of the long table. Their mother, now in her sixties, sat at the end nearest the stove so that she could attend to such cooking as continued during the meal, and at the other sat the oldest brother, Mahlon, a dark and gloomy man in his thirties, feeling dead.

When the six were seated, they bowed their heads for grace while Mahlon reviewed the evil state of the world and asked for forgiveness for such sins as his four younger brothers had committed during the interval since dinner: 'We are mindful of the fact that Brother Levi has been spending his afternoons on Hell Street, consorting in taverns and making acquaintances with the devil. Guide him to halt this infamous behavior and direct him to attend to his proper obligations.' Levi flushed and could feel the others looking at him from beneath lowered foreheads.

Mahlon had a long list of matters he desired God to take notice of, and at the end he repeated the rubric which had guided this family for the past hundred and fifty years: 'Help us so to live in Thy light that our name shall be respectable in all its doings.' From the five listeners rose a fervent 'Amen.'

It was curious that this supper table contained only one woman. Each of The Five Zendts, as they were called in Lancaster, was of marriageable age and each could be considered a catch. Many farm girls watched the Zendts, especially the four oldest; there was some talk that young Levi was not too stable.

But the Zendt family had always married late, when the stormy passions of youth had been suppressed and when the family as a whole had time to study contiguous farms to ascertain which had desirable fields that might accompany the girl of the family when she married. The Zendt farm had started with sixty acres in 1701 and now contained somewhat over three hundred, and you didn't augment a farm that way by marrying the first girl who came along when you were twenty. You did it by patient acquisition, and if fate determined that you must marry a girl who lived in another part of the county, you sold off her dowry immediately and bought land touching yours. In 1844 there was no better farm in Lancaster County than the Zendts', and with five marriageable sons, by 1854 it ought to be much better.

Mahlon, at thirty-three, had begun slowly to focus upon a certain girl who was likely to receive a substantial amount of land when her father died. He hadn't divulged his decision to anyone yet, least of all to the girl, because a man didn't want to rush into these things, but he kept his eye on her.

Tomorrow was Friday, the last of the three big days around which the Mennonite week revolved: Sunday for worship; Tuesday and Friday for market. At the conclusion of supper Levi shoved back his chair, saying brusquely, 'I'm goin' out to see the souse,' and when he was safely gone Mahlon told his brothers, 'We must all watch Levi. He's getting feisty.' The three other Zendts agreed. In their earlier days each of them had gone feisty at some time or other, had wanted to smoke tobacco, or taste beer at taverns along Hell Street, or ogle the girls, but each had suppressed these urges and had stuck to butchering. It was clear that now they would have to guide Levi through this dangerous period.

Out in the yard he lit a lantern and walked stolidly across the frozen snow to the small red building. Kicking open the door, he surveyed his little kingdom and found it in good order. The sausage machine was clean and placed against the wall. Six baskets of white sausage links were lined up and waiting. The twenty large flat scrapple pans were stacked, each filled nearly to the brim with a grayish delicacy hidden beneath a protecting layer of rich yellow fat. It, too, was ready. It was the souse that needed attention, and when he saw it still on the stove, he knew that he should have worked that afternoon instead of wandering down to Hell Street to watch the wagoners roar in.

Levi liked souse better than any of the other products he made, and he devoted extra attention to preparing it. Throughout the Lancaster area it was said, 'For souse, Levi Zendt.'

He went to the stove and dipped a long-handled ladle into the simmering pot. The thirty-six pigs' feet looked done. He picked up a bone from the ladle, and the well-cooked meat slid off.

'Good!' he said.

He lifted the kettle from the stove and with great skill extracted all the white bones of the hogs' feet, being careful to leave in the gristle, for that was what made Zendt souse so delectable. He then returned the kettle of hog meat to the fire, tossing in six pounds of the best lean pork, well chopped, and six hogs' tongues, also chopped. Throwing two chunks of wood into the stove, he allowed the mixture to cook while he prepared the broth which gave the souse its taste.

Extracting stock from the bubbling kettle, he poured it into a large crock to which he added twelve cups of the sourest cider vinegar the area could provide. 'That'll make 'em pucker,' he said. He then added twelve tablespoons of salt to give the souse a bite, three teaspoons of pepper to make it snap, and a handful of cloves and cinnamon bark to make it sweet. He placed the crock on the back of the stove, keeping it warm rather than hot. Twice he tasted it, smacking his lips over the acrid bite the vinegar and salt imparted, but he crushed two more cloves to give it better balance.

He now laid out twelve souse pans and placed in each of them round disks of the sourest Lancaster pickles and here and there a single small slice of pickled carrot. Then like an artist he adjusted various items to produce a more pleasing design.

After a few minutes he took the kettle of bubbling meat from the fire and with tongs began fishing out the larger pieces of meat, arranging them among the pickles and carrots in the bottom of the pans. It was here that Zendt souse achieved its visual distinction, because the meat came in two colors, white chunks from the fatty parts, red meat from the lean; he kept the two in balance, working rapidly, pulling up smaller and smaller pieces and distributing them evenly.

Finally, when little meat was left, he tipped the crock forward and strained the broth through a sieve, which removed the cloves and bits of cinnamon bark.

'Good!' he grunted.

With care he ladled the broth into the pans of meat, and he had calculated so neatly that when the last pan was filled, the kettle was empty. Before he had finished cleaning up, the gelatin from the hogs' feet had begun to set. By morning the souse would be shimmering hard, filled with tender pork and chewy gristle, clean and sour-tasting.

Links of sausage, pans of scrapple, flats of souse, that's what the people of Lancaster expected from the five Zendts and that's what they got.

When he left the red building he poked his lantern into the small black building, where a flood of acrid smoke greeted him. Covering his nose, he looked up at the rafters where great sausage links hung suspended, brown from the penetrating hickory fumes. They looked just right, but nevertheless he squeezed an end to satisfy himself. It was hard and firm, with just a little grease running out. He smelled it. A strong aroma of burnt hickory, one of the most enticing smells in the world, reassured him.

'It's ready,' he announced to his brothers as he rejoined them.

'We expected it to be,' Mahlon said. He had the Bible open and now asked his four brothers and his mother to join him in their nightly prayer. This being Thursday night, he intoned: 'And help us, O Lord, to be honest men tomorrow and to give good measure and to behave ourselves as Thou wouldst have us, and may no one who comes to us feel cheated or robbed or in any way set upon.' It was a prayer his father had uttered when the boys were young, and his father before him.

Closing the Bible reverently, he said, 'Breakfast at three, Momma,' and the five Zendts went to bed.

QUESTION

What are the key concepts of a folk society, and how do they affect the members of the primary group?

Vanished

Fletcher Knebel

In a modern society the bureaucracy has become one of the most important form of group. In fact it is so important that it can completely domi-
nate individuals with ease. In this selection from *Vanished,* the President
of the United States and his press secretary, Gene Culligan, are in conference with the Director of the Central Intelligence Agency (CIA), Arthur
Ingram, over the program Operation Flycatcher, an effort by the CIA to
use young atomic scientists as intelligence agents. During the course of
the conversation, the President finds himself up against not only the
Director but also the vast and well-organized bureaucracy. The question
of who dominates whom is significant both in the story and in society
today.

Arthur Ingram was already seated in the oval office when I entered. He
nodded to me, curtly, I thought. The CIA director disliked people like me
sitting in on conferences involving the Agency. I was half inside, because of
my service to the President, and half outside because of my obligations to
the press. Although I held top security clearance, I'm sure Ingram considered me a risk, emotional if not patriotic. He sat stiffly upright near a
corner of the President's desk. The No. 1 intelligence man was immacu-
lately groomed as always, his trousers sharply creased and his crossed feet
shod in cordovans with a gleaming polish. Ingram held his rimless spectacles in his hands, his fingers framing them in a precise semirectangle. The
narrow, tanned face wore an expression of wary confidence as though this
were his command post and the President and I were calling at his request.
Ingram was an adroit, intense, aloof man, even though he might conceal the
aloofness behind a shield of congeniality when he entertained legislators at
the Agency. He was also suspicious of others, whether innately or by the
nature of his current trade I did not know. His personality traits were the
opposite of Roudebush's candor, forthrightness, and warmth. I suppose
that is why I always felt on guard in Ingram's presence.

The President was leaning back in his chair, the big hands clasped on
his stomach. His glasses were pushed aloft in the thatch of gray hair. He
grinned at me, but it flashed off quickly. I sensed a tension in the room.

"Have a chair, Gene," he said. "I've merely told Arthur that I wanted
to discuss the Agency's operations among scientists. Why don't you just
sketch the affair as you did for me yesterday."

"Yes, sir," I said. "Yesterday noon I and Miguel Loomis, the son of the

Educational Micro president, had luncheon in the Ring Building with Steve, and—"

"Steve?" cut in Ingram. His thin eyebrows were arched.

"Stephen Greer."

"Oh," said Ingram. He managed to impart a dismissive inflection to the word as if to imply that anything involving a man who vanished in the night was subject to discount. I was puzzled, since I assumed Ingram had inquired sympathetically about Greer before I came into the room. Thus the name should have been fresh in his mind.

I told the story as Miguel related it the day before, adding for Ingram's benefit a few words about the political importance of Miguel's father, Barney. This last bit was perhaps gratuitous, for I knew that Ingram followed the nuances of politics as closely as we did in the White House.

When I finished, Ingram's eyes left mine and went inquiringly to those of the President. Roudebush lolled informally in his chair. Ingram sat stiffly erect.

"Well, Arthur," said the President in a pleasant tone, "what about it?"

"Except for a few unimportant details," said Ingram, "the story is correct as far as it goes. We initiated the atomic scientists' project last fall and used the Spruance Foundation as a conduit for funds."

"I see," said the President. "Does this project have an Agency name?"

"Yes," said Ingram. He colored slightly. "Operation Flycatcher."

I could understand his embarrassment. Both the Agency and the Defense Department had a gift for appending lilting names to their covert undertakings. The blacker the mission, the more euphemistic the label. In this case, one could picture a crested flycatcher standing on a birch limb and pealing his song of spring while young physicists skulked about and conversed in hooded whispers.

"And why was I not informed of this?" asked the President.

"Because of our quite explicit understanding at our first session after you took office," said Ingram swiftly. "I keep a memorandum of our discussion in my desk as a constant guideline. You said you wanted to be consulted on broad policy, on major new undertakings of a sensitive nature, but that you could not and would not deal in day-to-day details of Agency operation."

"Arthur, do you consider the manipulation of young atomic scientists to be a day-to-day detail?" The President's tone was low, curious, rather than hostile.

"I would take exception to the word 'manipulation,' Mr. President," said Ingram. "We supply funds to graduate students who inevitably will swell the nation's reservoir of skilled scientists. In return, we receive—or I should say we are beginning to receive—some valuable information on nuclear developments abroad."

"I don't recall that this ever came before the National Security Council," observed Roudebush.

"No, sir. As I say, I interpreted our understanding as applying to the Council as well."

"Is Operation . . . uh . . . Flycatcher confined to young men, or have you also tried to recruit some of the older nuclear scientists?" asked the President.

"So far," said Ingram, "we have confined it to men working on masters' and doctors' degrees. We hope, of course, that many of these men will continue to serve the Agency throughout their careers. But we did not deem it wise to approach the older physicists, chemists, and engineers at this time. In most cases, their attitudes have . . . well, hardened, shall we say."

"Did you weigh the consequences in the event the Agency's hand was exposed?" asked Roudebush. "The CIA isn't exactly loved abroad as it is."

"Of course, Mr. President." Ingram seldom groped for an answer. "Very few of our recruits yet know the exact connection between Spruance and the Agency, and those who suspect it are, I must say, the kind who place the national interest ahead of personal ambitions in science. Loomis is the first young man to raise a substantial question from an antagonistic viewpoint."

"Who is this Mr. Rimmel, who heads Spruance for you?" asked the President. "A Maury Rimmel is a member at Burning Tree, the one who searched for Steve last night. Is that the man?"

"Yes, sir." Ingram obviously did not intend to amplify that brief answer, but he saw the President's continuing look of inquiry. "A number of businessmen co-operate with us, as you know, some without compensation, some for a fee. Rimmel is paid a fee."

"How much?"

"I don't have the figure in my head, but I believe it is on the order of fourteen or fifteen thousand a year."

"Fifteen thousand to run a nonexistent foundation?" asked the President. "That seems more than ample, to put it mildly."

"He does have to fend off questions about the foundation," said Ingram. He looked down at his glasses as though measuring them. "That takes a certain brand of acumen."

"I see." The conversation lapsed for a moment.

It occurred to me that Ingram would find it quite handy to have a man on the CIA retainer circulating at Burning Tree among its members. The implication was Machiavellian, of course, and I wondered if I were being overly suspicious.

So the President's next comment surprised me.

"I suppose none of Rimmel's fellow members at Burning Tree are aware of his Agency connection," he said.

"I would doubt it," answered Ingram. "As you know, the basic law protects the identity of Agency personnel and, uh, consultants."

"I'm a member, you know," the President said dryly. He paused, then added: "Frankly, I thought the only mystery about Maury Rimmel was whether he really earned his pay as a steel lobbyist."

There was silence again, rather heavy this time. An ordinary American voter, I thought, would never credit this scene: The President of the United States informing his intelligence chief that he was unaware of the CIA connection of a fellow member in a private club. Ingram toyed with his glasses, betraying for the first time a dent in his self-assurance. But he made no comment. The President clasped his hands behind his head and stared up at the ceiling.

"Arthur," he said, "we have more than a question of Intelligence economics here—the value of information obtained per dollar spent, as it were. We have a moral question."

"Just what do you mean, Mr. President?"

"I mean you're in the covert business of twisting young American scientists into something they don't purport to be to their fellows. Science prides itself on open access to all knowledge, from whatever source. Scientists must share, seek, and exchange information in an atmosphere of mutual trust. Now you come along and turn these young men into secret agents whose real mission is to spy on their colleagues, both American and foreign. I'd say that raises a prime ethical issue."

"I disagree with you, Mr. President. The project differs but little from a dozen other highly successful operations of the Agency."

"I wonder." Roudebush studied Ingram for a moment, then he turned to me. "How did Mike Loomis put it yesterday, Gene?"

"He said American physics was being 'tainted and corrupted' by the CIA connection," I said. "He contended his friends were being bribed to inform on their colleagues."

Ingram flicked a hostile glance at me. I was the unbidden visitor. "I would say that's a highly emotional verb," he said. "Not very many young men, except perhaps the New Left radicals, would confuse service to their country with bribery. . . . And, of course, in this case, since the boy is half

Mexican, I'd say we'd have to consider a latent antipathy for the United States."

"Oh, come now, Arthur." The President smiled briefly. "I don't know the young man, but I do know his father. Miguel Loomis was born and reared here. He's an American who happens to be bilingual because his mother is from Mexico."

"I merely point a possibility," said Ingram coldly. "I may be doing him an injustice."

"Isn't that beside the point anyway, Arthur?" asked Roudebush. "If there had never been a Miguel Loomis, and I learned of this . . . this venture of yours . . . I'd have very grave reservations."

"I'm sorry we differ, Mr. President," said Ingram.

The President sighed, and I sensed that this abyss between viewpoints was an old one for these men.

"Arthur," said Roudebush, "I can't understand why I wasn't briefed on this operation along with other major Agency undertakings."

"I suppose, Mr. President, I didn't weight it on the same scales you do." A note of apology slid into Ingram's voice. "In a total budget of a half a billion dollars, some three or four hundred thousand over-all doesn't bulk very large. I assure you, sir, there was no intent to withhold information from you. Perhaps it would be better all around if my future briefings went more thoroughly into minor Agency operations." Ingram stressed the word "minor."

"Yes, I think so," said the President. There was silence again, definitely strained this time. Roudebush arose, pushed his hands into his coat pockets and walked to the French doors. He stood for a moment, gazing at the back of a Secret Service man on duty on the outside walkway.

"Arthur," he said when he turned to us again, "why isn't it possible to obtain the same information you get from the young scientists via normal embassy and Agency channels?"

"I just don't believe we'd get the same kind of result," said Ingram. "Mr. President, until last fall we had to rely on a rather limited structure for our information on foreign nuclear weapons. We do, of course, have a few—a precious few—agents in nuclear installations abroad. And a number of reputable scientists—again the number is deplorably small—have volunteered information to us after their travels abroad or attendance at international conferences."

Ingram's tone had become confidently professional. He was in his element now. "I am building for the future in Operation Flycatcher."

While I managed to retain a straight face, I wanted to laugh each time I heard that phrase. The thought was a droll one—flycatchers impressed into the muffled legions of espionage—and I wondered what brain at the Agency packaged these dark missions in such festive wrappings.

"I envision the day," Ingram continued, "when vital information will roll into the Agency from several hundred trained scientific agents who have reached top levels of their professions. You must remember, Mr. President, that many eminent American scientists today have a higher loyalty than to the United States. They regard the world of science as a kind of frontier-free society in which information should flow as easily as would commerce around a globe without tariff barriers. We have evidence of imprudent contacts between American and Communist scientists which appear to breach our own security regulations. Frankly, many of these men do not trust any government, including their own. And hundreds of them are still laboring under a guilt complex for having worked on the atomic bomb. I can appreciate this kind of emotional trap, but I can't sympathize with it."

Ingram paused and squared his shoulders. "In sum, Mr. President, I'm trying to indoctrinate a new breed of scientist, with first loyalty to the United States of America. Operation Flycatcher is our vehicle. I think it's an excellent investment of time, money, and energy."

The President had stood by the French doors as he listened. Now he returned to his desk.

"To use your words, Arthur," he said, "I can appreciate your viewpoint here, even if I cannot sympathize with it. Perhaps, from a cold intelligence appraisal, your Flycatcher project makes sense. But I have to look at this from a higher vantage point, one that takes in the whole scope of our relations with the rest of the world. And what I see, I do not like." He looked directly at Ingram. "To be blunt, Arthur, the CIA wouldn't be exactly crippled if we ended this operation?"

"Crippled, no." Ingram flushed under his tan. "Handicapped, yes."

"This thought has been running through my mind," said Roudebush. "Suppose I had a son, and suppose he, as a young physicist, had been approached by your people. What would my son say to me when he found out that the CIA was infiltrating the ranks of his colleagues? And, further, wouldn't he find it incredible when I denied knowledge of the operation? . . . Arthur, there is a corrupting aspect of this that I don't like at all. Not at all. These young men of science are exploring the wide world of knowledge, seeking the essence of matter, the precise nature of the universe. They must be free to test, probe, and weigh. If they are merely to be the subsidized front for old men and old ideas—and by that I mean you and me and our whole generation—then their careers become a sham." The President tilted back in his chair. "I think if I were in Miguel Loomis's shoes, I'd be just as disturbed as he is."

"I take it you want Operation Flycatcher dismantled," said Ingram quietly.

"I do." Roudebush smiled. "Actually, of course, Miguel Loomis has left us no alternative. If CIA support is not withdrawn, he plans to expose the connection publicly."

"He could be handled," said Ingram, leaving the clear implication that President Roudebush could not. "I respect your wishes, sir, and although I do not agree with you, the Spruance support of Flycatcher will be terminated and the project closed down."

Ingram sat perfectly straight in his chair, still framing his spectacles in that neat little half rectangle of fingers.

"Good," said the President. "I appreciate your co-operation, Arthur." The compartment door was closed.

Ingram, sensing it, arose from his chair and folded his unused glasses into the leather case at his breast pocket.

"I'm sorry about Stephen Greer," said Ingram. "I know it must be a shock to you, Mr. President."

I'm the one who felt the shock. It seemed inconceivable to me that Ingram would not have mentioned Greer the moment he entered the President's office.

"Sue Greer is the one I'm worried about," said Roudebush. "So far she's holding up. The whole business is extraordinary. The police don't have a solid clue."

"If the Agency can help in any way, please call me at once," said Ingram.

"Thank you, Arthur. For the moment, I think we should let the police handle the case."

As Roudebush walked Ingram to the door, he indicated by a nod that I was to remain. He returned to sit on the corner of his desk, his favorite informal roost beside the golden donkey pen set. His first remark was unexpected.

"Gene," he said, "I suppose you're going to write your version of this administration someday?"

"I had thought of it, Mr. President. No definite plans, but . . ."

He waved a hand. "I hope you do. You might be the best man. Your position, half fish of the media, half fowl of this office, ought to give you a fairly objective viewpoint. Personally, I can't stand these fawning memoirs that follow the late king like so many paid mourners. Jack Kennedy once said there was no such thing as history. I agree with what I think he meant. But you might come close."

I grinned in relief. "I'm not much for the establishment line anyway."

"Good, I hope you've been keeping notes. On this intelligence matter, you definitely should. I think we're in for quite a time. Who, for instance, would think the CIA director would keep secrets from his boss? . . . Or plant a shifty agent in his locker room?"

We eyed each other. Roudebush grinned, then we both broke into laughter. This man *is* different, I thought. I could imagine the irate explosion of a Dwight Eisenhower or a Lyndon Johnson at a similar revelation. But Roudebush, God bless him, also saw the irony. After our laughter quieted, he became serious again.

"Gene, can you give me one good reason why Ingram should be using graduate students in physics as servants of the Agency?"

"Ingram thinks it's sound," I replied. "But I sure don't. Frankly, Mr. President, in my book that Spruance-Flycatcher operation is a crude, cynical business."

He nodded. "I agree completely with young Loomis. This Flycatcher thing is repellent to me. It's the kind of operation that erodes faith in our own institutions. It is corrupting, and it's nasty, and the man who conceived the idea can't have much appreciation for the values of a free society." He shrugged. "But that's Arthur Ingram. . . . Damn it, just recalling what he said makes my blood pressure go up all over again."

"You didn't show it."

He shook his head. "No, anger is lost on Ingram. We've been over this ground before. He can't see that if we adopt Communist methods in our zeal to contain them, we wind up defeating ourselves, war or no war. What is left of our open society if every man has to fear a secret government agent at his elbow? Who can respect us or believe us when some of our best young scientists go abroad as the instruments of a hidden agency?"

He left the corner of the desk and walked back toward his chair, his head lowered as he scuffed at the carpet.

"The whole CIA has gotten out of hand," he continued. "Subsidizing intellectuals and labor leaders, buying up university research brains, fomenting revolutions, clandestine paramilitary operations—a whole ball of wax that was never contemplated when the Agency was set up to gather vital information abroad. That's its job, and that's all it should be doing. . . . Of course, it's partially my fault. I should have cracked down long ago.

But at this desk, there is always some other crisis, crying to be handled at once."

QUESTION

What are the main goals of a bureaucracy, and how do they relate to the way it operates?

Social Stratification

Social inequality is a reality within every society, and sociologists have spent a great deal of time studying this phenomenon in terms of social stratification. For the most part, social stratification refers to a group of people who share a similar ranking in a society in relationship to other groups in that society. These rankings are usually based upon a number of attributes that the group either does or does not have. Social stratification, in essence, is the division of society into various classes or stratas.

Two of the major factors involved in the stratification of society are wealth and power, and although they are at times interrelated and tend to reinforce one another, they can be seen as separate from each other. Wealth can be either one or several of the following: a significant income, the ownership of property, or the control of the productive resources of a society. Power, on the other hand, can be thought of as an ability to make something happen or to influence the decision-making processes within a society. In "Mammon and the Archer," wealth as a factor in social stratification is shown, while *The Iron Heel* reveals the influence of power.

Another concern of sociologists in the problem of social stratification is the movement between stratas or social mobility. The idea that one can rise from one class to another is portrayed by one of America's classic story writers, Horatio Alger, in *Julius*.

Mammon and the Archer

William S. Porter (O. Henry)

Wealth as a factor in the stratification of society is demonstrated in this short story by O. Henry, "Mammon and the Archer." Anthony Rockwall, a wealthy businessman, believes that money can do anything, and when his son tells him that money cannot buy the love of the young woman he is in love with, Mr. Rockwall acts in a very interesting manner.

Old Anthony Rockwall, retired manufacturer and proprietor of Rockwall's Eureka Soap, looked out the library window of his Fifth Avenue mansion and grinned. His neighbour to the right—the aristocratic clubman, G. Van Schuylight Suffolk-Jones—came out to his waiting motor-car, wrinkling a contumelious nostril, as usual, at the Italian renaissance scupture of the soap palace's front elevation.

"Stuck-up old statuette of nothing doing!" commented the ex-Soap King. "The Eden Musée'll get that old frozen Nesselrode yet if he don't watch out. I'll have this house painted red, white, and blue next summer and see if that'll make his Dutch nose turn up any higher."

And then Anthony Rockwall, who never cared for bells, went to the door of his library and shouted "Mike!" in the same voice that had once chipped off pieces of the welkin on the Kansas prairies.

"Tell my son," said Anthony to the answering menial, "To come in here before he leaves the house."

When young Rockwall entered the library the old man laid aside his newspaper, looked at him with a kindly grimness on his big, smooth, ruddy countenance, rumpled his mop of white hair with one hand and rattled the keys in his pocket with the other.

"Richard," said Anthony Rockwall, "what do you pay for the soap that you use?"

Richard, only six months home from college, was startled a little. He had not yet taken the measure of this sire of his, who was as full of unexpectedness as a girl at her first party.

"Six dollars a dozen, I think, dad."

"And your clothes?"

"I suppose about sixty dollars, as a rule."

"You're a gentleman," said Anthony, decidedly. "I've heard of these young bloods spending $24 a dozen for soap, and going over the hundred

William S. Porter (O. Henry), "Mammon and the Archer," from *The Four Million*, 1903.

mark for clothes. You've got as much money to waste as any of 'em, and yet you stick to what's decent and moderate. Now I use the old Eureka—not only for sentiment, but it's the purest soap made. Whenever you pay more than 10 cents a cake for soap you buy bad perfumes and labels. But 50 cents is doing very well for a young man in your generation, position and condition. As I said, you're a gentleman. They said it takes three generations to make one. They're off. Money'll do it as slick as soap grease. It's made you one. By hokey! it's almost made one of me. I'm nearly as impolite and disagreeable and ill-mannered as these two old knickerbocker gents on each side of me that can't sleep nights because I bought in between 'em."

"There are some things that money can't accomplish," remarked young Rockwall, rather gloomily.

"Now, don't say that," said old Anthony, shocked. "I bet my money on money every time. I've been through the encyclopædia down to Y looking for something you can't buy with it; and I expect to have to take up the appendix next week. I'm for money against the field. Tell me something money won't buy."

"For one thing," answered Richard, rankling a little, "it won't buy one into the exclusive circles of society."

"Oho! won't it?" thundered the champion of the root of evil. "You tell me where your exclusive circles would be if the first Astor hadn't had the money to pay for his steerage passage over?"

Richard sighed.

"And that's what I was coming to," said the old man, less boisterously. "That's why I asked you to come in. There's something going wrong with you, boy. I've been noticing it for two weeks. Out with it. I guess I could lay my hands on eleven millions within twenty-four hours, besides the real estate. If it's your liver, there's the *Rambler* down in the bay, coaled, and ready to steam down to the Bahamas in two days."

"Not a bad guess, dad; you haven't missed it far."

"Ah," said Anthony, keenly; "what's her name?"

Richard began to walk up and down the library floor. There was enough comradeship and sympathy in this crude old father of his to draw his confidence.

"Why don't you ask her?" demanded old Anthony. "She'll jump at you. You've got the money and the looks, and you're a decent boy. Your hands are clean. You've got no Eureka soap on 'em. You've been to college, but she'll overlook that."

"I haven't had a chance," said Richard.

"Make one," said Anthony. "Take her for a walk in the park, or a straw ride, or walk home with her from church. Chance! Pshaw!"

"You don't know the social mill, dad. She's part of the stream that turns it. Every hour and minute of her time is arranged for days in advance. I must have that girl, dad, or this town is a blackjack swamp forevermore. And I can't write it—I can't do that."

"Tut!" said the old man. "Do you mean to tell me that with all the money I've got you can't get an hour or two of a girl's time for yourself?"

"I've put it off too late. She's going to sail for Europe at noon day after to-morrow for a two years' stay. I'm to see her alone to-morrow evening for a few minutes. She's at Larchmont now at her aunt's. I can't go there. But I'm allowed to meet her with a cab at the Grand Central Station to-morrow evening at the 8.30 train. We drive down Broadway to Wallack's at a gallop, where her mother and a box party will be waiting for us in the lobby. Do you think she would listen to a declaration from me during that six or eight minutes under those circumstances? No. And what chance would I have in the theatre or afterward? None. No, dad, this is one tangle that your money can't unravel. We can't buy one minute of time with cash; if we could, rich people would live longer. There's no hope of getting a talk with Miss Lantry before she sails."

"All right, Richard, my boy," said old Anthony, cheerfully. "You may run along down to your club now. I'm glad it ain't your liver. But don't forget to burn a few punk sticks in the joss house to the great god Mazuma from time to time. You say money won't buy time? Well, of course, you can't order eternity wrapped up and delivered at your residence for a price, but I've seen Father Time get pretty bad stone bruises on his heels when he walked through the gold diggings."

That night came Aunt Ellen, gentle, sentimental, wrinkled, sighing, oppressed by wealth, in to Brother Anthony at his evening paper, and began discourse on the subject of lovers' woes.

"He told me all about it," said Brother Anthony, yawning. "I told him my bank account was at his service. And then he began to knock money. Said money couldn't help. Said the rules of society couldn't be bucked for a yard by a team of ten-millionaires."

"Oh, Anthony," sighed Aunt Ellen, "I wish you would not think so much of money. Wealth is nothing where a true affection is concerned. Love is all-powerful. If he only had spoken earlier! She could not have refused our Richard. But now I fear it is too late. He will have no opportunity to address her. All your gold cannot bring happiness to your son."

At eight o'clock the next evening Aunt Ellen took a quaint old gold ring from a moth-eaten case and gave it to Richard.

"Wear it to-night, nephew," she begged. "Your mother gave it to me. Good luck in love she said it brought. She asked me to give it to you when you had found the one you loved."

Young Rockwall took the ring reverently and tried it on his smallest finger. It slipped as far as the second joint and stopped. He took it off and stuffed it into his vest pocket, after the manner of man. And then he 'phoned for his cab.

At the station he captured Miss Lantry out of the grabbing mob at eight thirty-two.

"We mustn't keep mamma and the others waiting," said she.

"To Wallack's Theatre as fast as you can drive!" said Richard, loyally.

They whirled up Forty-second to Broadway, and then down the white starred lane that leads from the soft meadows of sunset to the rocky hills of morning.

At Thirty-fourth Street young Richard quickly thrust up the trap and ordered the cabman to stop.

"I've dropped a ring," he apologized, as he climbed out. "It was my mother's, and I'd hate to lose it. I won't detain you a minute—I saw where it fell."

In less than a minute he was back in the cab with the ring.

But within that minute a crosstown car had stopped directly in front of the cab. The cab-man tried to pass to the left, but a heavy express wagon cut him off. He tried the right and had to back away from a furniture van that had no business to be there. He tried to back out, but dropped his reins and swore dutifully. He was blockaded in a tangled mess of vehicles and horses.

One of those street blockades had occurred that sometimes tie up commerce and movement quite suddenly in the big city.

"Why don't you drive on?" said Miss Lantry impatiently. "We'll be late."

Richard stood up in the cab and looked around. He saw a congested flood of wagons, trucks, cabs, vans and street cars filling the vast space where Broadway, Sixth Avenue, and Thirty-fourth Street cross one another as a twenty-six inch maiden fills her twenty-two inch girdle. And still from all the cross streets they were hurrying and rattling toward the converging point at full speed, and hurling themselves into the straggling mass, locking wheels and adding their drivers' imprecations to the clamor. The entire traffic of Manhattan seemed to have jammed itself around them. The oldest

New Yorker among the thousands of spectators that lined the sidewalks had not witnessed a street blockade of the proportions of this one.

"I'm very sorry," said Richard, has he resumed his seat, "but it looks as if we are stuck. They won't get this jumble loosened up in an hour. It was my fault. If I hadn't dropped the ring we—"

"Let me see the ring," said Miss Lantry. "Now that it can't be helped, I don't care. I think theatres are stupid, anyway."

At 11 o'clock that night somebody tapped lightly on Anthony Rockwall's door.

"Come in," shouted Anthony, who was in a red dressing-gown, reading a book of piratical adventures.

Somebody was Aunt Ellen, looking like a gray-haired angel that had been left on earth by mistake.

"They're engaged, Anthony," she said, softly. "She has promised to marry our Richard. On their way to the theatre there was a street blockade, and it was two hours before their cab could get out of it.

"And oh, Brother Anthony, don't ever boast of the power of money again. A little emblem of true love—a little ring that symbolized unending and unmercenary affection—was the cause of our Richard finding his happiness. He dropped it in the street, and got out to recover it. And before they could continue the blockade occurred. He spoke of his love and won her there while the cab was hemmed in. Money is dross compared with true love, Anthony."

"All right," said old Anthony. "I'm glad the boy has got what he wanted. I told him I wouldn't spare any expense in the matter if—"

"But, Brother Anthony, what good could your money have done?"

"Sister," said Anthony Rockwall. "I've got my pirate in a devil of a scrape. His ship has just been scuttled, and he's too good a judge of the value of money to let drown. I wish you would let me go on with this chapter."

The story should end here. I wish it would as heartily as you who read it wish it did. But we must go to the bottom of the well for truth.

The next day a person with red hands and a blue polka-dot necktie, who called himself Kelly, called at Anthony Rockwall's house, and was at once received in the library.

"Well," said Anthony reaching for his check-book, "it was a good bilin' of soap. Let's see—you had $5,000 in cash."

"I paid out $300 more of my own," said Kelly. "I had to go a little above the estimate. I got the express wagons and cabs mostly for $5; but the trucks and two-horse teams mostly raised me to $10. The motormen wanted

$10, and some of the loaded teams $20. The cops stuck me hardest—$50 I paid two, and the rest $20 and $25. But didn't it work beautiful, Mr. Rockwall? I'm glad William A. Brady wasn't onto that little outdoor vehicle mob scene. I wouldn't want William to break his heart with jealousy. And never a rehearsal, either! The boys was on time to the fraction of a second. It was two hours before a snake could get below Greeley's statue."

"Thirteen hundred—there you are, Kelly," said Anthony, tearing off a check. "Your thousand, and the $300 you were out. You don't despise money, do you, Kelly?"

"Me?" said Kelly. "I can lick the man that invented poverty."

Anthony called Kelly when he was at the door.

"You didn't notice," said he, "anywhere in the tie-up, a kind of a fat boy without any clothes on shooting arrows around with a bow, did you?"

"Why, no," said Kelly, mystified. "I didn't. If he was like you say, maybe the cops pinched him before I got there."

"I thought the little rascal wouldn't be on hand," chuckled Anthony. "Good-by, Kelly."

QUESTION

What kind of opportunity does wealth give to those who have it as opposed to those wo do not?

The Iron Heel

Jack London

One basis that has been used to rank people in societies is the ability to make someone do something or the capability of influencing someone's decision-making process. This is the idea of power, and although it is usually conceived as being closely related to wealth as a factor in stratification, it is a separate entity. This point becomes very clear in this excerpt from Jack London's powerful novel *The Iron Heel*. Ernest, a labor organizer, is engaged in a heated debate with two businessmen, Mr. Calvin and Mr. Asmunsen, two middle-class members, and during the course of that debate, Ernest demonstrates that power can be and is a very significant factor in social stratification.

From Jack London, *The Iron Heel*, 1907.

"I'll show you something that isn't a dream, then," Ernest answered. "And that something I shall call the Oligarchy. You call it the Plutocracy. We both mean the same thing, the large capitalists or the trusts. Let us see where the power lies to-day. And in order to do so, let us apportion society into its class divisions.

"There are three big classes in society. First comes the Plutocracy, which is composed of wealthy bankers, railway magnates, corporation directors, and trust magnates. Second, is the middle class, your class, gentlemen, which is composed of farmers, merchants, small manufacturers, and professional men. And third and last comes my class, the proletariat, which is composed of the wage-workers.

"You cannot but grant that the ownership of wealth constitutes essential power in the United States to-day. How is this wealth owned by these three classes? Here are the figures. The Plutocracy owns sixty-seven billions of wealth. Of the total number of persons engaged in occupations in the United States, only nine-tenths of one per cent are from the Plutocracy, yet the Plutocracy owns seventy per cent of the total wealth. The middle class owns twenty-four billions. Twenty-nine per cent of those in occupations are from the middle class, and they own twenty-five per cent of the total wealth. Remains the proletariat. It owns four billions. Of all persons in occupations, seventy per cent come from the proletariat; and the proletariat owns four per cent of the total wealth. Where does the power lie, gentlemen?"

"From your own figures, we of the middle class are more powerful than labor," Mr. Asmunsen remarked.

"Calling us weak does not make you stronger in the face of the strength of the Plutocracy," Ernest retorted. "And furthermore, I'm not done with you. There is a greater strength than wealth, and it is greater because it cannot be taken away. Our strength, the strength of the proletariat, is in our muscles, in our hands to cast ballots, in our fingers to pull triggers. This strength we cannot be stripped of. It is the primitive strength, it is the strength that is to life germane, it is the strength that is stronger than wealth, and that wealth cannot take away.

"But your strength is detachable. It can be taken away from you. Even now the Plutocracy is taking it away from you. In the end it will take it all away from you. And then you will cease to be the middle class. You will descend to us. You will become proletarians. And the beauty of it is that you will then add to our strength. We will hail you brothers, and we will fight shoulder to shoulder in the cause of humanity.

"You see, labor has nothing concrete of which to be despoiled. Its

share of the wealth of the country consists of clothes and household furniture, with here and there, in very rare cases, an unencumbered home. But
you have the concrete wealth, twenty-four billions of it, and the Plutocracy
will take it away from you. Of course, there is the large likelihood that the
proletariat will take it away first. Don't you see your position, gentlemen?
The middle class is a wobbly little lamb between a lion and a tiger. If one
doesn't get you, the other will. And if the Plutocracy gets you first, why it's
only a matter of time when the Proletariat gets the Plutocracy.

"Even your present wealth is not a true measure of your power. The
strength of your wealth at this moment is only an empty shell. That is why
you are crying out your feeble little battle-cry, 'Return to the ways of our
fathers.' You are aware of your impotency. You know that your strength is
an empty shell. And I'll show you the emptiness of it.

"What power have the farmers? Over fifty per cent are thralls by virtue
of the fact that they are merely tenants or are mortgaged. And all of them
are thralls by virtue of the fact that the trusts already own or control (which
is the same thing only better)—own and control all the means of marketing
the crops, such as cold storage, railroads, elevators, and steamship lines.
And, furthermore, the trusts control the markets. In all this the farmers are
without power. As regards their political and governmental power, I'll take
that up later, along with the political and governmental power of the whole
middle class.

"Day by day the trusts squeeze out the farmers as they squeezed out
Mr. Calvin and the rest of the dairymen. And day by day are the merchants
squeezed out in the same way. Do you remember how, in six months, the
Tobacco Trust squeezed out over four hundred cigar stores in New York
City alone? Where are the old-time owners of the coal fields? You know
to-day, without my telling you, that the Railroad Trust owns or controls the
entire anthracite and bituminous coal fields. Doesn't the Standard Oil Trust
own a score of the ocean lines? And does it not also control copper, to say
nothing of running a smelter trust as a little side enterprise? There are ten
thousand cities in the United States to-night lighted by the companies
owned or controlled by Standard Oil, and in as many cities all the electric
transportation,—urban, suburban, and interurban,—is in the hands of
Standard Oil. The small capitalists who were in these thousands of enterprises are gone. You know that. It's the same way that you are going.

"The small manufacturer is like the farmer; and small manufacturers
and farmers to-day are reduced, to all intents and purposes, to feudal ten-
ure. For that matter, the professional men and the artists are at this present
moment villeins in everything by name, while the politicians are henchmen.

Why do you, Mr. Calvin, work all your nights and days to organize the farmers, along with the rest of the middle class, into a new political party? Because the politicians of the old parties will have nothing to do with your atavistic ideas; and with your atavistic ideas, they will have nothing to do because they are what I said they are, henchmen, retainers of the Plutocracy.

"I spoke of the professional men and the artists as villeins. What else are they? One and all, the professors, the preachers, and the editors, hold their jobs by serving the Plutocracy, and their service consists of propagating only such ideas as are either harmless to or commendatory of the Plutocracy. Whenever they propagate ideas that menace the Plutocracy, they lose their jobs, in which case, if they have not provided for the rainy day, they descend into the proletariat and either perish or become working-class agitators. And don't forget that it is the press, the pulpit, and the university that mould public opinion, set the thought-pace of the nation. As for the artists, they merely pander to the little less than ignoble tastes of the Plutocracy.

"But after all, wealth in itself is not the real power; it is the means to power, and power is governmental. Who controls the government to-day? The proletariat with its twenty millions engaged in occupations? Even you laugh at the idea. Does the middle class, with its eight million occupied members? No more than the proletariat. Who, then, controls the government? The Plutocracy, with its paltry quarter of a million of occupied members. But this quarter of a million does not control the government, though it renders yeoman service. It is the brain of the Plutocracy that controls the government, and this brain consists of seven small and powerful groups of men. And do not forget that these groups are working to-day practically in unison.

"Let me point out the power of but one of them, the railroad group. It employs forty thousand lawyers to defeat the people in the courts. It issues countless thousands of free passes to judges, bankers, editors, ministers, university men, members of state legislatures, and of Congress. It maintains luxurious lobbies at every state capital, and at the national capital; and in all the cities and towns of the land it employs an immense army of pettifoggers and small politicians whose business is to attend primaries, pack conventions, get on juries, bribe judges, and in every way to work for its interests.

"Gentlemen, I have merely sketched the power of one of the seven groups that constitute the brain of the Plutocracy. Your twenty-four billions of wealth does not give you twenty-five cents' worth of governmental power. It is an empty shell, and soon even the empty shell will be taken away from you. The Plutocracy has all power in its hands to-day. It to-day makes the laws, for it owns the Senate, Congress, the courts, and the state legislatures. And not only that. Behind law must be force to execute the law. To-day the Plutocracy makes the law, and to enforce the law it has at its beck and call the police, the army, the navy, and lastly, the militia, which is you and me and all of us."

Little discussion took place after this, and the dinner soon broke up. All were quiet and subdued, and leave-taking was done with low voices. It seemed almost that they were scared by the vision of the times they had seen.

"The situation is, indeed, serious," Mr. Calvin said to Ernest. "I have little quarrel with the way you have depicted it. Only I disagree with you about the doom of the middle class. We shall survive, and we shall overthrow the trusts."

"And return to the ways of your fathers," Ernest finished for him.

"Even so," Mr. Calvin answered gravely. "I know it's a sort of machine-breaking, and that it is absurd. But then life seems absurd to-day, what of the machinations of the Plutocracy. And at any rate, our sort of machine-breaking is at least practical and possible, which your dream is not. Your socialistic dream is . . . well, a dream. We cannot follow you."

"I only wish you fellows knew a little something about evolution and sociology," Ernest said wistfully, as they shook hands. "We would be saved so much trouble if you did."

QUESTION

In what ways do people who have power in a stratified society try to maintain their power?

Julius

Horatio Alger

One of the problems involved in social stratification is the movement between classes. If the class structure of a society is so rigid that it allows for no or little advancement, the society will be drastically affected, usually in a negative fashion. In America, however, social mobility between classes is relatively easy; in fact, it has become an integral part of American society. No author's work better illustrates social mobility than that of Horatio Alger, whose very name implies social mobility upward. In this chapter from his book *Julius,* Alger demonstrates the means by which a young man can advance in society.

Julius and his companions were readily excused by the superintendent, on explaining the cause of their delay.

After supper was over, Mr. O'Connor said, "Boys, this is the last time you will be all together. Tomorrow probably many of you will set out for new homes. Now, how shall we pass the time?"

"A speech from Corny Donovan!" cried one boy.

"Speech from Corny!" was heard from all parts of the hall.

"Corny, have you anything to say to the boys?" asked the superintendent, smiling.

Corny was a short, wiry little fellow, apparently twelve, but in reality two years older. He was noted among the boys for his drollery, and frequently amused them with his oratory. He came forward with a twinkle of merriment in his eye.

"The Honorable Corny Donovan will speak to the meetin'," said Julius, acting as temporary chairman.

Corny took his place on the platform, and with perfect gravity took out a small, red handkerchief, and blew his nose explosively, in imitation of a gentleman who once addressed the boys of the Lodging House. The boys greeted this commencement with vociferous applause.

"Go on Corny!" "Spit it out!" were heard from different parts of the hall.

"Boys," said Corny, extending his right arm horizontally, "I've come here from my manshun in Fifth Avenoo to give you some good advice. You're poor, miserable bummers, ivery mother's son of you. You don't know much anyhow. Once't I was as poor as you." ("Hi! hi!" shouted his

From Horatio Alger, *Julius,* 1874.

auditors.) "You wouldn't think to look at my good clo'es that I was once a poor bummer like the rest of yez." ("Yes we would. Where's your gold watch?") "Where's my gold watch? I left it at home on the pianner. Maybe you'd like to grow up gentlemen like me. But you can't do it. It aint in you." ("Oh, dry up!") "Boys, where's your manners? Don't you know no more'n to interrupt me in my speech? Me and Mr. O'Connor have brought you out here to make men of you. We want you to grow up 'spectable. Blackin' boots won't make men of you." ("You're only a bootblack yourself!") "I only blacked boots for amoosement, boys. I'd have you know I used to leave my Fifth Avenoo manshun in disguise, and pass the day round Printin' House Square, blackin' boots, 'cause my doctor told me I must have exercise, or I'd die of eatin' too much rich food." ("Rich hash, you mean!") "No, I don't. I never allow my cook to put hash on the table, 'cause you can't tell what it's made of, no more'n sassidges. There's lots of dogs and cats disappear in New York, and it's pop'larly supposed that they commits suicide; but the eatin'-house keepers know what 'comes of 'em." ("You bet! That's so, Corny!")

"Now I want you, boys, to leave off bummin', and try to be 'spectable members of s'ciety. I don't want yer to spend yer money for cigars, an' chew cheap tobaccer, just as ef you was men. Once't I saw a four-year-old bummer sittin' on a doorstep, smokin' a cigar that was half as big as he was. All at once't his rags took fire, and he went up in a balloon." ("Hi! Hi!")

"I tell you boys, the West is the place for you. Who knows but what you'll git to be Congressmen, or even President?" ("Hear the boy talk!") "I didn't mean you, Jim Malone, so you needn't say nothin'. They don't make Congressmen out'n sich crooked sticks as you be. Maybe you'll keep a corner grocery some time, or a whiskey-shop, an' lay on the floor drunk half the time." ("Pitch into him, Corny!") "But that aint what I was a goin' to say. You'll be great men, ef you don't miss it; and if you're good and honest and industrious like I am," ("Dry up! Simmer down!"), "you'll come to live in fine houses, and have lots of servants to wait on you, and black yer boots, instead of blackin' 'em yourself." ("I'll take you for my bootblack, Corny," interrupted Julius.) "No, you won't. I expect to be governor before that time, and maybe you'll be swallered by the bear that scared you so this afternoon." (Laughter from the boys.) "But I've most got through." ("Oh, drive ahead, Corny!") "If you want to be great men, all you've got to do is to imertate me. Me and Mr. Connor are goin' to watch you, to see that you behave the way you ought to. When you're rich you can come back to New York, and go to the Lodgin' House, and make a speech to the boys, and tell 'em you was once a poor bummer like they be, and advise 'em to go West, if they want to be somebody.

"Now, boys, I won't say no more, I'm afeared you won't remember what I've said already. I won't charge you nothin' for my advice."

Corny descended from the platform amid the laughter and applause of his comrades.

Mr. O'Connor said, "Boys, Corny's advice is very good, and I advise you to follow it, especially as to avoiding cigars and tobacco, which can only do boys harm. I am not sure that any of you stand a chance of becoming a Congressman or President, as he suggests, but there is one thing pretty certain—you can, if you are honest, industrious, and improve your opportunities at the schools which you will have a chance to attend, obtain a respectable position in society. Some of the boys who in former years have gone to the West have become prosperous, having farms or shops of their own. I don't see why you can't be just as successful as they. I hope you will be, and if, some years hence, you come to New York, I hope you will visit the Lodging House. If I am still there, I shall be glad to see you, and have you speak to the boys, and encourage them, by the sight of your prosperity, to work as you have done. Now I would suggest that you sing one or two of the songs we used to sing on Sunday evenings at the Lodging House. After that you may go out for an hour, but you must keep near this hall, as the evening is coming on."

QUESTION

What are the key aspects of social mobility, and how can they be a problem to the individual?

Chapter 6

Racial and Ethnic Groups

People as well as societies differ from one another, and these differences have become the basis for classifying people into larger groups. Race, religion, nationality, and other cultural distinctions are a few of these human differences that have been used to categorize people, and usually these classifications have been to the disadvantage of the individual as well as the group.

The result of this categorization has been prejudice and discrimination. Prejudice or a negative attitude underlies discrimination, which is an overt act against a group. In "A Short Wait between Trains" the practice of prejudice and discrimination that certain Americans have leveled against blacks is illustrated quite well.

Another process that has been used to keep minority groups from rising is the self-fulfilling prophecy. The basic idea of this theory is that a minority group is stereotyped in a certain way, primarily negative, and is constantly reminded of this stereotype to the point that the group begins to exhibit the stereotypes. The opening chapter from *Huckleberry Finn* is a good example of how the self-fulfilling prophecy works.

One of the major problem areas of racial and ethnic groups is formal and traditional institutions of society. For the most part, various social institutions, such as the education system, systematically eliminate a large number of minorities from advancing because of the major social and cultural foundations of the system, which are usually those of the white middle class. The short story "The Boy Who Painted Christ Black" is a classical example of what has been called institutional racism.

A Short Wait Between Trains

Robert McLaughlin

The expression of negative attitudes (prejudice) and the commission of overt acts against blacks (discrimination) are facts of American society and are shown in this short story, "A Short Wait Between Trains." Although the story takes place during World War II, it still is relevant today.

They came into Forrest Junction at eleven-thirty in the morning. Seen from the window of their coach, it wasn't much of a town. First there were the long rows of freight cars on sidings with green-painted locomotives of the Southern Railway nosing strings of them back and forth. Then they went past the sheds of cotton ginners abutting on the tracks. There were small frame houses with weed-choked lawns enclosed by broken picket fences, a block of frame stores with dingy windows and dark interiors, a small brick-and-concrete bank, and beyond that the angled roof and thin smokestacks of a textile mill.

The station was bigger than you would expect; it was of dirty brick and had a rolling, bungalow-type roof adorned with cupolas and a sort of desperate scroll-work. The grime of thousands of trains and fifty years gave it a patina suggesting such great age that it seemed to antedate the town.

Corporal Randolph, a big, sad Negro, said, "Here we is."

Private Brown, his pink-palmed hand closed over a comic book, looked out the window. "How long we here?" he asked.

"Until one o'clock," said Randolph, getting up. "Our train west is at one o'clock."

The two other privates—Butterfield and Jerdon—were taking down their barrack bags from the rack. Other passengers bunched in the aisles—two young colored girls in slacks; a fat, bespectacled mother and her brood, with the big-eyed child in her arms staring fixedly at the soldiers; tall, spare, colored farmers in blue overalls.

As they waited for the line to move, Jerdon said, "Who dat?"

Grinning, Brown answered, "Who dat say 'Who dat?' "

They both began to laugh and some of the passengers looked at them with half-smiles and uncertain eyes.

Butterfield said, "Even the kid thinks you're nuts."

The child in the fat woman's arms looked at him sharply as he spoke, then her eyes went back to Jerdon and Brown.

"You think I'm nuts, baby?" asked Jerdon. "Is it like the man say?"

The line of passengers began to move.

"That baby don't think I'm nuts," said Jerdon. "That baby is sure a smart baby."

Their coach was up by the engine, and they descended to the platform into a cloud of released steam, with the sharp pant of the engine seemingly at their shoulders.

A motor-driven baggage truck, operated by a colored man wearing an engineer's cap, plowed through them. The three privates, with their bags slung over their shoulders, stood watching the corporal. He was checking through the papers in a large manila envelope marked "War Department, Official Business." It contained their railway tickets and their orders to report to a camp in Arizona.

"Man," said Brown, "you better not lose anything. We don't want to stay in this place."

"This don't look like any town to me, either," said Jerdon.

Butterfield, slim, somewhat lighter in complexion, and a year or two older than the others, looked around him. "Hey," he said, "look what's up there."

The others turned. Down the platform they could see two white soldiers armed with carbines and what appeared to be a group of other white soldiers in fatigues. A crowd was forming around them.

"They're prisoners of war," said Butterfield. "You want to see some Germans, Brown? You say you're going to kill a lot of them: you want to see what they look like?"

Brown said, "That what they are?"

"Sure," said Butterfield. "See what they've got on their backs? 'P.W.' That means 'prisoner of war.'"

The four soldiers moved forward. They stood on the fringe of the crowd, which was mostly white, looking at the Nazi prisoners with wide-eyed curiosity. There were twenty Germans standing in a compact group, acting rather exaggeratedly unconscious of the staring crowd. A small mound of barracks bags was in the centre of the group, and the eyes of the prisoners looked above and through the crowd in quick glances at the station, the train, the seedy town beyond. They were very reserved, very quiet, and their silence put a silence on the crowd.

One of the guards spoke to a prisoner in German and the prisoner gave an order to his fellows. They formed up in a rough double column and moved off.

Little boys in the crowd ran off after them and the knot of watchers broke up.

When the four soldiers were alone again, Brown said, "They don't look like much. They don't look no different."

"What did you think they'd look like?" Butterfield asked.

"I don't know," said Brown.

"Man, you just don't know nothing," said Jerdon. "You're just plain ignorant."

"Well, what did you think they'd look like?" Butterfield asked Jerdon.

Jerdon shifted his feet and didn't look at Butterfield or answer him directly. "That Brown, he just don't know nothing," he repeated. He and Brown began to laugh; they were always dissolving in laughter at obscure jokes of their own.

A trainman got up on the steps of one of the coaches, moved his arm in a wide arc, the pant of the locomotive changed to a short puffing, and the train jerked forward.

The colored baggageman came trundling back in his empty truck and Corporal Randolph said to him, "They any place we can leave these bags?"

The baggageman halted. "You taking the one o'clock?"

"That's right."

"Dump them on the truck. I'll keep them for you."

Randolph said, "Any place we can eat around here?"

"No, they ain't."

"Where we have to go?"

"They ain't no place," the baggageman said, looking at them as though curious to see how they'd take it.

"Man," said Jerdon, "we're hungry. We got to eat."

"Maybe you get a handout someplace," said the baggageman, "but they sure no place for colored around here."

Butterfield said sourly, "We'll just go to the U.S.O."

"Oh, man, that's rich," Brown said, and he and Jerdon laughed.

"They got a U.S.O. in this here town?" Jerdon asked the baggageman.

"Man, ain't that the truth," replied Jerdon.

Randolph said stubbornly, "We got to get something to eat."

The baggageman said, "You want to walk to Rivertown you get something. That the only place, though."

"Where's Rivertown?" Butterfield asked.

"Take the main road down past the mill. It's about three, four miles."

"Hell, man," said Jerdon, "I'm hungry now. I don't have to walk no four miles to get hungry."

"You stay hungry then," said the baggageman, and went off.

"Well, ain't this just dandy?" said Brown.

The men all looked at Corporal Randolph, who transferred the manila envelope from one hand to the other, his heavy face wearing an expression of indecision.

Butterfield said, "There's a lunchroom in the station. You go tell them they've got to feed us."

Randolph said angrily, "You heard the man. You heard him say there's no place to eat."

"You're in charge of us," Butterfield said. "You've got to find us a place to eat."

"I can't find nothing that ain't there."

"You're just afraid to go talk to them," said Butterfield. "That's all that's the matter with you."

Brown said, "Corporal, you just let Mr. Butterfield handle this. He'll make them give us something to eat." He and Jerdon began to laugh.

"O.K.," said Butterfield. "I'll do it."

Brown and Jerdon looked at Randolph.

"My God," said Butterfield, "you even afraid to come with me while I ask them?"

"You're awful loud-talking—" Randolph began, angrily but defensively.

"You coming with me or not?" Butterfield asked.

"We're coming with you," Randolph said.

The four soldiers went into the colored section of the station and walked through it and into the passage that led to the main entrance. The lunchroom was right next to the white waiting room. The four men moved up to the door, bunching a little as though they were soldiers under fire for the first time.

Butterfield opened the screen door of the lunchroom and they followed him in. There were five or six tables and a lunch counter and, although it was around twelve, only a few diners. A cashier's desk and cigarette counter was by the door, and seated behind it was a gray-haired woman, stout and firm-chinned and wearing glasses.

Butterfield went up to her, rested his hands on the edge of the counter, and then hastily removed them.

She looked up.

Butterfield said quickly, "Is there any place we could get something to eat, Ma'am?"

She looked at him steadily, then her eyes shifted to the others, who were looking elaborately and with desperation at their shoes.

"This all of you?" asked the woman.

"Yes, Ma'am, there's just us four."

"All right," she said. "Go on to the kitchen. They'll feed you."

"Thank you, Ma'am." Butterfield, trailed by the others, started back toward the kitchen.

"Just a minute," said the woman. "Go out and around to the back."

They turned, bumping each other a little, and went back out the door.

Brown said, when they were outside, "Mr. Butterfield, he sure do it."

"That's right," said Jerdon. "You want to look out, Corporal. That Butterfield, he'll be getting your stripes."

Butterfield and Randolph didn't answer, didn't look at each other.

In the kitchen they found a thin, aged colored man in a white apron and a young, thick-bodied girl, who was washing dishes.

"What you want?" asked the cook. "Something to eat."

"Man, we're hungry," Jerdon told him. "We ain't put nothing inside us since before sunup. Ain't that right, Brown?"

"Since before sunup yesterday," said Brown.

"The lady say you come back here?" asked the cook.

"That's right."

The cook took their orders and, as he worked, asked them what camp they were from, where they were going, how long they'd been in the Army. He told them about his two sons, who were in the Engineers at Fort Belvoir.

"Labor troops," said Butterfield. "A bunch of ditch diggers and road menders."

The cook stared at him. "What the matter with you, man?"

Butterfield didn't answer. He lit a cigarette and walked to the serving window, looking out at the woman at the cashier's desk.

Brown and Jerdon went over to the girl washing dishes, and Corporal Randolph, his manila envelope under his arm, listened mournfully to the cook.

Suddenly, Butterfield threw away his half-smoked cigarette and called to the others, "Come here and look at this."

"What?" said Randolph.

"You come here and see this."

They all came over, the cook, the girl, the three other soldiers.

Sitting down at the tables in the lunchroom were the twenty German prisoners. One of their guards was at the door with his carbine slung over his shoulder, the other was talking to the cashier. The other diners were staring at the Nazis in fascination. The prisoners sat relaxed and easy at the tables, lighting cigarettes, drinking water, taking rolls from the baskets on their tables, and munching them unbuttered, their eyes incurious, their attitudes casual.

"God damn! Look at that," said Butterfield. "We don't amount to as much here as the men we're supposed to fight. Look at them, sitting there like kings, and we can't get a scrap to eat in this place without bending our knee and sneaking out to the kitchen like dogs or something."

The cook said severely, "Where you from, boy?"

"He from Trenton, New Jersey," said Brown.

Butterfield stared around at them and saw that only Randolph and the cook even knew what he was talking about and that they were both looking at him with troubled disapproval. Brown and Jerdon and the girl just didn't care. He turned and crossed the kitchen and went out the back door.

The cook said to Randolph, "I'll wrap some sandwiches for him and you give them to him on the train." He shook his head. "All the white folks around here is talking about all the nigger killing they going to do after the war. That boy, he sure to be one of them."

Randolph cracked his big knuckles unhappily. "We all sure to be one of them," he said. "The Lord better have mercy on us all."

QUESTION

What has been the result, both on individuals and society, of racial prejudice and discrimination in America?

Huckleberry Finn

Mark Twain

One form that racial discrimination can take is through what sociologists call the self-fulfilling prophecy. The main idea is that if a person is constantly told that he exhibits a certain behavior pattern, the individual will begin to believe and display that type of behavior. In Huck Finn's case, the widow Douglas and her sister, Miss Watson, tell Huck that he is bad, sinful, and dirty so much that he sees nothing else to do except be bad, sinful, and dirty. Huck's situation is similar to that of many minority groups in America who belong to an "outside" group and whose every move is being interpreted in a negative fashion.

You don't know about me without you have read a book by the name of *The Adventures of Tom Sawyer;* but that ain't no matter. That book was made by Mr. Mark Twain, and he told the truth, mainly. There was things

Mark Twain, *The Adventures of Huckleberry Finn,* 1912.

which he stretched, but mainly he told the truth. That is nothing. I never seen anybody but lied one time or another, without it was Aunt Polly, or the widow, or maybe Mary. Aunt Polly—Tom's Aunt Polly, she is—and Mary, and the Widow Douglas is all told about in that book, which is mostly a true book, with some stretchers, as I said before.

Now the way that the book winds up is this: Tom and me found the money that the robbers hid in the cave, and it made us rich. We got six thousand dollars apiece—all gold. It was an awful sight of money when it was piled up. Well, Judge Thatcher he took it and put it out at interest, and it fetched us a dollar a day apiece all the year round—more than a body could tell what to do with. The Widow Douglas she took me for her son, and allowed she would sivilize me; but it was rough living in the house all the time, considering how dismal regular and decent the widow was in all her ways; and so when I couldn't stand it no longer I lit out. I got into my old rags and my sugar-hogshead again, and was free and satisfied. But Tom Sawyer he hunted me up and said he was going to start a band of robbers, and I might join if I would go back to the widow and be respectable. So I went back.

The widow she cried over me, and called me a poor lost lamb, and she called me a lot of other names, too, but she never meant no harm by it. She put me in them new clothes again, and I couldn't do nothing but sweat and sweat, and feel all cramped up. Well, then, the old thing commenced again. The widow rung a bell for supper, and you had to come to time. When you got to the table you couldn't go right to eating, but you had to wait for the widow to tuck down her head and grumble a little over the victuals, though there warn't really anything the matter with them—that is, nothing only everything was cooked by itself. In a barrel of odds and ends it is different; things get mixed up, and the juice kind of swaps around, and the things go better.

After supper she got out her book and learned me about Moses and the Bulrushers, and I was in a sweat to find out all about him; but by and by she let it out that Moses had been dead a considerable long time; so then I didn't care no more about him, because I don't take no stock in dead people.

Pretty soon I wanted to smoke, and asked the widow to let me. But she wouldn't. She said it was a mean practice and wasn't clean, and I must try to not do it any more. That is just the way with some people. They get down on a thing when they don't know nothing about it. Here she was abothering about Moses, which was no kin to her, and no use to anybody, being gone, you see, yet finding a power of fault with me for doing a thing that had some good in it. And she took snuff, too; of course that was all right, because she done it herself.

Her sister, Miss Watson, a tolerable slim old maid, with goggles on, had just come to live with her, and took a set at me now with a spelling-book. She worked me middling hard for about an hour, and then the widow made her ease up. I couldn't stood it much longer. Then for an hour it was deadly dull, and I was fidgety. Miss Watson would say, "Don't put your feet up there, Huckleberry"; and "Don't scrunch up like that, Huckleberry—set up straight"; and pretty soon she would say, "Don't gap and stretch like that, Huckleberry—why don't you try to behave?" Then she told me all about the bad place, and I said I wished I was there. She got mad then, but I didn't mean no harm. All I wanted was to go somewheres; all I wanted was a change, I warn't particular. She said it was wicked to say what I said; said she wouldn't say it for the whole world; *she* was going to live so as to go to the good place. Well, I couldn't see no advantage in going where she was going, so I made up my mind I wouldn't try for it. But I never said so, because it would only make trouble, and wouldn't do no good.

Now she had got a start, and she went on and told me all about the good place. She said all a body would have to do there was to go around all day long with a harp and sing, forever and ever. So I didn't think much of it. But I never said so. I asked her if she reckoned Tom Sawyer would go there, and she said not by a considerable sight. I was glad about that, because I wanted him and me to be together.

Miss Watson she kept pecking at me, and it got tiresome and lonesome. By and by they fetched the niggers in and had prayers, and then everybody was off to bed. I went up to my room with a piece of candle, and put it on the table. Then I set down in a chair by the window and tried to think of something cheerful, but it warn't no use. I felt so lonesome I most wished I was dead. The stars were shining, and the leaves rustled in the woods ever so mournful; and I heard an owl, away off, who-whooing about somebody that was dead, and a whippowill and a dog crying about somebody that was going to die; and the wind was trying to whisper something to me, and I couldn't make out what it was, and so it made the cold shivers run over me. Then away out in the woods I heard that kind of a sound that a ghost makes when it wants to tell about something that's on its mind and can't make itself understood, and so can't rest easy in its grave, and has to go about that way every night grieving. I got so downhearted and scared I did wish I had some company. Pretty soon a spider went crawling up my shoulder, and I flipped it off and it lit in the candle; and before I could budge it was all shriveled up. I didn't need anybody to tell me that that was an awful bad sign and would fetch me some bad luck, so I was scared and most shook the clothes off of me. I got up and turned around in my tracks three times and crossed my breast every time; and then I tied up a little lock of my hair with a thread to keep witches away. But I hadn't no confidence. You do that when you've lost a horseshoe that you've found, instead of nailing it up over the door, but I hadn't ever heard anybody say it was any way to keep off bad luck when you'd killed a spider.

I set down again, a-shaking all over, and got out my pipe for a smoke; for the house was all as still as death now, and so the widow wouldn't know. Well, after a long time I heard the clock away off in the town go boom— boom—boom—twelve licks; and all still again—stiller than ever. Pretty soon I heard a twig snap down in the dark amongst the trees—something was a-stirring. I set still and listened. Directly I could just barely hear a *"me-yow! me-yow!"* down there. That was good! Says I, *"me-yow! me-yow!"* as soft as I could, and then I put out the light and scrambled out of the window on to the shed. Then I slipped down to the ground and crawled in among the trees, and, sure enough, there was Tom Sawyer waiting for me.

QUESTION

What are the key aspects of the self-fulfilling prophecy, and how has it been used in America against various minority groups?

The Boy Who Painted Christ Black

John Henrik Clarke

One neglected form of racial discrimination is institutional racism. While it is easy to detect individual discriminatory patterns, sometimes the structures and rules of institutions work against a minority group. In "The Boy Who Painted Christ Black," what institutional racism is and how it works is displayed quite appropriately.

He was the smartest boy in the Muskogee County School—for colored children. Everybody even remotely connected with the school knew this. The teacher always pronounced his name with profound gusto as she pointed him out as the ideal student. Once I heard her say: "If he were white he might, some day, become President." Only Aaron Crawford wasn't white; quite the contrary. His skin was so solid black that it glowed, reflecting an inner virtue that was strange, and beyond my comprehension.

In many ways he looked like something that was awkwardly put together. Both his nose and lips seemed a trifle too large for his face. To say he was ugly would be unjust and to say he was handsome would be gross exaggeration. Truthfully, I could never make up my mind about him. Sometimes he looked like something out of a book of ancient history . . . looked as if he was left over from that magnificent era before the machine age came and marred the earth's natural beauty.

His great variety of talent often startled the teachers. This caused his classmates to look upon him with a mixed feeling of awe and envy.

Before Thanksgiving, he always drew turkeys and pumpkins on the blackboard. On George Washington's birthday, he drew large American flags surrounded by little hatchets. It was these small masterpieces that made him the most talked-about colored boy in Columbus, Georgia. The Negro principal of the Muskogee County School said he would some day be a great painter, like Henry O. Tanner.

For the teacher's birthday, which fell on a day about a week before commencement, Aaron Crawford painted the picture that caused an uproar, and a turning point, at the Muskogee County School. The moment he entered the room that morning, all eyes fell on him. Besides his torn book holder, he was carrying a large-framed concern wrapped in old newspapers. As he went to his seat, the teacher's eyes followed his every motion, a curious wonderment mirrored in them conflicting with the half-smile that wreathed her face.

Aaron put his books down, then smiling broadly, advanced toward the teacher's desk. His alert eyes were so bright with joy that they were almost frightening. The children were leaning forward in their seats, staring greedily at him; a restless anticipation was rampant within every breast.

Already the teacher sensed that Aaron had a present for her. Still smiling, he placed it on her desk and began to help her unwrap it. As the last piece of paper fell from the large frame, the teacher jerked her hand away from it suddenly, her eyes flickering unbelieveingly. Amidst the rigid tension, her heavy breathing was distinct and frightening. Temporarily, there was no other sound in the room.

Aaron stared questioningly at her and she moved her hand back to the present cautiously, as if it were a living thing with vicious characteristics. I am sure it was the one thing she least expected.

With a quick, involuntary movement I rose up from my desk. A series

of submerged murmurs spread through the room, rising to a distinct mono-
tone. The teacher turned toward the children, staring reproachfully. They
did not move their eyes from the present that Aaron had brought her. . . .
It was a large picture of Christ—painted black!

Aaron Crawford went back to his seat, a feeling of triumph reflecting
in his every movement.

The teacher faced us. Her curious half-smile had blurred into a mild
bewilderment. She searched the bright faces before her and started to smile
again, occasionally stealing quick glances at the large picture propped on
her desk, as though doing so were forbidden amusement.

"Aaron," she spoke at last, a slight tinge of uncertainty in her tone,
"this is a most welcome present. Thanks. I will treasure it." She paused,
then went on speaking, a trifle more coherent than before. "Looks like you
are going to be quite an artist. . . . Suppose you come forward and tell the
class how you came to paint this remarkable picture."

When he rose to speak, to explain about the picture, a hush fell tightly
over the room, and the children gave him all of their attention . . . something they rarely did for the teacher. He did not speak at first; he just stood
there in front of the room, toying absently with his hands, observing his
audience carefully, like a great concert artist.

"It was like this," he said, placing full emphasis on every word. "You
see, my uncle who lives in New York teaches classes in Negro History at the
Y.M.C.A. When he visited us last year he was telling me about the many
great black folks who have made history. He said black folks were once the
most powerful people on earth. When I asked him about Christ, he said no
one ever proved whether he was black or white. Somehow a feeling came
over me that he was a black man, 'cause he was so kind and forgiving,
kinder than I have ever seen white people be. So, when I painted his picture
I couldn't help but paint it as I thought it was."

After this, the little artist sat down, smiling broadly, as if he had gained
entrance to a great storehouse of knowledge that ordinary people could
neither acquire nor comprehend.

The teacher, knowing nothing else to do under prevailing circumstances,
invited the children to rise from their seats and come forward so they could
get a complete view of Aaron's unique piece of art.

When I came close to the picture, I noticed it was painted with the
kind of paint you get in the five and ten cent stores. Its shape was blurred
slightly, as if someone had jarred the frame before the paint had time to

dry. The eyes of Christ were deep-set and sad, very much like those of Aaron's father, who was a deacon in the local Baptist Church. This picture of Christ looked much different from the one I saw hanging on the wall when I was in Sunday School. It looked more like a helpless Negro, pleading silently for mercy.

For the next few days, there was much talk about Aaron's picture.

The school term ended the following week and Aaron's picture, along with the best handwork done by the students that year, was on display in the assembly room. Naturally, Aaron's picture graced the place of honor.

There was no book work to be done on commencement day and joy was rampant among the children. The girls in their brightly colored dresses gave the school the delightful air of Spring awakening.

In the middle of the day all the children were gathered in the small assembly. On this day we were always favored with a visit from a man whom all the teachers spoke of with mixed esteem and fear. Professor Danual, they called him, and they always pronounced his name with reverence. He was supervisor of all the city schools, including those small and poorly equipped ones set aside for colored children.

The great man arrived almost at the end of our commencement exercises. On seeing him enter the hall, the children rose, bowed courteously, and sat down again, their eyes examining him as if he were a circus freak.

He was a tall white man with solid gray hair that made his lean face seem paler than it actually was. His eyes were the clearest blue I have ever seen. They were the only life-like things about him.

As he made his way to the front of the room the Negro principal, George Du Vaul, was walking ahead of him, cautiously preventing anything from getting in his way. As he passed me, I heard the teachers, frightened, sucking in their breath, felt the tension tightening.

A large chair was in the center of the rostrum. It had been daintily polished and the janitor had laboriously recushioned its bottom. The supervisor went straight to it without being guided, knowing that this pretty splendor was reserved for him.

Presently the Negro principal introduced the distinguished guest and he favored us with a short speech. It wasn't a very important speech. Almost at the end of it, I remember him saying something about he wouldn't be surprised if one of us boys grew up to be a great colored man, like Booker T. Washington.

After he sat down, the school chorus sang two spirituals and the girls in the fourth grade did an Indian folk dance. This brought the commencement program to an end.

After the supervisor came down from the rostrum, his eyes tinged with curiosity, and began to view the array of handwork on display in front of the chapel.

Suddenly his face underwent a strange rejuvenation. His clear blue eyes flickered in astonishment. He was looking at Aaron Crawford's picture of Christ. Mechanically he moved his stooped form closer to the picture and stood gazing fixedly at it, curious and undecided, as though it were a dangerous animal that would rise any moment and spread destruction.

We waited tensely for his next movement. The silence was almost suffocating. At last he twisted himself around and began to search the grim faces before him. The fiery glitter of his eyes abated slightly as they rested on the Negro principal, protestingly.

"Who painted this sacrilegious nonsense?" he demanded sharply.

"I painted it, sir." These were Aaron's words, spoken hesitantly. He wetted his lips timidly and looked up at the supervisor, his eyes voicing a sad plea for understanding.

He spoke again, this time more coherently. "Th' principal said a colored person have jes as much right paintin' Jesus black as a white person have paintin' him white. And he says . . . " At this point he halted abruptly, as if to search for his next words. A strong tinge of bewilderment dimmed the glow of his solid black face. He stammered out a few more words, then stopped again.

The supervisor strode a few steps toward him. At last color had swelled some of the lifelessness out of his lean face.

"Well, go on!" he said, enragedly, " . . . I'm still listening."

Aaron moved his lips pathetically but no words passed them. His eyes wandered around the room, resting finally, with an air of hope, on the face of the Negro principal. After a moment, he jerked his face in another direction, regretfully, as if something he had said had betrayed an understanding between him and the principal.

Presently the principal stepped forward to defend the school's prize student.

"I encouraged the boy in painting that picture," he said firmly. "And it was with my permission that he brought the picture into this school. I don't think the boy is so far wrong in painting Christ black. The artists of all other races have painted whatsoever God they worship to resemble themselves. I see no reason why we should be immune from that privilege. After all, Christ was born in that part of the world that had always been predominantly populated by colored people. There is a strong possibility that he could have been a Negro."

But for the monotonous lull of heavy breathing, I would have sworn that his words had frozen everyone in the hall. I had never heard the little principal speak so boldly to anyone, black or white.

The supervisor swallowed dumfoundedly. His face was aglow in silent rage.

"Have you been teaching these children things like that?" he asked the Negro principal, sternly.

"I have been teaching them that their race has produced great kinds and queens as well as slaves and serfs," the principal said. "The time is long overdue when we should let the world know that we erected and enjoyed the benefits of a splendid civilization long before the people of Europe had a written language."

The supervisor coughed. His eyes bulged menacingly as he spoke. "You are not being paid to teach such things in this school, and I am demanding your resignation for overstepping your limit as principal."

George Du Vaul did not speak. A strong quiver swept over his sullen face. He revolved himself slowly and walked out of the room towards his office.

The supervisor's eyes followed h. m until he was out of focus. Then he murmured under his breath: "There'll be a lot of fuss in this world if you start people thinking that Christ was a nigger."

Some of the teachers followed the principal out of the chapel, leaving the crestfallen children restless and in a quandary about what to do next. Finally we started back to our rooms. The supervisor was behind me. I heard him murmur to himself: "Damn, if niggers ain't getting smarter."

A few days later I heard that the principal had accepted a summer job as art instructor of a small high school somewhere in south Georgia and had gotten permission from Aaron's parents to take him along so he could continue to encourage him in his painting.

I was on my way home when I saw him leaving his office. He was carrying a large briefcase and some books tucked under his arm. He had already said good-by to all the teachers. And strangely, he did not look brokenhearted. As he headed for the large front door, he readjusted his horn-rimmed glasses, but did not look back. An air of triumph gave more dignity to his soldierly stride. He had the appearance of a man who had done a great thing, something greater than any ordinary man would do.

Aaron Crawford was waiting outside for him. They walked down the street together. He put his arms around Aaron's shoulder affectionately. He was talking sincerely to Aaron about something, and Aaron was listening, deeply earnest.

I watched them until they were so far down the street that their forms had begun to blur. Even from this distance I could see they were still walking in brisk, dignified strides, like two people who had won some sort of victory.

QUESTION

What are some of the effects of institutional racism upon the people who suffer from it?

Chapter 7

Deviance

In every society certain rules, norms, and values are established in order that the society continue to exist in an orderly fashion. Any violation of the social principles beyond a certain point cannot be tolerated, and such behavior is labeled as deviance.

However, the concept of deviance is not easily defined. Situations differ. For example, the killing of another human being is, in most societies, considered to be a deviant act; however, under certain circumstances it could be deemed appropriate, that is, self-defense. The question of whether or not a deed goes beyond society's boundaries of proper behavior is the main point in the book by Albert Camus, *The Stranger*, in which the court attempts to determine whether or not the accused acted in a deviant manner.

The causes of deviant behavior are many, but one aspect that sociologists have detected is that deviant behavior can be learned. In *One Flew over the Cuckoo's Nest* a mental hospital places people into deviant roles, and they act accordingly. However, the nonconforming McMurphy teaches the other inmates that they do not have to conform to the rules set up by the hospital.

Faced with the problem of deviance, societies have initiated various activities and/or programs to control and/or eliminate it altogether, for the fact that deviance continues to exist is a threat to society's viability. In George Orwell's society in *1984* a very elaborate and inclusive method of controlling deviance is used so as to maintain certain social and cultural attributes.

The Stranger

Albert Camus

The problem of defining deviant behavior is one that every society faces, and various institutions have been established to handle this problem. One means used by society to define deviance is the judicial process such as the one Albert Camus relates in *The Stranger*. In this particular section of the book, the main character, a young man, has been accused of a deviant act, murder. The two lawyers present their arguments, the prosecution maintaining that the deed was a deviant one and the defense that it was not. As the lawyers make their arguments, the defendant himself begins to wonder if there really is a "right" or "wrong."

He began by summing up the facts, from my mother's death onward. He stressed my heartlessness, my inability to state Mother's age, my visit to the swimming pool where I met Marie, our matinee at the pictures where a Fernandel film was showing, and finally my return with Marie to my rooms. I didn't quite follow his remarks at first, as he kept on mentioning "the prisoner's mistress," whereas for me she was just "Marie." Then he came to the subject of Raymond. It seemed to me that his way of treating the facts showed a certain shrewdness. All he said sounded quite plausible. I'd written the letter in collusion with Raymond so as to entice his mistress to his room and subject her to ill-treatment by a man "of more than dubious reputation." Then, on the beach, I'd provoked a brawl with Raymond's enemies, in the course of which Raymond was wounded. I'd asked him for his revolver and gone back myself with the intention of using it. Then I'd shot the Arab. After the first shot I waited. Then, "to be certain of making a good job of it," I fired four more shots deliberately, point-blank, and in cold blood, at my victim.

"That is my case," he said. "I have described to you the series of events which led this man to kill the deceased, fully aware of what he was doing. I emphasize this point. We are not concerned with an act of homicide committed on a sudden impulse which might serve as extenuation. I ask you to note, gentlemen of the jury, that the prisoner is an educated man. You will have observed the way in which he answered my questions; he is intelligent and he knows the value of words. And I repeat that it is quite impossible to assume that, when he committed the crime, he was unaware what he was doing."

I noticed that he laid stress on my "intelligence." It puzzled me rather why what would count as a good point in an ordinary person should be used against an accused man as an overwhelming proof of his guilt. While thinking this over, I missed what he said next, until I heard him exclaim indignantly: "And has he uttered a word of regret for his most odious crime? Not one word, gentlemen. Not once in the course of these proceedings did this man show the least contrition."

Turning toward the dock, he pointed a finger at me, and went on in the same strain. I really couldn't understand why he harped on this point so much. Of course, I had to own that he was right; I didn't feel much regret for what I'd done. Still, to my mind he overdid it, and I'd have liked to have a chance of explaining to him, in a quite friendly, almost affectionate way, that I have never been able really to regret anything in all my life. I've always been far too much absorbed in the present moment, or the immediate future, to think back. Of course, in the position into which I had been forced, there was no question of my speaking to anyone in that tone. I hadn't the right to show any friendly feeling or possess good intentions. And I tried to follow what came next, as the Prosecutor was now considering what he called my "soul."

He said he'd studied it closely—and had found a blank, "literally nothing, gentlemen of the jury." Really, he said, I had no soul, there was nothing human about me, not one of those moral qualities which normal men possess had any place in my mentality. "No doubt," he added, "we should not reproach him with this. We cannot blame a man for lacking what it was never in his power to acquire. But in a criminal court the wholly passive ideal of tolerance must give place to a sterner, loftier ideal, that of justice. Especially when this lack of every decent instinct is such as that of the man before you, a menace to society." He proceeded to discuss my conduct toward my mother, repeating what he had said in the course of the hearing. But he spoke at much greater length of my crime—at such length, indeed, that I lost the thread and was conscious only of the steadily increasing heat.

A moment came when the Prosecutor paused and, after a short silence, said in a low, vibrant voice: "This same court, gentlemen, will be called on to try tomorrow that most odious of crimes, the murder of a father by his son." To his mind, such a crime was almost unimaginable. But, he ventured to hope, justice would be meted out without paltering. And yet, he made bold to say, the horror that even the crime of parricide inspired in him paled beside the loathing inspired by my callousness.

"This man, who is morally guilty of his mother's death, is no less unfit to have a place in the community than that other man who did to death the father that begat him. And, indeed, the one crime led on to the other; the first of these two criminals, the man in the dock, set a precedent, if I may put it so, and authorized the second crime. Yes, gentlemen, I am convinced"—here he raised his voice a tone—"that you will not find I am exaggerating the case against the prisoner when I say that he is also guilty of the murder to be tried tomorrow in this court. And I look to you for a verdict accordingly."

The Prosecutor paused again, to wipe the sweat off his face. He then explained that his duty was a painful one, but he would do it without flinching. "This man had, I repeat, no place in a community whose basic principles he flouts without compunction. Nor, heartless as he is, has he any claim to mercy. I ask you to impose the extreme penalty of the law; and I ask it without a qualm. In the course of a long career, in which it has often been my duty to ask for a capital sentence, never have I felt that painful duty weigh so little on my mind as in the present case. In demanding a verdict of murder without extenuating circumstances, I am following not only the dictates of my conscience and a sacred obligation, but also those of the natural and righteous indignation I feel at the sight of a criminal devoid of the least spark of human feeling."

When the Prosecutor sat down there was a longish silence. Personally I was quite overcome by the heat and my amazement at what I had been hearing. The presiding judge gave a short cough, and asked me in a very low tone if I had anything to say. I rose, and as I felt in the mood to speak, I said the first thing that crossed my mind: that I'd had no intention of killing the Arab. The Judge replied that this statement would be taken into consideration by the court. Meanwhile he would be glad to hear, before my counsel addressed the court, what were the motives of my crime. So far, he must admit, he hadn't fully understood the grounds of my defense.

I tried to explain that it was because of the sun, but I spoke too quickly and ran my words into each other. I was only too conscious that it sounded nonsensical, and, in fact, I heard people tittering.

My lawyer shrugged his shoulders. Then he was directed to address the court, in his turn. But all he did was to point out the lateness of the hour and to ask for an adjournment till the following afternoon. To this the judge agreed.

When I was brought back next day, the electric fans were still churning up the heavy air and the jurymen plying their gaudy little fans in a sort of steady rhythm. The speech for the defense seemed to me interminable. At one moment, however, I pricked up my ears; it was when I heard him saying: "It is true I killed a man." He went on in the same strain, saying "I"

when he referred to me. It seemed so queer that I bent toward the policeman on my right and asked him to explain. He told me to shut up; then,
after a moment, whispered: "They all do that." It seemed to me that the
idea behind it was still further to exclude me from the case, to put me off
the map, so to speak, by substituting the lawyer for myself. Anyway, it
hardly mattered; I already felt worlds away from this courtroom and its
tedious "proceedings."

My lawyer, in any case, struck me as feeble to the point of being
ridiculous. He hurried through his plea of provocation, and then he, too,
started in about my soul. But I had an impression that he had much less
talent than the Prosecutor.

"I, too," he said, "have closely studied this man's soul; but, unlike my
learned friend for the prosecution, I have found something there. Indeed, I
may say that I have read the prisoner's mind like an open book." What he
had read there was that I was an excellent young fellow, a steady, conscientious worker who did his best by his employer; that I was popular with
everyone and sympathetic in others' troubles. According to him I was a
dutiful son, who had supported his mother as long as he was able. After
anxious consideration I had reached the conclusion that, by entering a
home, the old lady would have comforts that my means didn't permit me to
provide for her. "I am astounded, gentlemen," he added, "by the attitude
taken up by my learned friend in referring to this Home. Surely if proof be
needed of the excellence of such institutions, we need only remember that
they are promoted and financed by a government department." I noticed
that he made no reference to the funeral, and this seemed to me a serious
omission. But, what with his long-windedness, the endless days and hours
they had been discussing my "soul," and the rest of it, I found that my mind
had gone blurred; everything was dissolving into a grayish, watery haze.

Only one incident stands out; toward the end, while my counsel ram-
bled on, I heard the tin trumpet of an ice-cream vendor in the street, a
small, shrill sound cutting across the flow of words. And then a rush of
memories went through my mind—memories of a life which was mine no
longer and had once provided me with the surest, humblest pleasures:
warm smells of summer, my favorite streets, the sky at evening, Marie's
dresses and her laugh. The futility of what was happening here seemed to
take me by the throat, I felt like vomiting, and I had only one idea: to get
it over, to go back to my cell, and sleep . . . and sleep.

Dimly I heard my counsel making his last appeal.

"Gentlemen of the jury, surely you will not send to his death a decent,
hard-working young man, because for one tragic moment he lost his self-

control? Is he not sufficiently punished by the lifelong remorse that is to be his lot? I confidently await your verdict, the only verdict possible—that of homicide with extenuating circumstances."

QUESTION

Can you identify several kinds of behavior that could be considered deviant in one situation but normal in another?

One Flew over the Cuckoo's Nest
Ken Kesey

One explanation for deviant behavior within a society is that this kind of behavior is learned. In the novel One Flew over the Cuckoo's Nest, Mc-Murphy, the main character, has convinced the legal and medical authorities that he is insane so that he can serve out his sentence for breaking the law in a mental hospital rather than on a work farm. However, once inside the hospital he finds that the head nurse dominates everyone, the staff as well as the patients. McMurphy sees this situation as a challenge and sets about to change it by getting the other patients to rebel against the nurse, her rules and policies.

I know how they work it, the fog machine. We had a whole platoon used to operate fog machines around airfields overseas. Whenever intelligence figured there might be a bombing attack, or if the generals had something secret they wanted to pull—out of sight, hid so good that even the spies on the base couldn't see what went on—they fogged the field.

It's a simple rig: you got an ordinary compressor sucks water out of one tank and a special oil out of another tank, and compresses them together, and from the black stem at the end of the machine blooms a white cloud of fig that can cover a whole airfield in ninety seconds. The first thing I saw when I landed in Europe was the fog those machines make. There were some interceptors close after our transport, and soon as it hit ground the fog crew started up the machines. We could look out the transport's round, scratched windows and watch the jeeps draw the machines up close to the plane and watch the fog boil out till it rolled across the field and stuck against the windows like wet cotton.

You found your way off the plane by following a little referees' horn the lieutenant kept blowing, sounded like a goose honking. Soon as you were out of the hatch you couldn't see no more than maybe three feet in any direction. You felt like you were out on that airfield all by yourself. You were safe from the enemy, but you were awfully alone. Sounds died and dissolved after a few yards, and you couldn't hear any of the rest of your crew, nothing but that little horn squeaking and honking out of a soft furry whiteness so thick that your body just faded into white below the belt; other than that brown shirt and brass buckle, you couldn't see nothing but white, like from the waist down you were being dissolved by the fog too

And then some guy wandering as lost as you would all of a sudden be right before your eyes, his face bigger and clearer than you ever saw a man's face before in your life. Your eyes were working so hard to see in that fog that when something did come in sight every detail was ten times as clear as usual, so clear both of you had to look away. When a man showed up you didn't want to look at his face and he didn't want to look at yours, because it's painful to see somebody so clear that it's like looking inside him, but then neither did you want to look away and lose him completely. You had a choice: you could either strain and look at things that appeared in front of you in the fog, painful as it might be, or you could relax and lose yourself.

When they first used that fog machine on the ward, one they bought from Army Surplus and hid in the vents in the new place before we moved in, I kept looking at anything that appeared out of the fog as long and hard as I could, to keep track of it, just like I used to do when they fogged the airfields in Europe. Nobody'd be blowing a horn to show the way, there was no rope to hold to, so fixing my eyes on something was the only way I kept from getting lost. Sometimes I got lost in it anyway, got in too deep, trying to hide, and every time I did, it seemed like I always turned up at that same place, at the same metal door with the row of rivets like eyes and no number, just like the room behind the door drew me to it, no matter how hard I tried to stay away, just like the current generated by the fiends in that room was conducted in a beam along the fog and pulled me back along it like a robot. I'd wander for days in the fog, scared I'd never see another thing, then there'd be that door, opening to show me the mattress padding on the other side to stop out the sounds, the men standing in a line like zombies among shiny copper wires and tubes pulsing light, and the bright scrape of arcing electricity. I'd take my place in the line and wait my turn at the table. The table shaped like a cross, with shadows of a thousand murdered men printed on it, silhouette wrists and ankles running under leather straps sweated green with use, a silhouette neck and head running up to a silver band goes across the forehead. And a technician at the controls beside the table looking up from his dials and down the line and pointing at me with a rubber glove. "Wait, I *know* that big bastard there—better rabbit-punch him or call for some more help or something. He's an awful case for thrashing around."

So I used to try not to get in too deep, for fear I'd get lost and turn up at the Shock Shop door. I looked hard at anything that came into sight and hung on like a man in a blizzard hangs on a fence rail. But they kept making the fog thicker and thicker, and it seemed to me that, no matter how hard I tried, two or three times a month I found myself with that door opening in front of me to the acid smell of sparks and ozone. In spite of all I could do, it was getting tough to keep from getting lost.

Then I discovered something: I don't have to end up at that door if I stay still when the fog comes over me and just keep quiet. The trouble was I'd been finding that door my own self because I got scared of being lost so long and went to hollering so they could track me. In a way, I was hollering for them *to* track me; I had figured that anything was better'n being lost for good, even the Shock Shop. Now, I don't know. Being lost isn't so bad.

All this morning I been waiting for them to fog us in again. The last few days they been doing it more and more. It's my idea they're doing it on account of McMurphy. They haven't got him fixed with controls yet, and they're trying to catch him off guard. They can see he's due to be a problem; a half a dozen times already he's roused Cheswick and Harding and some of the others to where it looked like they might actually stand up to one of the black boys—but always, just the time it looked like the patient might be helped, the fog would start, like it's starting now.

I heard the compressor start pumping in the grill a few minutes back, just as the guys went to moving tables out of the day room for the therapeutic meeting, and already the mist is oozing across the floor so thick my pant legs are wet. I'm cleaning the windows in the door of the glass station, and I hear the Big Nurse pick up the phone and call the doctor to tell him we're just about ready for the meeting, and tell him perhaps he'd best keep an hour free this afternoon for a Staff meeting. "The reason being," she tells him, "I think it is past time to have a discussion of the subject of Patient Randle McMurphy and whether he should be on this ward or not." She listens a minute, and tells him, "I don't think it's wise to let him go on upsetting the patients the way he has the last few days."

That's why she's fogging the ward for the meeting. She don't usually do that. But now she's going to do something with McMurphy today, probably ship him to Disturbed. I put down my window rag and go to my chair at the end of the line of Chronics, barely able to see the guys getting into their chairs and the doctor coming through the door wiping his glasses like he thinks the blurred look comes from his steamed lenses instead of the fog.

It's rolling in thicker than I ever seen it before.

I can hear them out there, trying to go on with the meeting, talking some nonsense about Billy Bibbit's stutter and how it came about. The words come to me like through water, it's so thick. In fact it's so much like water it floats me right up out of my chair and I don't know which end is up for a while. Floating makes me a little sick to the stomach at first. I can't see a thing. I never had it so thick it floated me like this.

The words get dim and loud, off and on, as I float around, but as loud as they get, loud enough sometimes I know I'm right next to the guy that's talking. I still can't see a thing.

I recognize Billy's voice, stuttering worse than ever because he's nervous. ". . . fuh-fuh-flunked out of college be-be-cause I quit ROTC. I c-c-couldn't take it. Wh-wh-wh-whenever the officer in charge of class would call roll, call 'Bibbit,' I couldn't answer. You were s-s-supposed to say heh-heh-heh . . ." He's choking on the word, like it's a bone in his throat. I hear him swallow and start again. "You were supposed to say, 'Here sir,' and I never c-c-could get it out."

His voice gets dim; then the Big Nurse's voice comes cutting from the left. "Can you recall, Billy, when you first had speech trouble? When did you first stutter, do you remember?"

I can't tell is he laughing or what. "Fir-first stutter? First stutter? The first word I said I st-stut-tered:m-m-m-m-mamma."

Then the talking fades out altogether; I never knew that to happen before. Maybe Billy's hid himself in the fog too. Maybe all the guys finally and forever crowded back into the fog.

A chair and me float past each other. It's the first thing I've seen. It comes sifting out of the fog off to my right, and for a few seconds it's right beside my face, just out of my reach. I have been accustomed of late to just let things alone when they appear in the fog, sit still and not try to hang on. But this time I'm scared, the way I used to be scared. I try with all I got to pull myself over to the chair and get hold of it, but there's nothing to brace against and all I can do is thrash the air, all I can do is watch the chair come clear, clearer than ever before to where I can even make out the fingerprint where a worker touched the varnish before it was dry, looming out for a few seconds, then fading on off again. I never seen it where things floated around this way. I never seen it this thick before, thick to where I can't get down to the floor and get on my feet if I wanted to and walk around. That's why I'm so scared; I feel I'm going to float off someplace for good this time.

I see a Chronic float into sight a little below me. It's old Colonel Matterson, reading from the wrinkled scripture of that long yellow hand. I look close at him because I figure it's the last time I'll ever see him. His face is enormous, almost more than I can bear. Every hair and wrinkle of him is big, as though I was looking at him with one of those microscopes. I see him so clear I see his whole life. The face is sixty years of southwest Army camps, rutted by iron-rimmed caisson wheels, worn to the bone by thousands of feet on two-day marches.

He holds out that long hand and brings it up in front of his eyes and squints into it, brings up his other hand and underlines the words with a finger wooden and varnished the color of a gunstock by nicotine. His voice is deep and slow and patient, and I see the words come out dark and heavy over his brittle lips when he reads.

"No . . . The flag is . . . Ah-mer-ica. America is . . . the plum. The peach. The wah-ter-mel-on. America is . . . the gumdrop. The pump-kin seed. America is . . . tell-ah-vision."

It's true. It's all wrote down on that yellow hand. I can read it along with him myself.

"Now . . . The cross is . . . Mex-i-co." He looks up to see if I'm paying attention, and when he sees I am he smiles at me and goes on. "Mexico is . . . the wal-nut. The hazelnut. The ay-corn. Mexico is . . . the rain-bow. The rain-bow is . . . wooden. Mexico is . . . woo-den."

I can see what he's driving at. He's been saying this sort of thing for the whole six years he's been here, but I never paid him any mind, figured he was no more than a talking statue, a thing made out of bone and arthritis, rambling on and on with these goofy definitions of his that didn't make a lick of sense. Now, at last, I see what he's saying. I'm trying to hold him for one last look to remember him, and that's what makes me look hard enough to understand. He pauses and peers up at me again to make sure I'm getting it, and I want to yell out to him Yes, I see: Mexico *is* like a walnut; it's brown and hard and you feel it with your eye and it *feels* like the walnut! You're making sense, old man, a sense of your own. You're not crazy the way they think. Yes . . . I see . . .

But the fog's clogged my throat to where I can't make a sound. As he sifts away I see him bend back over that hand.

"Now . . . The green sheep is . . . Can-a-da. Canada is . . . the fir tree. The wheat field. The cal-en-dar . . ."

I strain to see him drifting away. I strain so hard my eyes ache and I have to close them, and when I open them again the colonel is gone. I'm floating by myself again, more lost than ever.

This is the time, I tell myself. I'm going for good.

There's old Pete, face like a searchlight. He's fifty yards off to my left, but I can see him plain as though there wasn't any fog at all. Or maybe he's up right close and real small, I can't be sure. He tells me once about how tired he is, and just his saying it makes me see his whole life on the railroad, see him working to figure out how to read a watch, breaking a sweat while he tries to get the right button in the right hole of his railroad overalls, doing his absolute damnedest to keep up with a job that comes so easy to the others they can sit back in a chair padded with cardboard and read mystery stories and girlie books. Not that he ever really figured to keep up—he knew from the start he couldn't do that—but he had to try to keep up, just to keep them in sight. So for forty years he was able to live, if not right in the world of men, at least on the edge of it.

I can see all that, and be hurt by it, the way I was hurt by seeing things in the Army, in the war. The way I was hurt by seeing what happened to Papa and the tribe. I thought I'd got over seeing those things and fretting over them. There's no sense in it. There's nothing to be done.

"I'm tired," is what he says.

"I know you're tired, Pete, but I can't do you no good fretting about it. You know I can't."

Pete floats on the way of the old colonel.

Here comes Billy Bibbit, the way Pete come by. They're all filing by for a last look. I know Billy can't be more'n a few feet away, but he's so tiny he looks like he's a mile off. His face is out to me like the face of a beggar, needing so much more'n anybody can give. His mouth works like a little doll's mouth.

"And even when I pr-proposed, I flubbed it. I said 'Huh-honey, will you muh-muh-muh-muh-muh . . . ' till the girl broke out l-laughing."

Nurse's voice, I can't see where it comes from: "Your mother has spoken to me about this girl, Billy. Apparently she was quite a bit beneath you. What would you speculate it was about her that frightened you so, Billy?"

"I was in luh-love with her."

I can't do nothing for you either, Billy. You know that. None of us can. You got to understand that as soon as a man goes to help somebody, he leaves himself wide open. He *has* to be cagey, Billy, you should know that as well as anyone. What could I do? I can't fix your stuttering. I can't wipe the razor-blade scars off your wrists or the cigarette burns off the back of your hands. I can't give you a new mother. And as far as the nurse riding you like this, rubbing your nose in your weakness till what little dignity you got left is gone and you shrink up to nothing from humiliation, I can't do anything about that, either. At Anzio, I saw a buddy of mine tied to a tree fifty yards from me, screaming for water, his face blistered in the sun. They wanted me to try to go out and help him. They'd of cut me in half from the farmhouse over there.

Put your face away, Billy.

They kept filing past.

It's like each face was a sign like one of those "I'm Blind" signs the dago accordion players in Portland hung around their necks, only these signs say "I'm tired" or "I'm scared" or "I'm dying of a bum liver" or "I'm all bound up with machinery and people *pushing* me alla time." I can read all the signs, it don't make any difference how little the print gets. Some of the faces are looking around at one another and could read the other fellow's if they would, but what's the sense? The faces blow past in the fog like confetti.

I'm further off than I've ever been. This is what it's like to be dead. I guess this is what it's like to be a Vegetable; you lose yourself in the fog. You don't move. They feed your body till it finally stops eating; then they burn it. It's not so bad. There's no pain. I don't feel much of anything other than a touch of chill I figure will pass in time.

I see my commanding officer pinning notices on the bulletin board, what we're to wear today. I see the US Department of Interior bearing down on our little tribe with a gravel-crushing machine.

I see Papa come loping out of a draw and slow up to try and take aim at a big six-point buck springing off through the cedars. Shot after shot puffs out of the barrel, knocking dust all around the buck. I come out of the draw behind Papa and bring the buck down with my second shot just as it starts climbing the rimrock. I grin at Papa.

I never knew you to miss a shot like that before, Papa.

Eye's gone, boy. Can't hold a bead. Sights on my gun just now was shakin' like a dog shittin' peach pits.

Papa, I'm telling you: that cactus moon of Sid's is gonna make you old before your time.

A man drinks that cactus moon of Sid's, boy, he's already old before his time. Let's go gut that animal out before the flies blow him.

That's not even happening now. You see? There's nothing you can do about a happening out of the past like that.

Look there, my man . . .

I hear whispers, black boys.

Look there, that old fool Broom, slipped off to sleep.

That's right, Chief Broom, that's right. You sleep an' keep outa trouble Yasss.

I'm not cold any more. I think I've about made it. I'm off to where the cold can't reach me I can stay off here for good. I'm not scared any more. They can't reach me. Just the words reach me, and those're fading.

Well . . . in as much as Billy has decided to walk out on the discussion, does anyone else have a problem to bring before the group?

As a matter of fact, ma'am, there does happen to be something . . .

That's that McMurphy. He's far away. He's still trying to pull people out of the fog. Why don't he leave me be?

" . . . remember that vote we had a day or so back—about the TV time? Well, today's Friday and I thought I might just bring it up again, just to see if anybody else has picked up a little guts."

"Mr. McMurphy, the purpose of this meeting is therapy, group therapy, and I'm not certain these petty grievances—"

"Yeah, yeah, the hell with that, we've heard it before. Me and some of the rest of the guys decided—"

"One moment, Mr. McMurphy, let me pose a question to the group: do any of you feel that Mr. McMurphy is perhaps imposing his personal desires on some of you too much? I've been thinking you might be happier if he were moved to a different ward."

Nobody says anything for a minute. Then someone says, "Let him vote, why dontcha? Why ya want to ship him to Disturbed just for bringing up a vote? What's so wrong with changing time?"

"Why, Mr. Scanlon, as I recall, you refused to eat for three days until we allowed you to turn the set on at six instead of six-thirty."

"A man needs to see the world news, don't he? God, they coulda bombed Washington and it'd been a week before we'd of heard."

"Yes? And how do you feel about relinquishing your world news to watch a bunch of men play baseball?"

"We can't have both, huh? No, I suppose not. Well, what the dickens—I don't guess they'll bomb us this week."

"Let's let him have the vote, Miss Ratched."

"Very well. But I think this is ample evidence of how much he is upsetting some of you patients. What is it you are proposing, Mr. Mc-Murphy?"

"I'm proposing a revote on watching the TV in the afternoon."

"You're certain one more vote will satisfy you? We have more important things—"

"It'll satisfy me. I just'd kind of like to see which of these birds has any guts and which doesn't."

"It's that kind of talk, Doctor Spivey, that makes me wonder if the patients wouldn't be more content if Mr. McMurphy were moved."

"Let him call the vote, why dontcha?"

"Certainly, Mr. Cheswick. A vote is now before the group. Will a show of hands be adequate, Mr. McMurphy, or are you going to insist on a secret ballot?"

"I want to see the hands. I want to see the hands that don't go up, too."

"Everyone in favor of changing the television time to the afternoon, raise his hand."

The first hand that comes up, I can tell, is McMurphy's, because the bandage where that control panel cut into him when he tried to lift it. And then off down the slope I see them, other hands coming up out of the fog. It's like . . . that big red hand of McMurphy's is reaching into the fog and dropping down and dragging the men up by their hands, dragging them blinking into the open. First one, then another, then the next. Right on down the line of Acutes, dragging them out of the fog till there they stand, all twenty of them, raising not just for watching TV, but against the Big Nurse, against her trying to send McMurphy to Disturbed, against the way she's talked and acted and beat them down for years.

Nobody says anything. I can feel how stunned everybody is, the patients as well as the staff. The nurse can't figure what happened; yesterday, before he tried lifting that panel, there wasn't but four or five men might of voted. But when she talks she don't let it show in her voice how surprised she is.

"I count only twenty, Mr. McMurphy."

"Twenty? Well, why not? Twenty is all of us there—" His voice hangs as he realizes what she means. "Now hold on just a goddamned minute, lady—"

"I'm afraid the vote is defeated."

"Hold on just one goddamned *minute!*"

"There are forty patients on the ward, Mr. McMurphy. Forty patients, and only twenty voted. You must have a majority to change the ward policy. I'm afraid the vote is closed."

The hands are coming down across the room. The guys know they're whipped, are trying to slip back into the safety of the fog. McMurphy is on his feet.

"Well, I'll be a sonofabitch. You mean to tell me that's how you're gonna pull it? Count the votes of those old birds over there too??"

"Didn't you explain the voting procedure to him Doctor?"

"I'm afraid—a majority *is* called for, McMurphy. She's right, she's right."

"A majority, Mr. McMurphy; it's in the ward constitution."

"And I suppose the way to change the damned constitution is with a majority vote. Of all the chicken-shit things I've ever seen, this by God takes the *cake!*"

"I'm sorry, Mr. McMurphy, but you'll find it written in the policy if you'd care for me to—"

"So this's how you work this democratic bullshit—hell's bells!"

"You seem upset, Mr. McMurphy. Doesn't he seem upset, Doctor? I want you to note this."

"Don't give me that noise, lady. When a guy's getting screwed he's got a right to holler. And we've been damn well screwed."

"Perhaps, Doctor, in view of the patient's condition, we should bring this meeting to a close early today—"

"Wait! Wait a minute, let me talk to some of those old guys."

"The vote is closed, Mr. McMurphy."

"Let me talk to 'em."

He's coming across the day room at us. He gets bigger and bigger, and he's burning red in the face. He reaches into the fog and tries to drag Ruckly to the surface because Ruckly's the youngest.

"What about you, buddy? You want to watch the World Series? Baseball? Baseball games? Just raise that hand up there—"

Fffffffuck da wife."

"All right, forget it. You, partner, how about you? What was your name—Ellis? What do you say, Ellis, to watching a ball game on TV? Just raise your hand. . . ."

Ellis's hands are nailed to the wall, can't be counted as a vote.

"I said the voting is closed, Mr. McMurphy. You're just making a spectacle of yourself."

He don't pay any attention to her. He comes down the line of Chronics. "C'mon, c'mon, just one vote from you birds, just raise a hand. Show her you can still do it."

"I'm tired," says Pete and wags his head.

"The night is . . . the Pacific Ocean." The Colonel is reading off his hand, can't be bothered with voting.

"*One* of you guys, for cryin' out loud! This is where you get the edge, don't you see that? We have to do this—or we're *whipped!* Don't a one of you clucks know what I'm talking about enough to give us a hand? You, Gabriel? George? No? You, Chief, what about you?"

He's standing over me in the mist. Why won't he leave me be?

"Chief, you're our last bet."

The Big Nurse is folding her papers; the other nurses are standing up around her. She finally gets to her feet.

"The meeting is adjourned, then," I hear her say. "And I'd like to see the staff down in the staff room in about an hour. So, if there is nothing el—"

It's too late to stop it now. McMurphy did something to it that first day, put some kind of hex on it with his hand so it won't act like I order it. There's no sense in it, any fool can see; I wouldn't do it on my own. Just by the way the nurse is staring at me with her mouth empty of words I can see I'm in for trouble, but I can't stop it. McMurphy's got hidden wires hooked to it, lifting it slow just to get me out of the fog and into the open where I'm fair game. He's doing it, wires . . .

No. That's not the truth. I lifted it myself.

McMurphy whoops and drags me standing, pounding my back.

"Twenty-one! The Chief's vote makes it twenty-one! And by God if that ain't a majority I'll eat my hat!"

"Yippee," Cheswick yells. The other Acutes are coming across toward me.

"The meeting was closed," she says. Her smile is still there, but the back of her neck as she walks out of the day room and into the Nurses' Station, is red and swelling like she'll blow apart any second.

But she don't blow up, not right off, not until about an hour later. Behind the glass her smile is twisted and queer, like we've never seen before. She just sits. I can see her shoulders rise and fall as she breathes.

McMurphy looks up at the clock and he says it's time for the game. He's over by the drinking fountain with some of the other Acutes, down on his knees scouring off the baseboard. I'm sweeping out the broom closet for the tenth time that day. Scanlon and Harding, they got the buffer going up and down the hall, polishing the new wax into shining figure eights. Mc-Murphy says again that he guesses it must be game time and he stands up, leaves the scouring rag where it lies. Nobody else stops work. McMurphy walks past the window where she's glaring out at him and grins at her like he knows he's got her whipped now. When he tips his head back and winks at her she gives that little sideways jerk of her head.

Everybody keeps on at what he's doing, but they all watch out of the corners of their eyes while he drags his armchair out to in front of the TV set, then switches on the set and sits down. A picture swirls onto the screen of a parrot out on the baseball field singing razorblade songs. McMurphy gets up and turns up the sound to drown out the music coming down from the speaker in the ceiling, and he drags another chair in front of him and sits down and crosses his feet on the chair and leans back and lights a cigarette. He scratches his belly and yawns.

"How-*weee!* Man, all I need me now is a can of beer and a red-hot."

We can see the nurse's face get red and her mouth work as she stares at him. She looks around for a second and sees everybody watching what she's going to do—even the black boys and the little nurses sneaking looks at her, and the residents beginning to drift in for the staff meeting, they're watching. Her mouth clamps shut. She looks back at McMurphy and waits till the razor-blade song is finished; they she gets up and goes to the steel door where the controls are, and she flips a switch and the TV picture swirls back into the gray. Nothing is left on the screen but a little eye of light beading right down on McMurphy sitting there.

That eye don't faze him a bit. To tell the truth, he don't even let on he knows the picture is turned off; he puts his cigarette between his teeth and pushes his cap forward in his red hair till he has to lean back to see out from under the brim.

And sits that way, with his hands crossed behind his head and his feet stuck out in a chair, a smoking cigarette sticking out from under his hat-brim—watching the TV screen.

The nurse stands this as long as she can; then she comes to the door of the Nurses' Station and calls across to him he'd better help the men with the housework. He ignores her.

"I said, Mr. McMurphy, that you are supposed to be working during these hours." Her voice has a tight whine like an electric saw ripping through pine. "Mr. McMurphy, I'm *warning* you!"

Everybody's stopped what he was doing. She looks around her, then takes a step out of the Nurses' Station toward McMurphy.

"You're committed, you realize. You are . . . under the *jurisdiction* of me . . . the staff." She's holding up a fist, all those red-orange fingernails burning into her palm. "Under jurisdiction and *control—*"

Harding shuts off the buffer, and leaves it in the hall, and goes pulls him a chair up alongside McMurphy and sits down and lights him a cigarette too.

"Mr. Harding! You return to your scheduled duties!"

I think how her voice sounds like it hit a nail, and this strikes me so funny I almost laugh.

"Mr. Har-*ding!*"

Then Cheswick goes and gets him a chair, and then Billy Bibbit goes, and then Scanlon and then Fredrickson and Sefelt, and then we all put down our mops and brooms and scouring rags and we all go pull us chairs up.

"You *men*—Stop this. *Stop!*"

And we're all sitting there lined up in front of that blanked-out TV set, watching the gray screen just like we could see the baseball game clear as day, and she's ranting and screaming behind us.

If somebody'd of come in and took a look, men watching a blank TV, a fifty-year-old woman hollering and squealing at the back of their heads about discipline and order and recriminations, they'd of thought the whole bunch was crazy as loons.

QUESTION

What are some forms of deviant behavior that could be taught to you?

1984

George Orwell

No other work demonstrates more vividly a society dominated by a single force than George Orwell's *1984*. In this society the Party completely controls everything, and no form of deviance is tolerated. Winston, a member of the underground that wants to overthrow the Party, is apprehended and brought before a Party leader, O'Brien, for punishment. O'Brien, while punishing Winston, explains to him why deviance cannot be tolerated and why the Party must win.

"I told you, Winston," he said, "that metaphysics is not your strong point. The word you are trying to think of is solipsism. But you are mistaken. This is not solipsism. Collective solipsism, if you like. But that is a different thing; in fact, the opposite thing. All this is a digression," he added in a different tone. "The real power, the power we have to fight for night and day, is not power over things, but over men." He paused, and for a moment assumed again his air of a schoolmaster questioning a promising pupil: "How does one man assert his power over another, Winston?"

Winston thought. "By making him suffer," he said.

"Exactly. By making him suffer. Obedience is not enough. Unless he is suffering, how can you be sure that he is obeying your will and not his own?

Power is in inflicting pain and humiliation. Power is in tearing human minds to pieces and putting them together again in new shapes of your own choosing. Do you begin to see, then, what kind of world we are creating? It is the exact opposite of the stupid hedonistic Utopias that the old reformers imagined. A world of fear and treachery and torment, a world of trampling and being trampled upon, a world which will grow not less but *more* merciless as it refines itself. Progress in our world will be progress toward more pain. The old civilizations claimed that they were founded on love and justice. Ours is founded upon hatred. In our world there will be no emotions except fear, rage, triumph, and self-abasement. Everything else we shall destroy—everything. Already we are breaking down the habits of thought which have survived from before the Revolution. We have cut the links between child and parent, and between man and man, and between man and woman. No one dares trust a wife or a child or a friend any longer. But in the future there will be no wives and no friends. Children will be taken from their mothers at birth, as one takes eggs from a hen. The sex instinct will be eradicated. Procreation will be an annual formality like the renewal of a ration card. We shall abolish the orgasm. Our neurologists are at work upon it now. There will be no loyalty, except loyalty toward the Party. There will be no love, except the love of Big Brother. There will be no laughter, except the laugh of triumph over a defeated enemy. There will be no art, no literature, no science. When we are omnipotent we shall have no more need of science. There will be no distinction between beauty and ugliness. There will be no curiosity, no employment of the process of life. All competing pleasures will be destroyed. But always—do not forget this, Winston—always there will be the intoxication of power, constantly increasing and constantly growing subtler. Always, at every moment, there will be the thrill of victory, the sensation of trampling on an enemy who is helpless. If you want a picture of the future, imagine a boot stamping on a human face—forever."

He paused as though he expected Winston to speak. Winston had tried to shrink back into the surface of the bed again. He could not say anything. His heart seemed to be frozen. O'Brien went on:

"And remember that it is forever. The face will always be there to be stamped upon. The heretic, the enemy of society, will always be there, so that he can be defeated and humiliated over again. Everything that you have undergone since you have been in our hands—all that will continue, and worse. The espionage, the betrayals, the arrests, the tortures, the executions, the disappearances will never cease. It will be a world of terror as much as a world of triumph. The more the Party is powerful, the less it will be tolerant; the weaker the opposition, the tighter the despotism. Goldstein and his heresies will live forever. Every day, at every moment, they will be defeated, discredited, ridiculed, spat upon—and yet they will always survive. This drama that I have played out with you during seven years will be played out over and over again, generation after generation, always in subtler forms. Always we shall have the heretic here at our mercy, screaming with pain, broken up, contemptible—and in the end utterly penitent, saved from himself, crawling to our feet of his own accord. That is the world that we are preparing, Winston. A world of victory after victory, triumph after triumph after triumph: an endless pressing, pressing, pressing upon the nerve of power. You are beginning, I can see, to realize what that world will be like. But in the end you will do more than understand it. You will accept it, welcome it, become part of it."

Winston had recovered himself sufficiently to speak. "You can't!" he said weakly.

"What do you mean by that remark, Winston?"

"You could not create such a world as you have just described. It is a dream. It is impossible."

"Why?"

"It is impossible to found a civilization on fear and hatred and cruelty. It would never endure."

"Why not?"

"It would have no vitality. It would disintegrate. It would commit suicide."

"Nonsense. You are under the impression that hatred is more exhausting than love. Why should it be? And if it were, what difference would that make? Suppose that we choose to wear ourselves out faster. Suppose that we quicken the tempo of human life till men are senile at thirty. Still what difference would it make? Can you not understand that the death of the individual is not death? The Party is immortal."

As usual, the voice had battered Winston into helplessness. Moreover he was in dread that if he persisted in his disagreement O'Brien would twist the dial again. And yet he could not keep silent. Feebly, without arguments, with nothing to support him except his inarticulate horror of what O'Brien had said, he returned to the attack.

"I don't know—I don't care. Somehow you will fail. Something will defeat you. Life will defeat you."

"We control life, Winston, at all its levels. You are imagining that there is something called human nature which will be outraged by what we do and will turn against us. But we create human nature. Men are infinitely malleable. Or perhaps you have returned to your old idea that the proletarians or the slaves will arise and overthrow us. Put it out of your mind. They are helpless, like the animals. Humanity is the Party. The others are outside—irrelevant."

QUESTION

If deviance is controlled too rigidly, what happens to the role of the individual in society?

Chapter 8

Collective Behavior

Riots, mobs, social movements, and public opinion that crowd the mass media are all examples of what sociologists call collective behavior. For the most part this concept refers to a noninstitutionalized form of behavior in which large numbers of people act together with respect to some common goal or object of interest. Its form may differ from a revolutionary social movement to a small crowd. As such, the role of collective behavior is very important in any study of society.

Perhaps the most elementary form of collective behavior is that of a crowd. In a crowd people are anonymous and have little or no fear of doing things that they would not normally do as individuals or in a small group. One explanation given for this phenomenon is called social contagion or circular reaction. This idea expresses the view that people in a crowd are more susceptible to suggestions of any kind due to the fact that there is an air of excitement and undefined rules of behavior. This idea of social contagion or circular reaction is vividly portrayed in the excerpt from *The Ox-Bow Incident*.

Another type of collective behavior is the charismatic leader of a social movement. Society has many ills, and there are people who want to correct them but lack the leadership necessary to accomplish that goal. A leader emerges and, by the force of his personality and some bold and dramatic acts, he becomes the symbol of the movement. *The Minister* by Charles Mercer is a novel about such a leader and his quest to eradicate the evils of society.

The Ox-Bow Incident

Walter Van Tilburg Clark

The concept of social contagion or circular reaction is plainly demonstrated in this scene from *The Ox-Bow Incident*. Art Croft and his friend
Gil, a couple of drifters, find themselves involved in a lynching party
which was precipitated by the announcement of the presumed murder of
Larry Kincaid. With emotions running high, the crowd sets out to find
those responsible for this deed and hang them. They are successful in
their quest and, despite the protests and pleas of the three men they
captured, nothing can change or deter the crowd from carrying out the
previously determined verdict and sentence.

The Mexican's courage, and even, in a way, young Martin's pride in the
matter of the letter, had won them much sympathy, and I think we all
believe now that the old man was really a pitiful fool, but whatever we
thought, there was an almost universal determination to finish the job now.
The gun was a clincher with us.

All but Davies. Davies was trying to get other men to read the letter.
He maintained stronger than ever that young Martin was innocent, that
Martin was not the kind of a man who could either steal or kill. He worked
on those of us who had shown some sympathy with his ideas before. He
tried hard not to let Tetley notice what he was doing, to stand naturally
when he talked, and not to appear too earnest to a person who couldn't
hear him. But he didn't make much headway. Most of the men had made
up their minds, or felt that the rest had and that their own sympathy was
reprehensible and should be concealed. That was the way I felt. None of us
would look at the letter. When he came to us, telling us to read the letter,
Gil said, "I don't want to read the letter. It's none of my business. You
heard the kid; you ought to remember if anybody does."

"Do you suppose it matters to his wife who sees this letter?" Davies
said. "In her place which would you rather have, a live husband with some
of his secrets with you revealed, or a dead husband and all your secrets still?

"I don't like to pry any more than you do," he insisted, "but you can't
put a life against a scruple. I tell you, if you'll read this letter you'll know he
couldn't have done it; not any of it. And if the letter's a fake we have only
to wait to know, don't we?"

It wasn't long until daylight, and the men hadn't really settled down

again, but were moving around in groups, talking and smoking. Still, I
thought Tetley was watching us.

"That must be some letter." Gil was saying.

Davies held it out to him. "Read it," he pleaded.

"You get Martin to ask me to read it and I will," Gil told him, grinning.

"Then you read it," Davies said, turning to me. Gil was watching me
still grinning.

"No," I said, "I'd rather not." I was curious to read that letter, but I
couldn't, there, like that.

Davies stood and looked from one to the other of us, despairingly.

"Do you want that kid to hang?" he asked finally.

"You can't change rustlin' and murder," Gil said.

"Never mind that," Davies said. "Don't think about anything but the
way you really feel about it. Do you feel that you'd like to have that kid
hanged; any of them, for that matter?"

"My feelings haven't got anything to do with it," Gil said.

Davies began to argue to show us that feelings did; that they were the
real guide in a thing like this, when Tetley called out to him by name.
Everyone looked at Tetley and Davies, and stopped moving around or
talking.

"Don't you know a trick when you see one, Davies?" Tetley asked him,
for all of us to hear. "Or are you in on this?"

Davies retorted that he knew a trick as well as the next man, and that
Tetley himself knew that this wasn't any trick; yes, and that Tetley knew
he'd had no part in any such games himself. He was defiant, and stated
again, defiantly, his faith in the innocence of the three men. But he talked
hurriedly, defensively, and finally stopped of his own accord at a point that
was not a conclusion. Whatever else was weakening him, I believe he felt all
the time that it was ugly to talk so before the men themselves, that his own
defense sounded no prettier there than Tetley's side. Then too, he had little
support, and he knew it. He knew it so well that, when he had faltered to
silence, and Tetley asked him, "Are you alone in this, Davies?" he said
nothing.

"I think we'd better get this settled," Tetley said. "We must act as a
unit in a job like this. Then we need fear no mistaken reprisal. Are you
content to abide by a majority decision, Davies?"

Davies looked him in the face, but even that seemed to be an effort. He
wouldn't say anything.

"How about the rest of you men?" Tetley asked, "Majority rule?"

There were sounds of assent. Nobody spoke out against it.

"It has to," Ma said. "Among a bunch of pigheads like this you'd never get everybody to agree to anything."

"We'll vote," Tetley said. "Everybody who is with Mr. Davies for putting this thing off and turning it over to the courts, step out here." He pointed to a space among us on the south side of the fire.

Davies walked out there and stood. Nobody else came for a moment, and he flushed when Tetley smiled at him. Then Sparks shambled out too, but smiling apologetically. Then Gerald Tetley joined them. His fists were clenched as he felt the watching, and saw his father's sardonic smile disappear slowly until his face was a stern mask. There was further movement, and some muttering, as Carl Bartlett and Moore stood out with them also. No more came.

"Five," said Tetley. "Not a majority, I believe, Mr. Davies."

He was disappointed that anyone had ventured to support Davies; I'm sure he hadn't expected as many as four others. I know I hadn't. And he was furious that Gerald had been among them. But he spoke quietly and ironically, as if his triumph had been complete.

Davies nodded, and slowly put Martin's letter away in his shirt pocket, under his waistcoat.

It was already getting light; the cabin and the trees could be seen clearly. There was no sunrise, but a slow leaking in of light from all quarters. The firelight no longer colored objects or faces near it. The faces were gray and tired and stern. We knew it was going to happen now, and yet, I believe, most of us still had a feeling it couldn't. It had been delayed so long; we had argued so much. Only Tetley seemed entirely self-possessed; his face showed no signs of weariness or excitement.

He asked Martin if there was any other message he wished to leave. Martin shook his head. In this light his face looked hollow, pale, and without individuality. His mouth was trembling constantly, and he was careful not to talk. I hoped, for our sake as much as his, that he'd make the decent end he now had his will set on.

Sparks was talking to the old fool again, but he, seeing the actual preparations begin, was frightened sick once more, and babbled constantly in a hoarse, worn-out voice, about his innocence, his age and his not wanting to die. Again and again he begged Martin to do something. This, more than anything else, seemed to shake Martin. He wouldn't look at old Hardwick, and pretended not to hear him.

We were surprised that the Mex wanted to make a confession, but he did. There wasn't any priest, so Amigo was to hear the confession, and carry it to a priest the first time he could go himself. There couldn't be any forgiveness, but it was the best they could do. They went down to the place where the sheds had stood, the Mex limping badly, and Amigo half carrying him along. Bartlett was stationed at a respectful distance as sentinel. We saw the Mex try to kneel, but he couldn't, so he stood there confessing with his back to us. Occasionally his hands moved in gestures of apology, which seemed strange from him. Amigo was facing us; but, when he wants, Amigo has a face like a wooden Indian. If the Mex was saying anything we ought to know now, which was what we were all thinking, we couldn't tell it from watching Amigo. He appeared merely to be intent upon remembering, in order that all the Mex's sins might be reported and forgiven.

In his field-officer manner Tetley was directing. Farnley knotted and threw up three ropes, so they hung over the long branch with the three nooses in a row. Then others staked down the ends of the ropes. The three horses were brought up again, and held under the ropes.

Tetley appointed Farnley, Gabe Hart and Gerald to whip the horses out. It was all right with Farnley, but Gabe refused. He gave no excuse, but stood there immovable, shaking his head. I was surprised Tetley had picked him.

"Gabe's not agin us, Mr. Tetley," Winder apologized,—"he can't stand to hurt anything. It would work on his mind."

Tetley asked for a volunteer, and when no one else came forward Ma took the job. She was furious about it, though. Moore looked at Smith, and so did Tetley, but Smith pretended to be drunker than he really was. Really he was scared sober now.

When it seemed all settled, young Tetley, nearly choking, refused also.

"You'll do it," was all Tetley told him.

"I can't, I tell you."

"We'll see to it you can."

The boy stood there, very white, still shaking his head.

"It's a necessary task," Tetley told him, evenly. "Someone else must perform it if you fail. I think you owe it to the others, and to yourself, on several scores."

The boy still shook his head stubbornly.

Moore, although he had refused on his own account, came over to Tetley and offered to relieve Gerald. "The boy's seen too much already. You shouldn't press him, man."

Tetley's face abruptly became bloodless; his mouth stretched downward, long and thin and hard, and his eyes glimmered with the fury he restrained. It was the first time I'd ever seen him let that nature show through, though I had felt always that it was there. He still spoke quietly though, and evenly.

"This is not your affair, Moore. Thank you just the same."

Moore shrugged and turned his back on him. He was angry himself.

Tetley said to Gerald, "I'll have no female boys bearing my name. You'll do your part, and say nothing more." He turned away, giving the boy no opportunity to reply.

"That must have been a very busy life," he remarked, looking down where the Mex was still confessing to Amigo.

When at last the Mex was done and they came back up, and the three prisoners were stood in a row with their hands tied down, Martin said,

"I suppose it's no use telling you again that we're innocent?"

"No good," Tetley assured him.

"It's not for myself I'm asking," Martin said.

"Other men have had families and have had to go for this sort of thing," Tetley told him. "It's too bad, but it's not our fault."

"You don't care for justice," Martin flared. "You don't even care whether you've got the right men or not. You want your way, that's all. You've lost something and somebody's got to be punished; that's all you know."

When Tetley just smiled, Martin's control broke again. "There's nobody to take care of them; they're in a strange place, they have nothing, and there's nobody to take care of them. Can't you understand that, you butcher? You've got to let me go; if there's a spot of humanity in you, you've got to let me go. Send men with me if you want to; I'm not asking you to trust me; you wouldn't trust anybody; your kind never will. Send men with me, then, but let me see them, let me arrange for them to go somewhere, for somebody to help them."

Old Hardwick began to whimper and jabber aloud again, and finally buckled in the knees and fell forward on his face. The Mex looked straight ahead of him and spit with contempt. "This is fine company for a man to die with," he said.

Martin started to yell something at the Mex, who was right beside him, but Mapes walked up to him and slapped him in the face. He slapped him hard, four times, so you could hear it like the crack of a lash. He paid no attention to protests or to Davies trying to hold his arm. After the fourth blow he waited to see if Martin would say anything more. He didn't, but stood there, crying weakly and freely, great sobs heaving his chest up and making him lift his chin to catch his breath because of the bonds.

Others put the old man back on his feet, and a couple of shots of whisky were given to each of the three. Then they walked them over to the horses. The old man went flabby on them, and they had nearly to carry him.

I saw Davies keeping Amigo behind, holding him by the arm and talking. Amigo's face was angry and stubborn, and he kept shaking his head. Tetley saw it too, and guessed what I had. Smiling, he told Davies that a confession was a confession, and not evidence, even in a court.

"He doesn't have to tell us," Davies said. "All he has to do is say whether we'd better wait; then we could find out."

Amigo looked worried.

Tetley said, "Men have been known to lie, even in confession, under pressure less than this." Amigo looked at him as if for the first time he questioned his divinity, but then he said, "It wasn't a priest; I don't know."

"Even if it had been," Tetley said, eying the Mex. "I'll give you two minutes to pray," he told the three. They were standing by the horses now, under the branch with the ropes hanging down from it.

Martin was chewing his mouth to stop crying. He looked around at us quickly. We were in a fairly close circle; nobody would face him, man after man looked down. Finally, like he was choking, he ducked his head, then, awkwardly because of the rope, got to his knees. The Mex was still standing, but had his head bent and was moving his lips rapidly. The old man was down in a groveling heap with Sparks beside him; Sparks was doing the praying for him. Moore took off his hat, and then the rest of us did the same. After a moment Davies and some of the others knelt also. Most of us couldn't bring ourselves to do that, but we all bowed and kept quiet. In the silence, in the gray light slowly increasing, the moaning of the old man, Sparks' praying and the Mex going again and again through his rapid patter sounded very loud. Still you could hear every movement of the horses, leather creaking, the little clinks of metal.

"Time's up," Tetley said, and the old man wailed once, as if he'd been hit. The Mex lifted his head and glanced around quickly. His face had a new expression, the first we'd seen of it in him. Martin rose slowly to his feet, and looked around slowly. The moments of silence and the crisis had had the reverse effect on him. He no longer appeared desperate or incoherent, but neither did he look peaceful or resigned. I have never seen another face so bitter as his was then, or one that showed its hatred more clearly. He spoke to Davies, but even his voice proved the effort against his pride and detestation.

"Will you find someone you can trust to look out for my wife and children?" he asked. "In time she will repay anything it puts you out."

Davies' eyes were full of tears. "I'll find someone," he promised.

"You'd better take some older woman along," Martin said. "It's not going to be easy."

"Don't worry," Davies said, "your family will be all right."

"Thanks," Martin said. Then he said, "My people are dead, but Miriam's are living. They live in Ohio. And Drew didn't want to sell his cattle; he'll buy them back for enough to cover their travel."

Davies nodded.

"Better not give her my things," Martin said, "just this ring, if you'll get it."

Davies fumbled at the task. He had trouble with the rope, and his hands were shaking, but he got the ring, and held it up for Martin to see. Martin nodded. "Just give her that and my letter first. Don't talk to her until she's read my letter." He didn't seem to want to say any more.

"That all?" Tetley asked.

"That's all, thanks," Martin said.

They asked the Mex, and he suddenly started speaking very rapidly. He was staring around as if he couldn't quite see us. It had got to him finally, all right. Then he stopped speaking just as suddenly and kept shaking his head in little short shakes. He'd been talking in Spanish. They didn't ask the old man.

The three of them were lifted onto the horses and made to stand on them. Two men had to support old Hardwick.

"Tie their ankles," Mapes ordered.

"God," Gil whispered, "I was afraid they weren't going to." He felt it a great relief that their ankles were going to be tied.

Farnley got up on a horse and fixed the noose around each man's neck. Then he and Ma got behind two of the horses with quirts in their hands. Young Tetley had to be told twice to get behind his. Then he moved to his place like a sleepwalker, and didn't even know he had taken the quirt somebody put in his hand.

The old man, on the inside, was silent, staring like a fish, and already hanging on the rope a little in spite of the men holding him up. The Mex had gone to pieces too, buckling nearly as badly as Hardwick, and jabbering rapid and panicky in Spanish. When the horses sidled under him once, tightening the rope, he screamed. In the pinch Martin was taking it the best of the three. He kept his head up, not looking at any of us, and even the bitterness was gone from his face. He had a melancholy expression, such as goes with thinking of an old sorrow.

Tetley moved around behind the horses, and directed Mapes to give the signal. We all moved out of the circle to give the horses room. In the last second even the Mex was quiet. There was no sound save the shifting of the three horses, restless at having been held so long. A feathery, wide-apart snow was beginning to sift down again; the end of a storm, not the beginning of another, though. The sky was becoming transparent, and it was full daylight.

Mapes fired one shot, and we heard it echo in the mountain as Ma and Farnley cut their horses sharply across the haunches and the holders let go and jumped away. The horses jumped away too, and the branch creaked under the jerk. The old man and the Mex were dead at the fall, and just swung and spun slowly. But young Tetley didn't cut. His horse just walked out from under, letting Martin slide off and dangle, choking to death, squirming up and down like an impaled worm, his face bursting with compressed blood. Gerald didn't move even then, but stood there shaking all over and looking up at Martin fighting the rope.

After a second Tetley struck the boy with the butt of his pistol, a back-handed blow that dropped him where he stood.

"Shoot him," he ordered Farnley, pointing at Martin. Farnley shot. Martin's body gave a little leap in the air, then hung slack, spinning slowly around and back, and finally settling into the slowing pendulum swing of the others.

Gil went with Davies to help young Tetley up. Nobody talked much, or looked at anybody else, but scattered and mounted. Winder and Moore caught up the rustlers' ponies. The Bartlett boys and Amigo remained to drive the cattle, and to do the burying before they started. All except Mapes and Smith shied clear of Tetley, but he didn't seem to notice. He untied his big palomino, mounted, swung him about and let off toward the road. His face was set and white; he didn't look back.

Most of the rest of us did, though, turn once or twice to look. I was glad when the last real fall of the snow started, soft and straight and thick. It lasted only a few minutes, but it shut things out.

QUESTION

Had you been in the lynching party would you have done what they did, or how would you have stopped them?

The Minister

Charles Mercer

A social movement, one form of collective behavior, is sometimes hampered by a lack of a force to unify and lead the movement. Often this force can come in the form of a charismatic leader, a person whose personality ignites and stimulates the movement. More often than not, this type of person becomes the personification of the movement.

Such a person is David Murchison in *The Minister*. While leading a civil rights crusade in Alabama, David manages to keep the workers' morale up, particularly Kathy Judson's, a new recruit, by his spiritual, physical, and mental powers. Note, too, how the movement and Murchison become one and the same.

Name: Katherine Judson. Age: twenty-one. Home: New York City. Occupation: junior, Wellesley College, Wellesley, Massachusetts. Affiliation: Student Nonviolent Coordinating Committee.

In the heat and turmoil of the Nashville bus terminal the young, bespectacled black took down the information carefully, then looked Kathy up and down. "Honey, you sure you're twenty-one?"

"I will be in a few days."

He grinned. "So you want to spend your birthday in jail. You doing this to duck your year's finals?"

"I finished them yesterday," Kathy said. "I had to fly to get here on time."

"Plenty of time," the black said. "This bus don't keep much of a schedule. The drivers keep funkin' out. So you're a SNICK." Thus the Student Nonviolent Coordinating Committee was called. "We got five SNICK's, eight CORE's, three SCLC's, seven independents, and not a single N double ACP." He looked around at the next bench. "Suzie Polk over there's a SNICK from Howard. Hey, Suzie!" he yelled above the din at a stout young Negro woman. "Here's an ofay to keep you company."

Suzie Polk treated Kathy coolly. What was SNICK doing at Wellesley? Kathy sometimes had wondered herself. A gang of Nashville white youths, jeering and yelling obscenities at the group planning an integrated bus ride to Montgomery, Alabama, made conversation almost impossible anyway. When a couple of youths began throwing tomatoes, shirt-sleeved sheriff's deputies stepped in front of the gang and said, "Cut it out, boys, now just take it easy." Kathy wanted to tell Suzie that *this* was why she had come here, that they were sisters, that all citizens must have equal rights. But of course, those sentiments, which had seemed convincing on the Wellesley campus, would have sounded banal in the Nashville bus terminal.

"There's Dave Murchison." Suzie pointed to a tall, husky-looking young white man who had just come in carrying an airline flight bag and was being greeted warmly by a couple of the black leaders. "He's one ofay Dr. King trusts. Last year during the Greensboro sit-ins he spent a week in jail."

Kathy found it hard to believe. She thought him sort of handsome in an Ivy League biscuit-cutter way: cropped hair, lean face, deadpan demeanor. He stared at her over the heads of the blacks, then made his way to her.

"I'm Dave Murchison. Who are you?"

"Kathy Judson, New York."

He sat down beside her. "I'm at Union Seminary."

Suddenly he interested her. "My father's a minister in New York."

He looked at her more closely. "Martin Judson?" Yes. "Martin Judson of Old Fourth," he said slowly. "So we have a daughter of the Protestant Establishment with us."

She narrowed her eyelids at him. "What Establishment are you talking about, preacher boy?"

He grinned suddenly. "The New York Protestant Establishment begins at the Cathedral and goes south to Trinity at Wall, then curves through the prettier parts of Long Island and up into Westchester. They wear the sword of liberalism but take care never to join any expedition south of the Mason-Dixon Line."

Father a member of the Protestant Establishment? It was ridiculous. Because he had pulled Old Fourth up by its bootstraps and built it into a strong church, he apparently had become a target for the little preacher boys. Good heavens, Father was a radical! When she had phoned him from Wellesley and asked for money to join the freedom ride, he had not demurred for an instant. "I'll send a check right away, Kathy. Glad you want to act on your convictions. Just do me one favor. If you land in jail and SNICK doesn't have the bail money promptly, send me a wire."

At last they climbed on the bus, and Kathy sat down beside Suzie. David Murchison took the seat across the aisle from Kathy. As the bus rolled through the suburbs of Nashville, he talked endlessly, practically telling her the story of his life.

He had been graduated from the University of Michigan, where he had worked at trying to be a writer. "Only thing wrong with that is I don't have any real talent for it." Then why Union Theological? His answer to her question was vague.

"Well, maybe just to irritate my old man. He's dead and doesn't know it. Dead and buried in Scarsdale. I hadn't seen him in three years when I tried to raise some money from him to go to Union. Gosh, it made him mad. He hates Christianity—everything, me included. Says I'm a goddamn Communist."

His father and mother had divorced when he was fifteen, and now she was married to a kooky art dealer and living in Paris. It was his mother who financed him at Union. "She'd like to spoil me. Compensation, I suppose, for walking out on the old bastard in Scarsdale and going off with the art dealer." Did he hate her, too? "No. I sort of like her and feel sorry for her."

There were six white and seventeen black passengers on the bus which sped south through a parched-looking land of yellow clay. The country was as Kathy had expected from her reading about the South. But the atmosphere in the bus was wholly unexpected. In Wellesley and Boston she had heard much about the warm fraternity of fighters for civil rights, but on this bus there was a restraint amounting to coolness between blacks and whites. Dave, a veteran of the new civil war, was the only white whom the blacks trusted fully.

Early in the afternoon the bus stopped where there was a roadside stand, a dilapidated house above a clay bank, a mangy dog asleep in the dust. An old man began padlocking an outhouse as Kathy walked to the stand where a thin woman with a weathered face stared at her grimly. There was nothing to eat, nothing to drink, the woman cried shrilly.

Dave shared his sandwiches and thermos of iced tea with Kathy, who had not thought to bring food or drink. After they climbed onto the bus, he sat down beside her and at once fell asleep. She marveled at him. When she remembered having read that instant sleep was a capacity possessed by most persons who fought oppressive society, she even began to admire him. In midafternoon the black leader called to him, and he awakened as instantaneously as he had slept.

Following a short conference with Dave, the leader addressed the riders. Montgomery was their destination, but first they must pass through Birmingham. He advised them to segregate themselves by color, remain passive, and not try to leave the bus when it paused at the Birmingham terminal. "But Dave has other ideas. He's going to tell you his, and you're free to act as you please. After all, this is a *freedom* ride."

Dave's voice rose easily, and Kathy realized he must be a persuasive public speaker. "My thought is that the Battle of Montgomery is no more important than the Battle of Birmingham. In fact, the more Southern battlefields the better. I think the police may stop us at the Birmingham city limits and arrest any who refuse to segregate their seats. Personally, this ofay plans to get arrested. They say the Birmingham city jail has nice clean sheets and ice cold drinks." There were jeering cheers. "Is there a black man on this bus willing to go to jail with me?" After a lengthy silence a young CORE man said he would be honored. "Anybody else want to see how the better half lives in a Southern jail?"

Kathy wondered if he was gazing at her. Remembering suddenly a line from one of her childhood prayers—"Let's get on with it, Lord"—she stood up.

Dave smiled at her and called, "Bless thee, Katherine, in the names of Peter, Titus and Paul. Kathy Judson of New York is looking for a cellmate. Any takers?"

Suzie looked around at her and exclaimed, "Well, I'll be! Come sit with me, Kathy."

"You're a pretty dispirited-looking bunch," Dave said. "Let's put some oil on this tired machine. Let's *lubricate* democracy and make freedom hum. Everybody remembers that rascal John Brown. . . ."

As he led them in the well-known song, Kathy thought: *My gosh, an old-time Gospel singing preacher, turned inside out and twisted all around, with different aims and a language part new, part old, but all tuned to strange ears.*

Half an hour later, as they entered Birmingham, the wailing of a police siren made her neck chill. The driver pulled to the side and stopped the bus. Kathy, thinking of what she had heard about Southern police brutality, was scared. Yet she had asked for whatever might happen to her, so there was no reason to William Blake it and think with the poet: "and the bitter groan of a martyr's woe/Is an arrow from the Almighty's bow."

To her surprise, the policeman who stepped onto the bus was young, good-looking. In a courteous tone he said they had entered the city limits of Birmingham. Then he recited the local ordinance on segregation of bus riders and asked them to conform with the law. When Kathy, Dave and their black seat partners failed to move, the policeman said he would have to take them into custody. Unprotesting, they left the bus with him. Kathy and Suzie rode to police headquarters in the rear seat of one squad car while Dave and his companion rode in another.

At headquarters they pleaded guilty and were booked. After searching through a sheaf of papers, a lieutenant said Dave and his seat companion had criminal records; if they could not post bail of one thousand dollars each, they would be remanded to jail. Dave laughed, and they were led away. Suzie's bail was set at five hundred dollars, and she left with a matron.

"Now look here," the lieutenant said to Kathy. Why should a nice girl like her mess around in things that didn't affect her? It was the most paternal lecture she ever had received. Repent—and go home. She thought of a couple of eloquent remarks but could not bring herself to make them. Instead, she insisted she was guilty, and lacking five hundred dollars' bail, she followed the matron to a reasonably clean cell in the women's block.

A drunken woman yammered down the block, and two cockroaches paraded on the ceiling. After a while Suzie called out her name, and Kathy answered. Having anticipated arrest, Kathy had brought along a paperback edition of *Walden,* which she had started twice in years past but never finished. Now, beginning it again while curled up on her cot, she found herself understanding for the first time why Thoreau went to the pond.

Around six o'clock the matron brought her corned-beef hash, bread, and canned peaches. When she came for the dishes, she lingered for a long time—not to converse, but to lecture. What did Kathy think she was accomplishing? On and on the matron ranted. Didn't she at least want to notify her parents so they could bail her out? No, she had given the lieutenant money for a telegram notifying SNICK headquarters of Suzie's and her arrests, but she was beginning to wonder if the telegram had been sent.

Later in the evening five women who had been on the bus were brought into the block. They said there had been roughing at the bus terminal, and they had been put under something called protective custody. Kathy slept poorly, and the next day she began to understand why the verb "languish" applied to jail. After finishing *Walden,* she started it again and found that the pond had grown stagnant to her.

On the second morning, following a breakfast of bread, powdered eggs, and coffee, she and the six black women riders were taken to the room where they had been arraigned. Two black men riders were brought from their cells and joined them. Kathy inquired about Dave, but the men did not know what had become of him. When the nine were led out and placed by threes in three police cars, she assumed they were being taken to court.

But the cars sped north out of Birmingham along the highway which the freedom riders had followed into the city two days previously. At last Kathy asked, "Where are we going?" Neither of the two policemen in the front seat answered her. It was bewildering and a little frightening, like being caught up in a Kafka creation in which the subject could not relate to the object. She had been arrested and jailed under due process of law, but now the authorities were violating law as flagrantly as the freedom riders. On the police cars raced for what seemed hours.

At last the car began to slow down on a lonely stretch of road fringed by clay banks and pine barrens. When they stopped, one of the policemen spoke for the first time: "Get out!" The woman beside Kathy began to shake and weep. Her terror was infectious, raising unreasonable images of the law gone berserk, of massacre by police guns on the hot and piny clay. Kathy's legs shook as she climbed out.

The policemen stared out at her contemptuously, ignoring the blacks. "This is the state line," one said. "Start walking, and never come back to Alabama."

As they walked north in the heat, cars passed them in both directions. Drivers stared at them curiously, but none stopped. Eventually, Kathy thought, they would reach a town where they could board a bus back to Nashville. It was a sad, a ridiculous ending to her brave protest, her great adventure. Before long the heat began to dissipate her anger into a sullen weariness.

The blaring of a horn behind them warned of some new danger. She looked around at an old outsized limousine such as served airport passengers. Seated beside the black driver was David Murchison, who managed to look at the same time surprised, pleased, sad and angry. Thus possibly General Nathan Bedford Forrest had looked when surrounded in these parts before issuing his famous order: "We'll charge both ways!" But when Dave climbed out of the swaybacked limousine, his order was: "Hop in! Back to Birmingham!"

Not Bedford Forest, but Tom Sawyer, Kathy thought. Into jail, out of jail, back to jail again—and like Huck Finn, she wondered to what purpose. "Now wait a minute," she said.

You've had enough?"

"Not necessarily. I'd just like some explanation of what's being accomplished."

"We've got 'em on the run."

"I'd say they had us on the walk. How did you get out of jail?"

"My outfit raised bail. Reinforcements are pouring in. Our intelligence network is really cracking. We knew the minute you people were run out of town. Both President Kennedy and the Attorney General are trying to get the governor of Alabama on the phone. We're gathering strength at the Birmingham bus terminal. Before long they'll weaken, and we'll bus it on to Montgomery. Climb in!"

After they climbed into the swaybacked limousine and headed back to

Birmingham, Kathy asked him, "Have you ever considered an Army career?"

"No dice. I'm a pacifist."

Some pacifist! Like Uncle Tubby, with his medals, or Father, with his Korean adventures. Onward, Christian soldiers, marching on to jail.

More than a score of freedom riders were gathered at the Birmingham bus terminal when they arrived there. Kathy expected momentarily that they would be arrested, but General Bedford Forrest Murchison proved himself the wiser tactician. They were too numerous now; such a large number of arrests would flood the jail and draw more national attention to Birmingham than the city authorities cared to receive.

Now the police gave them a protective screen against the toughs who wanted to assault them. Now, too, Kathy began to realize that patience was the most important weapon of the resistance fighter. As the hours crept by, she struggled against boredom, fatigue, and—worst of all—a feeling of personal uncleanliness. She would have given almost anything for a shower, a change of clothing a few quiet moments away from the din—anything, of course, except giving up the effort and going home.

It was a long night on benches which seemed to grow harder as time passed. Their effort to integrate the terminal lunchroom failed when the employees closed it and left. Dave and a white professor from Princeton attempted a sortie out for coffee and food, but they were attacked by a gang of youths and retreated to the terminal somewhat battered. At an early hour of morning, however, a strong force of allies brought them coffee and dry bologna sandwiches.

Wheels were turning in other places, Dave maintained cheerfully. Eventually the governor of Alabama would have to pick up the phone and answer the President of the United States. Eventually something must indeed have happened someplace else, for, about ten o'clock in the morning, they climbed onto a bus and set out for Montgomery.

Ah, Montgomery, first capital of the Old Confederacy, rising from the Alabama River, white columns gleaming through catalpa, sweet gum and magnolia, haunt of Jefferson Davis and the professional auctioneers wearing beaver hats and black tailcoats as they cried, "Niggers is cheap, niggers is cheap . . ." swollen now to one hundred and thirty-four thousand black and white skins, industries capitalized by the North, yet still unreconstructed Confederate. Thus Kathy tried to alleviate her weariness. Thus, too, a black man ahead of her said, "We'll bring those bastards to their knees."

It happened with terrifying suddenness after the bus pulled into the Montgomery terminal. The mob gathered there was much larger, its outraged cries more menacing than the crowds had been in Nashville and Birmingham. Dave led the way off the bus. Kathy, not far behind, saw him suddenly engulfed by several youths. He disappeared, as if the earth had swallowed him. Those behind him began trying to struggle back on, but those still aboard were screaming that the mob was trying to set fire to the bus. Kathy found herself flung into the roaring crowd as by a kind of centrifugal force. She glimpsed a man swing a baseball bat at her and tried to dodge, but someone else shoved her into its arc. There was a numbing pain in her right side, and she went down, struggling for consciousness. . . .

The events that followed always remained vague to her. Somehow she struggled free of the fierce riot and finally was seized by two policemen. When arraigned the pain in her chest was so severe that she begged for the attention of a doctor. What bail was set she could not remember, neither could she recall whether she gave Father's name and address. She kept asking about Dave, but no one seemed to understand her. And then she found herself in a cell with two Negro women.

Perhaps it was that day, perhaps the next, that a doctor came to her cell. Almost at once he had her carried out on a stretcher and transported by ambulance to a women's ward of a hospital. After a time she was rolled off for X rays, and eventually, at some hour of daylight or darkness, a physician came to her bedside. He was a kindly, competent man named Grey, who talked with her as if she were a close friend. She had four broken ribs and a torn liver, besides cuts and contusions about the head and both arms. Her ribs would heal; so would her liver without surgery if she remained immobile, Dr. Grey believed. She gave him Father's name, and he promised to find out what had happened to Dave.

The next afternoon she awakened from a doze to see Dave standing beside her bed. Both his eyes were blackened, his lip cut, his jaw swollen.

He said something corny: "But you ought to see those other guys." He assumed a John L. Sullivan stance and swung his fists. "Take that, Jeff Davis! Take that, Pierre Beauregard! And you that, Braxton Bragg! Not a scratch on 'em." Incredibly, his eyes filled with tears. Even more incredibly, he leaned over and kissed her gently on the forehead. "Kathy, I'm so sorry about that beautiful face of yours. But the doctor says you're going to be all right." Blinking back his tears, he pulled up a chair and sat down gingerly, wincing. "The greatest indignity came when somebody gave me a tremendous boot in the ass."

Why aren't you in jail?" she asked.

"Released on bail again. Things are really popping. . . ." Montgomery was under martial law. Martin Luther King, Jr., had arrived from Chicago, and when he tried to address a black mass meeting at a church, there had been an even worse riot than at the bus terminal. Reinforcements for the freedom riders were pouring in from the North, as were federal marshals.

QUESTION

What are the overpowering traits that a leader such as David Murchison has, and why are those traits valuable to a social movement?

Chapter 9

The Family

One of the longest-standing institutions of man is the family. To adequately define what a family is is a difficult problem because of the many forms it takes; however, a list of some of the family's more important functions can be made. First, the family is the unit where reproduction takes place; second, it is the place where the physical and psychological needs of the offspring are met; and third, it is a major agent in the process of socialization. It is the operation of the traditional family structure that provides for the reproducing, maintenance, and socialization of the succeeding generation. An example of the traditional family structure is illustrated in Mario Puzo's *The Godfather,* in which the Corleone family members are tied together through birth and deeds to perform such familial functions as are needed.

As time has passed, the insitution of the family has been undergoing some pressure to change. Technology and economics have placed great strains on the traditional family, and there are today a significant number of people who are seeking alternatives to it. Communes, trial marriages, no marriages at all are but a few attempts to find solutions to the family. In

The Dharma Bums a group of people try to form a group effort to find a more desirable way to answer the needs formerly met by the traditional family structure.

The Godfather

Mario Puzo

In this selection from the novel *The Godfather,* Michael Corleone, the
heir apparent to the Corleone family, tries to explain to his girl friend,
Kay, the importance of his family. The issue involved is a marriage proposal, and Michael tries to explain to Kay not only the rewards and benefits of the marriage but also of the responsibilities and commitments she
will have to make to the family if she accepts his proposal. The lecture-
proposal is punctuated with exhortations of loyality between various relationships, father-son, husband-wife, and parent-child, and on the family unit as being paramount for the existence of the Corleones.

Michael held the handkerchief in his hand. "OK," he said, "this one time.
You are the only person I felt any affection for, that I care about. I didn't
call you because it never occurred to me that you'd still be interested in me
after everything that's happened. Sure, I could have chased you, I could
have conned you, but I didn't want to do that. Now here's something I'll
trust you with and I don't want you to repeat it even to your father. If
everything goes right, the Corleone Family will be completely legitimate in
about five years. Some very tricky things have to be done to make that
possible. That's when you may become a wealthy widow. Now what do I
want you for? Well, because I want you and I want a family. I want kids;
it's time. And I don't want those kids to be influenced by me the way I was
influenced by my father. I don't mean my father deliberately influenced
me. He never did. He never even wanted me in the family business. He
wanted me to become a professor or a doctor, something like that. But
things went bad and I had to fight for my Family. I had to fight because I
love and admire my father. I never knew a man more worthy of respect. He
was a good husband and a good father and a good friend to people who
were not so fortunate in life. There's another side to him, but that's not
relevant to me as his son. Anyway I don't want that to happen to our kids.
I want them to be influenced by you. I want them to grow up to be All-
American kids, real All-American, the whole works. Maybe they or their
grandchildren will go into politics." Michael grinned. "Maybe one of them
will be President of the United States. Why the hell not? In my history
course at Dartmouth we did some background on all the Presidents and
they had fathers and grandfathers who were lucky they didn't get hanged.

But I'll settle for my kids being doctors or musicians or teachers. They'll never be in the Family business. By the time they are that old I'll be retired anyway. And you and I will be part of some country club crowd, the good simple life of well-to-do Americans. How does that strike you for a proposition?"

"Marvelous," Kay said. "But you sort of skipped over the widow part."

"There's not much chance of that. I just mentioned it to give a fair presentation." Michael patted his nose with the handkerchief.

"I can't believe it, I can't believe you're a man like that, you're just not," Kay said. Her face had a bewildered look. "I just don't understand the whole thing, how it could possibly be."

"Well, I'm not giving any more explanations," Michael said gently. "You know, you don't have to think about any of this stuff, it has nothing to do with you really, or with our life together if we get married."

Kay shook her head. "How can you want to marry me, how can you hint that you love me, you never say the word but you just now said you loved your father, you never said you loved me, how could you if you distrust me so much you can't tell me about the most important things in your life? How can you want to have a wife you can't trust? Your father trusts your mother. I know that."

"Sure," Michael said. "But that doesn't mean he tells her everything. and, you know, he has reason to trust her. Not because they got married and she's his wife. But she bore him four children in times when it was not that safe to bear children. She nursed and guarded him when people shot him. She believed in him. He was always her first loyalty for forty years. After you do that maybe I'll tell you a few things you really don't want to hear."

"Will we have to live in the mall?" Kay asked.

Michael nodded. "We'll have our own house, it won't be so bad. My parents don't meddle. Our lives will be our own. But until everything gets straightened out, I have to live in the mall."

"Because it's dangerous for you to live outside it," Kay said.

For the first time since she had come to know him, she saw Michael angry. It was cold chilling anger that was not externalized in any gesture or change in voice. It was a coldness that came off him like death and Kay knew that it was this coldness that would make her decide not to marry him if she so decided.

"The trouble is all that damn trash in the movies and the newspapers," Michael said. "You've got the wrong idea of my father and the Corleone Family. I'll make a final explanation and this one will be really final. My father is a businessman trying to provide for his wife and children and those friends he might need someday in a time of trouble. He doesn't accept the rules of the society we live in because those rules would have condemned him to a life not suitable to a man like himself, a man of extraordinary force and character. What you have to understand is that he considers himself the equal of all those great men like Presidents and Prime Ministers and Supreme Court Justices and Governors of the States. He refused to live by rules set up by others, rules which condemn him to a defeated life. But his ultimate aim is to enter that society with a certain power since society doesn't really protect its members who do not have their own individual power. In the meantime he operates on a code of ethics he considers far superior to the legal structures of society."

Kay was looking at him incredulously. "But that's ridiculous," she said. "What if everybody felt the same way? How could society ever function, we'd be back in the times of the cavemen. Mike, you don't believe what you're saying, do you?"

Michael grinned at her. "I'm just telling you what my father believes. I just want you to understand that whatever else he is, he's not irresponsible, or at least not in the society which he has created. He's not a crazy machine-gunning mobster as you seem to think. He's a responsible man in his own way."

"And what do you believe?" Kay asked quietly.

Michael shrugged. "I believe in my family," he said. "I believe in you and the family we may have. I don't trust society to protect us, I have no intention of placing my fate in the hands of men whose only qualification is that they managed to con a block of people to vote for them. But that's for now. My father's time is done. The things he did can no longer be done except with a great deal of risk. Whether we like it or not the Corleone Family has to join that society. But when they do I'd like us to join it with plenty of our own power; that is, money and ownership of other valuables. I'd like to make my children as secure as possible before they join that general destiny."

"But you volunteered to fight for your country, you were a war hero," Kay said. "What happened to make you change?"

Michael said, "This is really getting us no place. But maybe I'm just one of those real old-fashioned conservatives they grow up in your hometown. I take care of myself, individual. Governments really don't do much for their people, that's what it comes down to, but that's not it really. All I can say, I have to help my father, I have to be on his side. And you have to make your decision about being on my side." He smiled at her. "I guess getting married was a bad idea."

QUESTION

What are the main functions of the traditional family, and how were they performed for Michael Corleone?

The Dharma Bums

Jack Kerouac

As societies change, pressure is placed upon certain social institutions to change too. Even the family, one of society's most basic units, has not escaped the pressure to change in some way. Two proposed alternatives to the traditional family structure have been trial and group marriages. Another alternative—communal living—is presented in this selection from *The Dharma Bums*. A group of young people have banded together in order to provide the members of the commune with all of the needs that had been previously been met by the traditional family. Close attention should be paid to the form and structure of this particular style of communal living.

If the Dharma Bums ever get lay brothers in America who live normal lives with wives and children and homes, they will be like Sean Monahan.

Sean was a young carpenter who lived in an old wooden house far up a country road from the huddled cottages of Corte Madera, drove an old jalopy, personally added a porch to the back of the house to make a nursery for later children, and had selected a wife who agreed with him in every detail about how to live the joyous life in America without much money. Sean liked to take days off from his job to just go up the hill to the shack, which belonged to the property he rented, and spend a day of meditation and study of the Buddhist sutras and just brewing himself pots of tea and taking naps. His wife was Christine, a beautiful young honey-haired girl, her hair falling way down over her shoulders, who wandered around the house and yard barefooted hanging up wash and baking her own brown bread and cookies. She was an expert on making food out of nothing. The year before Japhy had made them an anniversary gift which was a huge ten-pound bag of flour, and they were very glad to receive it. Sean in fact was just an oldtime patriarch; though he was only twenty-two he wore a full beard like Saint Joseph and in it you could see his pearly white teeth smiling and his young blue eyes twinkling. They already had two little daughters, who also wandered around barefooted in the house and yard and were brought up to take care of themselves. Sean's house had woven straw mats on the floor and there too when you came in you were required to take off your shoes. He had lots of books and the only extravagance was a hi-fi set so he could play his fine collection of Indian records and Flamenco records and jazz. He even had Chinese and Japanese records. The dining table was a low, black-lacquered, Japanese style table, and to eat in Sean's house you not only had to be in your socks but sitting on mats at this table, any way you could. Christine was a great one for delicious soups and fresh biscuits.

When I arrived there at noon that day, getting off the Greyhound bus and walking up the tar road about a mile, Christine immediately had me sit down to hot soup and hot bread with butter. She was a gentle creature. "Sean and Japhy are both working on his job at Sausalito. They'll be home about five."

"I'll go up to the shack and look at it and wait up there this afternoon."

"Well, you can stay down here and play records."

"Well, I'll get out of your way."

"You won't be in my way, all I'm gonna do is hang out the wash and bake some bread for tonight and mend a few things." With a wife like that Sean, working only desultorily at carpentry, had managed to put a few thousand dollars in the bank. And like a patriarch of old Sean was generous, he always insisted on feeding you and if twelve people were in the house he'd lay out a big dinner (a simple dinner but delicious) on a board outside in the yard, and always a big jug of red wine. It was a communal arrangement, though, he was strict about that: we'd make collections for the wine, and if people came, as they all did, for a long weekend, they were expected to bring food or food money. Then at night under the trees and the stars of his yard, with everybody well fed and drinking red wine, Sean would take out his guitar and sing folksongs. Whenever I got tired of it I'd climb my hill and go sleep.

After eating lunch and talking awhile to Christine, I went up the hill. It climbed steeply right at the back door. Huge ponderosas and other pines, and in the property adjoining Sean's a dreamy horse meadow with wild flowers and two beautiful bays with their sleek necks bent to the butterfat grass in the hot sun. "Boy, this is going to be greater than North Carolina woods!" I thought, starting up. In the slope of grass was where Sean and Japhy had felled three huge eucalyptus trees and had already bucked them (sawed whole logs) with a chain saw. Now the block was set and I could see where they had begun to split the logs with wedges and sledgehammers and doublebitted axes. The little trail up the hill went so steeply that you almost had to lean over and walk like a monkey. It followed a long cypress row that had been planted by the old man who had died on the hill a few years ago. This prevented the cold foggy winds from the ocean from blasting across the property unhindered. There were three stages to the climb: Sean's backyard; then a fence, forming a little pure deer park where I actually saw deer one night, five of them, resting (the whole area was a game refuge); then the final fence and the top grassy hill with its sudden hollow on the right where the shack was barely visible under trees and flowery bushes. Behind the shack, a well-built affair actually of three big rooms but only one room occupied by Japhy, was plenty of good firewood and a saw horse and axes and an outdoor privy with no roof, just a hole in the ground and a board. It was like the first morning in the world in fine yard, with the sun streaming in through the dense sea of leaves, and birds and butterflies jumping around, warm, sweet, the smell of higher-hill heathers and flowers beyond the barbed-wire fence which led to the very top of the mountain and showed you a vista of all the Marin County area. I went inside the shack.

On the door was a board with Chinese inscriptions on it; I never did find out what it meant: probably "Mara stay away" (Mara the Tempter). Inside I saw the beautiful simplicity of Japhy's way of living, neat, sensible, strangely rich without a cent having been spent on the decoration. Old clay jars exploded with bouquets of flowers picked around the yard. His books were neatly stacked in orange crates. The floor was covered with inexpensive straw mats. The walls, as I say, were lined with burlap, which is one of the finest wallpapers you can have, very attractive and nice smelling. Japhy's mat was covered with a thin mattress and a Paisley shawl over that, and at the head of it, neatly rolled for the day, his sleeping bag. Behind burlap drapes in a closet his rucksack and junk were put away from sight. From the burlap wall hung beautiful prints of old Chinese silk paintings and maps of Marin County and northwest Washington and various poems he'd written and just stuck on a nail for anybody to read. The latest poem superimposed over others on the nail said: "It started just now with a hummingbird stopping over the porch two yards away through the open door, then gone, it stopped me studying and I saw the old redwood post leaning in clod ground, tangled in a huge bush of yellow flowers higher than my head, through which I push every time I come inside. The shadow network of the sunshine through its vines. White-crowned sparrows make tremendous singings in the trees, the rooster down the valley crows and crows. Sean Monahan outside, behind my back, reads the Diamond Sutra in the sun. Yesterday I read Migration of Birds. The Golden Plover and the Arctic Tern, today that big abstraction's at my door, for juncoes and the robins soon will leave, and nesting scrabblers will pick up all the string, and soon in hazy day of April summer heat across the hill, without a book I'll know, the seabirds'll chase spring north along the coast: they'll be nesting in Alaska in six weeks." And it was signed: "Japheth M. Ryder, Cypress-Cabin, 18:III: 56."

I didn't want to disturb anything in the house till he got back from work so I went out and lay down in the tall green grass in the sun and waited all afternoon, dreaming. But then I realized, "I might as well make a nice supper for Japhy" and I went down the hill again and down the road to the store and bought beans, saltpork, various groceries and came back and lit a fire in the woodstove and boiled up a good pot of New England beans, with molasses and onions. I was amazed at the way Japhy stored his food: just on a shelf by the woodstove: two onions, an orange, a bag of wheat germ, cans of curry powder, rice, mysterious pieces of dried Chinese seaweed, a bottle of soy sauce (to make his mysterious Chinese dishes). His salt and pepper was all neatly wrapped up in little plastic wrappers bound with elastic. There wasn't anything in the world Japhy would ever waste, or lose. Now I was introducing into his kitchen all the big substantial pork-and-beans of the world, maybe he wouldn't like it. He also had a big chunk of Christine's fine brown bread, and his bread knife was a dagger simply stuck into the board.

It got dark and I waited in the yard, letting the pot of beans keep warm on the fire. I chopped some wood and added it to the pile behind the stove. The fog began to blow in from the Pacific, the trees bowed deeply and roared. From the top of the hill you could see nothing but trees, trees, a roaring sea of trees. It was paradise. As it got cold I went inside and stoked up the fire, singing, and closed the windows. The windows were simply removable opaque plastic pieces that had been cleverly carpentered by Whitey Jones, Christine's brother, they let in light but you couldn't see anything outdoors and they cut off the cold wind. Soon it was warm in the cozy cabin. By and by I heard a "Hoo" out in the roaring sea of fog trees and it was Japhy coming back.

I went out to greet him. He was coming across the tall final grass, weary from the day's work, clomping along in his boots, his coat over his back. "Well, Smith, here you are."

"I cooked up a nice pot of beans for you."

"You did?" He was tremendously grateful. "Boy, what a relief to come home from work and don't have to cook up a meal yourself. I'm starved." He pitched right into the beans with bread and hot coffee I made in a pan on the stove, just French style brewing coffee stirred with a spoon. We had a great supper and them lit up our pipes and talked with the fire roaring. "Ray, you're going to have a great summer up on that Desolation Peak. I'll tell you all about it."

"I'm gonna have a great spring right here in this shack."

"Durn right, first thing we do this weekend is invite some nice new girls I know, Psyche and Polly Whitmore, though wait a minute, hmm. I can't invite both of them they both love me and'll be jealous. Anyway we'll have big parties every weekend, starting downstairs at Sean's and ending up here. And I'm not workin tomorrow so we'll cut some firewood for Sean. That's all he wants you to do. Though, if you wanta work on that job of ours in Sausalito next week, you can make ten bucks a day."

QUESTION

What are the merits and demerits to alternative families such as communes, group marriage, and trial marriage?

Chapter 10

Religion

Ever since people have been living together in groups, they have attempted to explain the unexplainable or the ultimate questions of life such as Where did man come from? In speculating about these questions, man has created a body of beliefs and knowledge which has formed the basis for religion.

However, religion does more than just explain the unexplainable; it also assigns people to certain roles in society. An individual could be assigned to a place of high esteem like the Pope in Catholicism or to a position of insignificance like the "untouchables" in Hinduism. Furthermore, religion can reconcile a person to his or her station in life, as Christianity does by rewarding him or her with a good afterlife while various hardships are suffered on earth. It is to these same points that the selection from *The Dune Messiah* addresses itself, namely, the function of religion.

In modern society, religion has been undergoing a great amount of change: attention is now being focused on the secular rather than the religious life of the individual. The secularization of religion cannot be shown in a better way than in the activity of contemporary religious leaders, for they are becoming more and more involved in the issues of the day. The civil rights movement, the anti-Vietnam struggle, and the abortion fight are just a few examples of the issues that ministers, priests, and rabbis have taken stands on. And, with this activity by their religious leaders, many of the faithful are questioning their religion.

However, the questioning of religion is not limited to any particular group, although young people are among the leaders. They are no longer satisfied with accepting ideas on the basis of faith along; they want to be shown that religion is relevant and meaningful to them. Thus, it has fallen to religious leaders like Rabbi David Wise in *Tuesday the Rabbi Saw Red* to convince them of the value of religion

The Dune Messiah

Frank Herbert

Religion or a system of beliefs is present in almost every society, although its function may differ from society to society. It may be used to interpret the phenomenon of nature, provide a code of personal conduct, express a general philosophy of life, or for all three of these uses. Within a society, then, religion has many functions and dimensions.

The question emerges: Why the need for religion? Scientists can explain natural occurrences, society can dictate for itself a code of conduct, and philosophers can devise some general concepts of life. Why then religion? This is the issue that Paul, a leader of a futuristic society, and Edric, an ambassador from another world, are analyzing in this selection from *The Dune Messiah,* and their conclusions are quite relevant to the question Why religion?

The most dangerous game in the universe is to govern from an oracular base. We do not consider ourselves wise enough or brave enough to play that game. The measures detailed here for regulation in lesser matters are as near as we dare venture to the brink of government. For our purposes, we borrow a definition from the Bene Gesserit and we consider the various worlds as gene pools, sources of teachings and teachers, sources of the possible. Our goal is not to rule, but to tap these gene pools, to learn, and to free ourselves from all restraints imposed by dependency and government.

—"The Orgy as a Tool of Statecraft,"
Chapter Three of The Steersman's Guide

"Is that where your father died?" Edric asked, sending a beam pointer from his tank to a jeweled marker on one of the relief maps adorning the wall of Paul's reception salon.

"That's the shrine of his skull," Paul said. "My father died a prisoner on a Harkonnen frigate in the sink below us."

"Oh, yes: I recall the story now," Edric said. "Something about killing the old Baron Harkonnen, his mortal enemy." Hoping he didn't betray too much of the terror which small enclosures such as this room imposed upon him, Edric rolled over in the orange gas, directed his gaze at Paul, who sat alone on a long divan of striped gray and black.

"My sister killed the Baron," Paul said, voice and manner dry, "just before the battle of Arrakeen."

And why, he wondered, did the Guild man-fish reopen old wounds in this place and at this time?

The Steersman appeared to be fighting a losing battle to contain his

nervous energies. Gone were the languid fish motions of their earlier en-
counter. Edric's tiny eyes jerked here . . . there, questing and measuring.
The one attendant who had accompanied him in here stood apart near the
line of houseguards ranging the end wall at Paul's left. The attendant worried Paul—hulking, thick-necked, blunt and vacant face. The man had entered the salon, nudging Edric's tank along on its supporting field, walking
with a strangler's gait, arms akimbo.

Scytale, Edric had called him. *Scytale, an aide.*

The aide's surface shouted stupidity, but the eyes betrayed him. They
laughed at everything they saw.

"Your concubine appeared to enjoy the performance of the Face
Dancers," Edric said. "It pleases me that I could provide that small entertainment. I particularly enjoyed her reaction to seeing her own features
simultaneously repeated by the whole troupe."

"Isn't there a warning against Guildsmen bearing gifts?" Paul asked.

And he thought of the performance out there in the Great Hall. The
dancers had entered in the costumes and guise of the Dune Tarot, flinging
themselves about in seemingly random patterns that devolved into fire ed-
dies and ancient prognostic designs. Then had come the rulers—a parade of
kings and emperors like faces on coins, formal and stiff in outline, but
curiously fluid. And the jokes: a copy of Paul's own face and body, Chani
repeated across the floor of the Hall, even Stilgar, who had grunted and
shuddered while others laughed.

"But our gifts have the kindest intent," Edric protested.

"How kindly can you be?" Paul asked. "The ghola you gave us believes
he was designed to destroy us."

"Destroy you, Sire?" Edric asked, all bland attention. "Can one destroy a god?"

Stilgar, entering on the last words, stopped, glared at the guards. They
were much farther from Paul than he liked. Angrily he motioned them
closer.

"It's all right, Stil," Paul said, lifting a hand. "Just a friendly discussion. Why don't you move the Ambassador's tank over by the end of my
divan?"

Stilgar, weighing the order, saw that it would put the Steersman's tank
between Paul and the hulking aide, much too close to Paul, but . . .

"It's all right, Stil," Paul repeated, and he gave the private hand-signal
which made the order an imperative.

Moving with obvious reluctance, Stilgar pushed the tank closer to Paul.
He didn't like the feel of the container or the heavily perfumed smell of

melange around it. He took up a position at the corner of the tank beneath the orbiting device through which the Steersman spoke.

"To kill a god," Paul said. "That's very interesting. But who says I'm a god?"

"Those who worship you," Edric said, glancing pointedly at Stilgar.

"Is that what you believe?" Paul asked.

"What I believe is of no moment, Sire," Edric said. "It seems to most observers, however, that you conspire to make a god of yourself. And one might ask if that is something any mortal can do . . . safely?"

Paul studied the Guildsman. Repellent creature, but perceptive. It was a question Paul had asked himself time and again. But he had seen enough alternate Timelines to know of worse possibilities than accepting godhead for himself. Much worse. These were not, however, the normal avenues for a Steersman to probe. Curious. Why had that question been asked? What could Edric hope to gain by such effrontery? Paul's thoughts went *flick* (the association of Tleilaxu would be behind this move)—*flick* (the Jihad's recent Sembou victory would bear on Edric's action)—*flick* (various Ben Gesserit credos showed themselves here) *flick* . . .

A process involving thousands of information bits poured flickering though his computational awareness. It required perhaps three seconds.

"Does a Steersman question the guidelines of prescience?" Paul asked, putting Edric on the weakest ground.

This disturbed the Steersman, but he covered well, coming up with what sounded like a long aphorism: "No man of intelligence questions the fact of prescience, Sire. Oracular vision has been known to men since most ancient times. It has a way of entangling us when we least suspect. Luckily, there are other forces in our universe."

"Greater than prescience?" Paul asked, pressing him.

"If prescience alone existed and did everything, Sire, it would annihilate itself. Nothing but prescience? Where could it be applied except to its own degenerating movements?"

"There's always the human situation," Paul agreed.

"A precarious thing at best," Edric said, "without confusing it by hallucinations."

"Are my visions no more than hallucinations?" Paul asked, mock sadness in his voice. "Or do you imply that my worshippers hallucinate?"

Stilgar, sensing the mounting tensions, moved a step nearer Paul, fixed his attention on the Guildsman reclining in the tank.

"You twist my words, Sire," Edric protested. An odd sense of violence lay suspended in the words.

Violence here? Paul wondered. *They wouldn't dare! Unless* (and he glanced at his guards) *the forces which protected him were to be used in replacing him.*

"But you accuse me of conspiring to make a god of myself," Paul said, pitching his voice that only Edric and Stilgar might hear. "Conspire?"

"A poor choice of word, perhaps, my Lord," Edric said.

"But significant," Paul said. "It says you expect the worst of me."

Edric arched his neck, stared sideways at Stilgar with a look of apprehension. "People always expect the worst of the rich and powerful, Sire. It is said one can always tell an aristocrat: he reveals only those of his vices which will make him popular."

A tremor passed across Stilgar's face.

Paul looked up at the movement, sensing the thoughts and angers whispering in Stilgar's mind. How dared this Guildsman talk thus to Maud'dib?

"You're not joking, of course," Paul said.

"Joking, Sire?"

Paul grew aware of dryness in his mouth. He felt that there were too many people in this room, that the air he breathed had passed through too many lungs. The taint of melange from Edric's tank felt threatening.

"Who might my accomplices be in such a conspiracy?" Paul asked presently. "Do you nominate the Qizarate?"

Edric's shrug stirred the orange gas around his head. He no longer appeared concerned by Stilgar, although the Fremen continued to glare at him.

"Are you suggesting that my missionaries of the Holy Orders, *all of them,* are preaching subtle falsehood?" Paul insisted.

"It could be a question of self-interest and sincerity," Edric said.

Stilgar put a hand to the crysknife beneath his robe.

Paul shook his head, said: "Then you accuse me of insincerity."

"I'm not sure that *accuse* is the proper word, Sire."

The boldness of this creature! Paul thought. And he said: "Accused or not, you're saying my bishops and I are no better than power-hungry brigands."

"Power-hungry, Sire?" Again, Edric looked at Stilgar. "Power tends to isolate those who hold too much of it. Eventually, they lose touch with reality . . . and fall."

"M'Lord," Stilgar growled, "you've had men executed for less!"

"Men, yes," Paul agreed. "But this is a Guild Ambassador."

"He accuses you of an unholy fraud!" Stilgar said.

"His thinking interest me, Stil," Paul said. "Contain your anger and remain alert."

"As Muad'dib commands."

"Tell me, Steersman," Paul said, "how could we maintain this hypothetical fraud over such enormous distances of space and time without the means to watch every missionary, to examine every nuance in every Qizarate priory and temple?"

"What is time to you?" Edric asked.

Stilgar frowned in obvious puzzlement. And he thought: *Muad'dib has often said he sees past the veils of time. What is the Guildsman really saying?*

"Wouldn't the structure of such a fraud begin to show holes?" Paul asked. "Significant disagreements, schisms . . . doubts, confessions of guilt—surely fraud could not suppress all these."

"What religion and self-interest cannot hide, governments can," Edric said.

"Are you testing the limits of my tolerance?" Paul asked.

"Do my arguments lack all merit?" Edric countered.

Does he want us to kill him? Paul wondered. *Is Edric offering himself as a sacrifice?*

"I prefer the cynical view," Paul said, testing. "You obviously are trained in all the lying tricks of statecraft, the double meanings and the power words. Language is nothing more than a weapon to you and, thus, you test my armor."

"The cynical view," Edric said, a smile stretching his mouth. "And rulers are notoriously cynical where religions are concerned. Religion, too, is a weapon. What manner of weapon is religion when it becomes the government?"

Paul felt himself go inwardly still, a profound caution gripping him. To whom was Edric speaking? Damnable clever words, heavy with manipulation leverages—the undertone of comfortable humor, the unspoken air of shared secrets: his manner said he and Paul were two sophisticates, men of a wider universe who understood things not granted common folk. With a feeling of shock, Paul realized that he had not been the main target for all this rhetoric. This affliction visited upon the court had been speaking for the benefit of others—speaking to Stilgar, to the household guards . . . perhaps even to the hulking aide.

"Religious *mana* was thrust upon me," Paul said. "I did not seek it." And he thought: *There! Let this manfish think himself victorious in our battle of words!*

"Then why have you not disavowed it, Sire?" Edric asked.

"Because of my sister Alia," Paul said, watching Edric carefully. "She is a goddess. Let me urge caution where Alia is concerned lest she strike you dead with her glance."

A gloating smile began forming on Edric's mouth, was replaced by a look of shock.

"I am deadly serious," Paul said, watching the shock spread, seeing Stilgar nod.

In a bleak voice, Edric said: "You have mauled my confidence in you, Sire. And no doubt that was your intent."

"Do not be certain you know my intent," Paul said, and he signaled Stilgar that the audience was at an end.

To Stilgar's questioning gesture asking if Edric were to be assassinated, Paul gave a negative hand-sign, amplified it with an imperative lest Stilgar take matters into his own hands.

Scytale, Edric's aide, moved to the rear corner of the tank, nudged it toward the door. When he came opposite Paul, he stopped, turned that laughing gaze on Paul, said: "If my Lord permits?"

"Yes, what is it?" Paul asked, noting how Stilgar moved close in answer to the implied menace from this man.

"Some say," Scytale said, "that people cling to Imperial leadership because space is infinite. They feel lonely without a unifying symbol. For a lonely people, the Emperor is a definite place. They can turn toward him and say: 'See, there He is. He makes us one.' Perhaps religion serves the same purpose, m'Lord."

Scytale nodded pleasantly, gave Edric's tank another nudge. They moved out of the salon, Edric supine in his tank, eyes closed. The Steersman appeared spent, all his nervous energies exhausted.

Paul stared after the shambling figure of Scytale, wondering at the man's words. A peculiar fellow, that Scytale, he thought. While he was speaking, he had radiated a feeling of many people—as though his entire genetic inheritance lay exposed on his skin.

"That was odd," Stilgar said, speaking to no one in particular.

Paul arose from the divan as a guard closed the door behind Edric and the escort.

"Odd," Stilgar repeated. A vein throbbed at his temple.

Paul dimmed the salon's lights, moved to a window which opened onto an angled cliff of his Keep. Lights glittered far below—pigmy movement. A work gang moved down there bringing giant plasmeld blocks to repair a facade of Alia's temple which had been damaged by a freak twisting of a sandblast wind.

"That was a foolish thing, Usul, inviting that creature into these chambers," Stilgar said.

Usul, Paul thought. *My sietch name. Stilgar reminds me that he ruled over me once, that he saved me from the desert.*

"Why did you do it?" Stilgar asked, speaking from close behind Paul.

"Data," Paul said. "I need more data."

"Is it not dangerous to try meeting this threat *only* as a mentat?"

That was perceptive, Paul thought.

Mentat computation remained finite. You couldn't say something boundless within the boundaries of any language. Mentat abilities had their uses, though. He said as much now, daring Stilgar to refute his argument.

"There's always something outside," Stilgar said. "Some things best *kept* outside."

"Or inside," Paul said. And he accepted for a moment his own oracular/mentat summation. Outside, yes. And inside: here lay the true horror. How could he protect himself from himself? They certainly were setting him up to destroy himself, but this was a position hemmed in by even more terrifying possibilities.

His reverie was broken by the sound of rapid footsteps. The figure of Korba the Qizara surged through the doorway backlighted by the brilliant illumination in the hallways. He entered as though hurled by an unseen force and came to an almost immediate halt when he encountered the salon's gloom. His hands appeared to be full of shigawire reels. They glittered in the light from the hall, strange little round jewels that were extinguished as a guardsman's hand came into view, closed the door.

"Is that you, m'Lord?" Korba asked, peering into the shadows.

"What is it?" Stilgar asked.

"Stilgar?"

"We're both here. What is it?"

"I'm disturbed by this reception for the Guildsman."

"Disturbed?" Paul asked.

"The people say, m'Lord, that you honor our enemies."

"Is that all?" Paul said. "Are those the reels I asked you to bring earlier?" He indicated the shigawire orbs in Korba's hands.

"Reels . . . oh! Yes, m'Lord. These are the histories. Will you view them here?"

"I've viewed them. I want them for Stilgar here."

"For me?" Stilgar asked. He felt resentment grow at what he interpreted as caprice on Paul's part. Histories! Stilgar had sought out Paul earlier to discuss the logistics computations for the Zabulon conquest. The Guild Ambassador's presence had intervened. And now—Korba with histories!

"How much history do you know?" Paul mused aloud, studying the shadowy figure beside him.

"M'Lord, I can name every world our people touched in their migration. I know the reaches of Imperial . . ."

"The Golden Age of Earth, have you ever studied that?"

"Earth? Golden Age?" Stilgar was irritated and puzzled. Why would Paul wish to discuss myths from the dawn of time? Stilgar's mind still felt crammed with Zabulon data—computations from the staff mentats: two hundred and five attack frigates with thirty legions, support battalions, pacification cadres, Qizarate missionaries . . . the food requirements (he had the figures right here in his mind) and melange . . . weaponry, uniforms, medals . . . urns for the ashes of the dead . . . the number of specialists— men to produce raw materials of propaganda, clerks, accountants . . . spies . . . and spies upon the spies . . .

"I brought the pulse-synchronizer attachment, also, m'Lord," Korba ventured. He obviously sensed the tensions building between Paul and Stilgar and was disturbed by them.

Stilgar shook his head from side to side. *Pulse-synchronizer?* Why would Paul wish him to use a mnemonic flutter-system on a shigawire projector? Why scan for specific data in histories? This was mentat work! As usual, Stilgar found he couldn't escape a deep suspicion at the thought of using a projector and attachments. The thing always immersed him in disturbing sensations, an overwhelming shower of data which his mind sorted out later, surprising him with information he had not known he possessed.

"Sire, I came with the Zabulon computations," Stilgar said.

"Dehydrate the Zabulon computations!" Paul snapped, using the obscene Fremen term which meant that here was moisture no man could demean himself by touching.

"M'Lord!"

"Stilgar," Paul said, "you urgently need a sense of balance which can come only from an understanding of long-term effects. What little information we have about the old times, the pittance of data which the Butlerians left us, Korba has brought it for you. Start with the Genghis Khan."

"Genghis . . . Khan? Was he of the Sardaukar, m'Lord?"

"Oh, long before that. He killed . . . perhaps four million."

"He must've had formidable weaponry to kill that many, Sire. Lasbeams, perhaps, or . . ."

"He didn't kill them himself, Stil. He killed the way I kill, by sending out his legions. There's another emperor I want you to note in passing—a Hitler. He killed more than six million. Pretty good for those days."

"Killed . . . by his legions?" Stilgar asked.

"Yes,"

"Not very impressive statistics, m'Lord."

"Very good, Stil." Paul glanced at the reels in Korba's hands. Korba stood with them as though he wished he could drop them and flee. "Statistics: at a conservative estimate, I've killed sixty-one billion, sterilized ninety planets, completely demoralized five hundred others. I've wiped out the followers of forty religions which had existed since—"

"Unbelievers!" Korba protested. "Unbelievers all!"

"No," Paul said. "Believers."

"My Liege makes a joke," Korba said, voice trembling. "The Jihad has brought ten thousand worlds into the shining light of—"

"Into the darkness," Paul said. "We'll be a hundred generations recovering from Muad'dib's Jihad. I find it hard to imagine that anyone will ever surpass this." A barking laugh erupted from his throat.

"What amuses Muad'dib?" Stilgar asked.

"I am not amused. I merely had a sudden vision of the Emperor Hitler saying something similar. No doubt he did."

"No other ruler ever had your powers," Korba argued. "Who would dare challenge you? Your legions control the known universe and all the—"

"The legions control," Paul said. "I wonder if they know this?"

"You control your legions, Sire," Stilgar interrupted, and it was obvious from the tone of his voice that he suddenly felt his own position in that chain of command, his own hand guiding all that power.

Having set Stilgar's thoughts in motion along the track he wanted, Paul turned his full attention to Korba, said: "Put the reels here on the divan." As Korba obeyed, Paul said: "How goes the reception, Korba? Does my sister have everything well in hand?"

"Yes, m'Lord." Korba's tone was wary. "And Chani watches from the spy hole. She suspects there may be Sardaukar in the Guild entourage."

"No doubt she's correct," Paul said. "The jackals gather."

"Bannerjee," Stilgar said, naming the chief of Paul's Security detail, "was worried earlier that some of them might try to penetrate the private areas of the Keep."

"Have they?"

"Not yet."

"But there was some confusion in the formal gardens," Korba said.

"What sort of confusion?" Stilgar demanded.

Paul nodded.

"Strangers coming and going," Korba said, "trampling the plants, whispered conversations—I heard reports of some disturbing remarks."

"Such as?" Paul asked.

"Is this the way our taxes are spent? I'm told the Ambassador himself asked that question."

"I don't find that surprising," Paul said. "Were there many strangers in the gardens?"

"Dozens, m'Lord."

"Bannerjee stationed picked troopers at the vulnerable doors, m'Lord," Stilgar said. He turned as he spoke, allowing the salon's single remaining light to illuminate half his face. The peculiar lighting, the face, all touched a node of memory in Paul's mind—something from the desert. Paul didn't bother bringing it to full recall, his attention being focused on how Stilgar had pulled back mentally. The Fremen had a tight-skinned forehead which mirrored almost every thought flickering across his mind. He was suspicious now, profoundly suspicious of his Emperor's odd behavior.

"I don't like the intrusion into the gardens," Paul said. "Courtesy to guests is one thing, and the formal necessities of greeting an envoy, but this . . ."

"I'll see to removing them," Korba said. "Immediately."

"Wait!" Paul ordered as Korba started to turn.

In the abrupt stillness of the moment, Stilgar edged himself into a position where he could study Paul's face. It was deftly done. Paul admired the way of it, an achievement devoid of any forwardness. It was a Fremen thing: slyness touched by respect for another's privacy, a movement of necessity.

"What time is it?" Paul asked.

"Almost midnight, Sire," Korba said.

"Korba, I think you may be my finest creation," Paul said.

"Sire!" There was injury in Korba's voice.

"Do you feel awe of me?" Paul asked.

"You are Paul-Muad'dib who was Usul in our sietch," Korba said. "You know my devotion to—"

"Have you ever felt like an apostle?" Paul asked.

Korba obviously misunderstood the words, but correctly interpreted the tone. "My Emperor knows I have a clean conscience!"

"Shai-hulud save us," Paul murmured.

The questioning silence of the moment was broken by the sound of someone whistling as he walked down the outer hall. The whistling was stilled by a guardsman's barked command as it came opposite the door.

"Korba, I think you may survive all this," Paul said. And he read the growing light of understanding in Stilgar's face.

"The strangers in the gardens, Sire?" Stilgar asked.

"Ahh, yes," Paul said. "Have Bannerjee put them out, Stil. Korba will assist."

"Me, Sire?" Korba betrayed deep disquiet.

"Some of my friends have forgotten they once were Fremen," Paul said, speaking to Korba, but designing his words for Stilgar. "You will mark down the ones Chani identifies as Sardaukar and you will have them killed. Do it yourself. I want it done quietly and without undue disturbance. We must keep in mind that there's more to religion and government than approving treaties and sermons."

QUESTION

What are the arguments that could made for the continued existence of religion in a modern, scientifically oriented society?

Tuesday the Rabbi Saw Red

Harry Kemelman

While religion played a significant role in earlier societies, it has been dwindling in its influence in modern society due to a number of factors. One of these factors is the increased secularization or the involvement of religious leaders in issues which have usually been viewed as being political in nature rather than religious. The consequence of this and other factors has been a questioning of religion and its relevance by many segments of American society.

In this chapter from *Tuesday the Rabbi Saw Red,* Rabbi David Wise is trying to explain to his students some of the misconceptions they have about Judaism and how it differs from Christianity. During the course of the discussion the Rabbi demonstrates that religion can still offer something in a modern society.

WHY DON'T JEWS EAT HAM? WHY DO JEWS WEAR BLACK BEANIES WHEN THEY PRAY? GOD IS DEAD. TRUE OR FALSE? WHY . . .?
WHY . . .?

The rabbi stood in the doorway of the classroom, bemused, as he looked over the blackboard with its long list of questions, each written in a different hand.

"You said we could ask questions today," said Harvey Shacter.

"So I did, Mr. Shacter." He came into the room, his eye still on the board. "And with a list that long, we'd better get started. We'll take them in order. Now the first question, about ham: that involves our dietary laws. Briefly, we may eat only the flesh of an animal which has cloven hooves and chews its cud. It must satisfy both conditions to qualify as kosher, that is, ritually fit to eat. Fish must have both scales and fins, which rules out shellfish; and fowl with curved beaks and talons—that is, birds of prey—are taboo. Some try to justify these laws on scientific grounds—healthy and nourishing animals are permitted, those liable to disease and hence less fit for human consumption are taboo—but that's a modern rationalization. Traditionally, we observe the dietary laws because we have been so commanded in the Bible. Now since the pig does not chew its cud, it is considered unclean, and so ham is forbidden."

"But don't we have a special thing about the pig that we don't have about other non-kosher animals?" asked Leventhal.

"Yes, that's true, Mr. Leventhal. We have a special aversion for the pig, possibly because it was an object of worship among many pagan peoples. But I am inclined to think it is for a more fundamental reason. All the other domestic animals have some utility for man while they are alive: the cow gives milk, the sheep produces wool, the horse performs work and transportation, the dog guards the house, the cat controls mice. Only the pig, of all domestic animals, kosher and non-kosher, serves no purpose except to be slaughtered and eaten. Now our religion forbids cruelty to animals. In fact, there are dozens of regulations in the Bible and in the interpretations of the rabbis that require us to treat the lower animals with kindness: one must not muzzle the ox that treads corn; a donkey and an ox may not be yoked together; beasts of burden must be rested on the Sabbath; hunting for sport is forbidden. With that as our tradition, you can readily understand how raising an animal solely for slaughter would be repugnant to us."

The rabbi made a checkmark against the question on the board. "All right, let's go on to the next, the black beanie. Whose is that, by the way?"

Harvey Shacter raised his hand.

"I've never heard the *kipoh* referred to that way," said the rabbi smiling, "but it's a good enough description. Why do we wear it? It's just a matter of custom, Mr. Shacter. There's no biblical regulation, although I might point out that with us custom takes on the force of law. It doesn't

have to be black and it doesn't have to be a beanie. Any head covering will
do. At times it was the custom to go bareheaded, at other times to be
covered, and the latter custom seems to have won out except in Reform
temples where they usually pray bareheaded."

He checked off the question, and then after a moment's hesitation,
checked off the next one, remarking, " 'God is dead' concerns Protestant
theologians rather than Jewish rabbis."

"Why is that?" called out Henry Luftig.

"Yours, Mr. Luftig?"

"Yes, sir."

"Well, it's a theological question, and we have no theology, at least not
in the generally accepted sense."

"Why not?"

"Because we don't need one," said the rabbi simply. "Our religion is
based on the idea of a single God, a God of Justice. If you think about it,
the concept of justice demands a single God because it implies a single
standard. And because He is infinite, He is unknowable to finite minds. We
don't forbid the study of Him, you understand, but we consider it pointless.
Much as an engineer would who sees a young colleague trying to construct
a perpetual motion machine. He might say: 'You can work on it if you like,
but you're wasting your time because it's theoretically impossible.' So because we believe it's pointless to try to know the unknowable, we have no
theology."

"Then why do the Christians have one?" demanded Luftig.

"I had intended this session to deal with your questions on Judaism,
not Christianity," the rabbi said reprovingly.

"How can we know about Judasim if we don't have something to
compare it to?" asked Shacter.

The rabbi pursed his lips and considered. "You're quite right, Mr.
Shacter. All right, I'll try to explain. Like us, the Christians also believe in a
single God. But in addition they have another divine being in the form of
Jesus as a son of God. And since a son implies a mother, they also have
Mary, who is at least semi-divine. Now these familial relationships, between
God and Jesus, Mary and Jesus, Mary and God, and all the other possible
permutations, to say nothing of the human-divine nature of Jesus—these
are not easy to explain."

"Is that what they call the Holy Trinity?"

"No," said the rabbi, "that's the Holy Family. The trinity consists of
the Father, the Son, and the Holy Ghost, and their relationship to each
other is the concern of Christian theology. There are very fine distinctions
on these matters between the various Christian sects."

"Yeah, but aren't those just word games played by priests and ministers?"

"Tens of thousands have been killed in religious wars, from the time of Constantine in the fourth century down to modern times, all because of these so-called word games," said the rabbi. "No, Mr. Luftig, the arguments of theologians are not to be dismissed lightly."

Lillian Dushkin waved her hand. "This boy I know, he's into this Jews for Jesus thing, and he says that Jesus is the Messiah Jews believe in and that he came to save mankind."

"Save them from what?" It was a young man who took copious notes, and it flicked across the rabbi's mind that for once, like most of the others, he had been listening rather than writing.

"Saved from hell, of course," said Mazelman scornfully. "Isn't that right, Rabbi?"

"Yes, that's the idea," he said. "Hell was an attempt to answer the age-old question: why do good men suffer while evil men frequently triumph and prosper? All religions have wrestled with that problem. The Hindus solve it by the doctrine of reincarnation. You get your just deserts in the next life for what you have done in this life. Christian doctrine holds that the wicked burn everlastingly in hell while the virtuous are rewarded by everlasting life in heaven."

"Pie in the sky," said Luftig sarcastically.

"That's a rather irreverent way of putting it, Mr. Luftig."

"What's the Jewish answer?" asked Lillian Dushkin. "Don't we believe in heaven and hell?"

"Not really, Miss Dushkin. Oh, the concept has crept in from time to time, but it's never really taken hold. Our 'answer,' as you put it, is best expressed in the Book of Job, and I'm afraid it is not very comforting. We say it's just the nature of the world—the sun shines as brightly on the wicked as it does on the good and just—but that goodness is its own reward, while evil carries its own punishment. At least it has the virtue of being realistic and of focusing our attention on this world, and trying to improve it, whereas the Christian view can be said to focus on the next world, regarding this one as a mere stopping-off place. Of course, it developed at a time when the world was troubled, and traditional ideas and institutions were crumbling, much like the present."

"Like the present?"

"Yes, Mr. Luftig. Just look at the world-wide revolt of young people against what they call the Establishment."

"Well, maybe that does prove God is dead!" challenged Luftig. "I don't notice any movement to religion or any new cults—"

"No?" said the rabbi. "Then how would you describe your generation's sudden fascination with astrology and yoga and Zen and I Ching and Tarot cards and the macrobiotic diet and drugs and communes—Shall I go on?—all of them offering escape or instant knowledge or instant mystical ecstasy."

He realized from the tense silence that he had spoken with some feeling. To reestablish the easy informality, he went on in his normal voice: "Basically, Christianity is a mystical religion and offers the psychological satisfactions mysticism affords. It is other-worldly, heaven-oriented, while our religion is this-world oriented. We oppose what is evil in the world and enjoy the good things, spiritual and material, it has to offer. We do not shun the world by asceticism or try to rise above it by mysticism, which has no following among the main body of Jews."

"What about Hassidim?" ventured Mark Leventhal.

The rabbi nodded. "Yes, they lean in that direction, but I would not say the Hassidic movement is central to our tradition. It's significant that Martin Buber, the chief modern apologist for Hassidism, was a lot more influential with Christian theologians that he was with Jews. We do not believe that the single ecstatic moment of near union with God ensures virtue forever after. With us, it has to be a day-by-day conscious practice of justice and virtue. But it is human virtue we require, not the superhuman virtue of the saint. Our religion calls for us to make a practical adjustment to the world as it it. It is a religion of work and rest, of life and death, of marriage and children, and their training and education, of the joys of living and the necessity to make a living."

"Well, their religion must work," said Shacter. "They're doing a lot more business than we are."

The class laughed and the rabbi joined in, relieving the tension. "Yes, Mr. Shacter, Christianity is a very pleasant religion. It offers a number of highly desirable responses to questions that have beset man down through the ages. He fears death and finds life too short, and the church offers him a world after death with a life everlasting. All we can offer in that respect is the hope that he will live on in his children and in the memory of his friends. He sees the good man suffering and the wicked prospering, and the church assures him that in the next world all will be redressed. And all we can say is that this is the nature of the world. For the everyday trials and tribulations of life, the church offers him the peace that comes with surrender to the mercy of Christ and the good offices of countless saints to whom he can pray for assistance, even for miracles. And periodically he can renew his faith through communion with his Lord by a magical act. And for us there is no magic, no short-cut, only a lifetime of effort. I suppose that gives another shade of meaning to the saying that it is hard to be a Jew."

Lillian Dushkin was bewildered. "But if theirs is so much better, why don't we go in for it?"

The rabbi smiled. "There's just one little hitch, Miss Dushkin. You have to believe. And we cannot believe."

"So then what's in it for us?"

"What's in it, as you put it so bluntly, is the satisfaction of facing reality." He saw the class were all attentive now. "It doesn't permit us to dodge problems, but it does help us to solve them, if only by recognizing they exist. And, after all, isn't that what the modern world is beginning to do? So after thousands of years it appears our way is at last coming into style. As for who's doing more business, Mr. Shacter, look about you and you will find that the great changes in thought and attitude that produced modern Western civilization are paralleled in Jewish religious thought—the equality of people, the rights of women, the right of all men to the good things of this life, the improvement of conditions on earth, respect for life in the treatment of the lower animals, the importance of learning."

"You mean they got them all from us?"

"Whether they did or whether they finally developed them on their own is not particularly important. What is important is that these were inherent in our religion from the beginning, which suggests it accords with reality."

The bell rang, and with a start the rabbi realized that the hour was over. He realized, too, that he had not made his usual head count, and as he glanced about he saw there were twenty-one present, more than ever before on a Friday. He smiled and nodded to them in dismissal.

QUESTION

In what ways has religion affected your ideas about what you should or should not do?

Chapter 11

Education

In Chapter 2, the process of socialization was shown as the means by which an individual learns values and norms. Put under a more generic term, this entire process of learning can be more aptly entitled education.

Education or the cultural transmission of knowledge can take place anywhere and anytime, but it is usually thought of as being performed in a formal setting, namely, the classroom. Here the teacher employs any technique that he or she can in order to accomplish the task of transmitting some knowledge to the students. Sometimes this process can be very trying, and the experience of Mr. Hart in *The Paper Chase* is not unusual.

Because education is such an important part of society, it is usually scrutinized very closely, particularly at the college level. In recent years college students along with others have been questioning not only teachers and their techniques but also courses of studies, course content, and the goals of education. Relevance is what these critics are seeking, and the effect of this demand has had some impact on the educational process, as the two professors in *Tuesday the Rabbi Saw Red* reveal.

The Paper Chase

John Osborn

For a society to continue to exist, it must educate its youth into the accepted ways of the society. This can be accomplished through a multiplicity of means, either formal (the classroom situation) or informal (experience). While the primary agent of educating the young belongs to the family, a significant influence is the school, and thus cultural transmission is a main function of the schools.

The novel *The Paper Chase* is a good example of how the transmission of one of society's more important elements: the law. Mr. Hart, the central figure of the story, is a first-year law student at Harvard Law School and is about to attend his first class. His introduction into the educational process at law school is quite revealing.

In the few days between arrival at Harvard Law School and the first classes, there are rumors. And stories. About being singled out, made to show your stuff.

Mostly, they're about people who made some terrible mistake. Couldn't answer a question right.

One concerns a boy who did a particularly bad job. His professor called him down to the front of the class, up the podium, gave the student a dime and said, loudly:

"Go call your mother, and tell her you'll never be a lawyer."

Sometimes the story ends here, but the way I heard it, the crushed student bowed his head and limped slowly back through the one hundred and fifty students in the class. When he got to the door, his anger exploded. He screamed:

"You're a son of a bitch, Kingsfield."

"That's the first intelligent thing you've said," Kingsfield replied. "Come back. Perhaps I've been too hasty."

Professor Kingsfield, who should have been reviewing the cases he would offer his first class of the year, stared down from the window forming most of the far wall of his second story office in Langdell Hall and watched the students walking to class.

He was panting. Professor Kingsfield had just done forty push-ups on his green carpet. His vest was pulled tight around his small stomach and it seemed, each time his heart heaved, the buttons would give way.

A pyramid-shaped wooden box, built for keeping time during piano lessons, was ticking on his desk and he stopped its pendulum. Professor Kingsfield did his push-ups in four-four time.

His secretary knocked on the door and reminded him that if he didn't get moving he'd be late. She paused in the doorway, watching his heaving chest. Since Crane had broken his hip in a fall from the lecture platform, Professor Kingsfield was the oldest active member of the Harvard Law School faculty.

He noticed her concern and smiled, picked up the casebook he had written thirty years before, threw his jacket over his shoulder and left the office.

Hart tried to balance the three huge casebooks under one arm, and with the other hold up his little map. He really needed two hands to carry the casebooks—combined, they were more than fifteen inches thick, with smooth dust jackets that tended to make the middle book slide out—and he stumbled along, trying to find Langdell North and avoid bumping into another law student.

Everything would have been easy if he had known which direction was North. He had figured out that the dotted lines didn't represent paths, but instead tunnels, somewhere under his feet, connecting the classrooms, the library, the dorms and the eating hall in Harkness. He knew that the sharp red lines were the paths—little asphalt tracks widing along through the maze of granite buildings.

Some of the buildings were old. Langdell was old: a three story dark stone building, built in neoclassical renaissance. It stretched for a block in front of and behind him, with the library on the third floor. Hart had been circling it for ten minutes trying to find an entrance that would lead to his classroom.

The other buildings he'd passed were more modern but in an attempt to compromise with Langdell had been given the library's worst features. They were tall concrete rectangles, broken by large dark windows, woven around Langdell like pillboxes, guarding the perimeter of the monolith. It seemed that everything was interconnected, not only by the tunnels, but also by bridges which sprung out from the second and third floors of Langdell like spider legs, gripping the walls of the outposts.

Hart took a reading on the sun, trying to remember from his Boy Scout days where it rose. He absolutely refused to ask anyone the way. He disliked being a first year student, disliked not knowing where things were. Most of all, he disliked feeling unorganized, and he was terribly unorganized on this first day of classes. He couldn't read his map, he couldn't carry his casebooks. His glasses had fallen down over his nose, and he didn't have a free hand to lift them up.

He had expected to have these troubles, and knew from experience that he wouldn't want to ask directions. Thus, he had allowed a full twenty minutes to find the classroom. His books were slowly sliding forward from under his arm, and he wondered if he should reconsider his vow never to buy a briefcase.

He moved into a flow of red books, tucked on top of other casebooks. Red. His contracts book was red. He followed the flow to one of the stone entrances to Langdell, up the granite steps. In the hallway, groups of students pushed against each other, as they tried to squeeze through the classroom door. Every now and then books hit the floor when students bumped. A contagious feeling of tension hung in the corridor. People were overly polite or overly rude. Hart pulled his books to his chest, let his map drop to the floor, and started pushing toward the red door of the classroom.

Most of the first year students, in anticipation of their first class at the Harvard Law School, were already seated as Professor Kingsfield, at exactly five minutes past nine, walked purposefully through the little door behind the lecture platform. He put his books and notes down on the wooden lectern and pulled out the seating chart. One hundred and fifty names and numbers: the guide to the assigned classroom seats. He put the chart on the lectern, unbuttoned his coat, exposing the gold chain across his vest, and gripped the smooth sides of the stand, feeling for the identations he had worn into the wood. He did not allow his eyes to meet those of any student—his face had a distant look similar to the ones in the thirty or so large gilt-framed portraits of judges and lawyers that hung around the room.

Professor Kingsfield was at ease with the room's high ceiling, thick beams, tall thin windows. Though he knew the room had mellowed to the verge of decay, he disliked the new red linoleum bench tops. They hid the mementos carved by generations of law students, and accented the fact that the wooden chairs were losing their backs, the ceiling peeling, and the institutional light brown paint on the walls turning the color of mud. He could have taught in one of the new classrooms with carpets and programmed acoustics designed to hold less than the full quota of a hundred and fifty students. But he had taught in this room for thirty years, and felt at home.

At exactly ten past nine, Professor Kingsfield picked a name from the seating chart. The name came from the left side of the classroom. Professor Kingsfield looked off to the right, his eyes following one of the curving benches to where it ended by the window.

Without turning, he said crisply, "Mr. Hart, will you recite the facts of *Hawkins* versus *McGee?*"

When Hart, seat 259, heard his name, he froze. Caught unprepared, he simply stopped functioning. Then he felt his heart beat faster than he could ever remember its beating and his palms and arms broke out in sweat.

Professor Kingsfield rotated slowly until he was staring down at Hart. The rest of the class followed Kingsfield's eyes.

"I have got your name right?" Kingsfield asked. "You are Mr. Hart?" He spoke evenly, filling every inch of the hall.

A barely audible voice floated back: "Yes, my name is Hart."

"Mr. Hart, you're not speaking loud enough. Will you speak up?"

Hart repeated the sentence, no louder than before. He tried to speak loudly, tried to force the air out of his lungs with a deep push, tried to make his words come out with conviction. He could feel his face whitening, his lower lip beat against his upper. He couldn't speak louder.

"Mr. Hart, will you stand?"

After some difficulty, Hart found, to his amazement, he was on his feet.

"Now, Mr. Hart, will you give us the case?"

Hart had his book open to the case: he had been informed by the student next to him that a notice on the bulletin board listed *Hawkins* v. *McGee* as part of the first day's assignment in contracts. But Hart had not known about the bulletin board. Like most of the students, he had assumed that the first lecture would be an introduction.

His voice floated across the classroom: "I . . . I haven't read the case. I only found out about it just now."

Kingsfield walked to the edge of the platform.

"Mr. Hart, I will myself give you the facts of the case. *Hawkins* versus *McGee* is a case in contract law, the subject of our study. A boy burned his hand by touching an electric wire. A doctor who wanted to experiment in skin grafting asked to operate on the hand, guaranteeing that he would restore the hand 'one hundred percent.' Unfortunately, the operation failed to produce a healthy hand. Instead, it produced a hairy hand. A hand not only burned, but covered with dense matted hair."

"Now, Mr. Hart, what sort of damages do you think the doctor should pay?"

Hart reached into his memory for any recollections of doctors. There were squeaks from the seats as members of the class adjusted their positions. Hart tried to remember the summation he had just heard, tried to think about it in a logical sequence. But all his mental energy had been expended in pushing back shock waves from the realization that, though

Kingsfield had appeared to be staring at a boy on the other side of the room, he had in fact called out the name Hart. And there was the constant strain of trying to maintain his balance because the lecture hall sloped toward the podium at the center, making him afraid that if he fainted he would fall on the student in front of him.

Hart said nothing.

"As you remember, Mr. Hart, this was a case involving a doctor who promised to restore an injured hand."

That brought it back. Hart found that if he focused on Kingsfield's face, he could imagine there was no one else in the room. A soft haze formed around the face. Hart's eyes were watering, but he could speak.

"There was a promise to fix the hand back the way it was before," Hart said.

Kingsfield interruped: "And what in fact was the result of the operation?"

"The hand was much worse than when it was just burned . . ."

"So the man got less than he was promised, even less than he had when the operation started?"

Kingsfield wasn't looking at Hart now. He had his hands folded across his chest. He faced out, catching as many of the class's glaces as he could.

"Now, Mr. Hart," Kingsfield said, "how should the court measure the damages?"

"The difference between what he was promised and what he got, a worse hand?" Hart asked.

Kingsfield stared off to the right, picked a name from the seating chart.

"Mr. Pruit, perhaps you can tell the class if we should give the boy the difference between what he was promised and what he got, as Mr. Hart suggests, or the difference between what he got, and what he had."

Hart fell back into his seat. He blinked, trying to erase the image of Kingsfield suspended in his mind. He couldn't. The lined white skin, the thin rusty lips grew like a balloon until the image seemed to actually press against his face, shutting off everything else in the classroom.

Hart blinked again, felt for his pen and tried to focus on his clean paper. His hand shook, squiggling a random line. Across the room, a terrified, astonished boy with a beard and wire-rimmed glasses was slowly talking about the hairy hand.

QUESTION

What are the areas in which the cultural transmission of knowledge takes place in the educational process?

Tuesday the Rabbi Saw Red

Harry Kemelman

During the 1960s and now in the 1970s, the educational system is subject to a great deal of criticism, particularly at the college level. Students complain about the lack of relevance in their education, while teachers assert that students are not in college to learn but are there because they have nothing else to do or because they are expected to go to college. Both of these views have had some effect on the college environment, and the points that Professor Hendryx makes in *Tuesday the Rabbi Saw Red* are quite incisive.

"Look Rabbi, let me tell you the facts of academic life. The dean doesn't give a damn if you walk out on a class occasionally, or even if you meet with them at all. What you do in your classroom is your business. Last year, Professor Tremayne announced a three-week reading period in the middle of February and took off for Florida. Of course, Tremayne is the kind of teacher who may provide greater benefit to his students by his absence than his presence."

"Nevertheless, I think I'll tell her about it anyway. Besides, I've got to turn in my mid-semester failure notices."

Hendryx whistled. "You mean you're really sending out flunk notices after all I told you?"

"But last week I received a notice that the lists were due Monday, the sixteenth."

"Rabbi, Rabbi," Hendryx, "when was the last time you had any connection with a college?"

"I've lectured to Hillel groups."

"No, I mean a real connection."

"Not since I was a student, I suppose, fifteen or sixteen years ago. Why?"

"Because in the last sixteen years—hell, in the last six—things have changed. Where have you been? Don't you read the papers?"

"But the students—"

"Students!" Hendryx said scornfully. "What in the world to you think college cares about students? The primary purpose of college nowadays is to support the faculty, presumably a society of learned men, in some degree of comfort and security. It's society's way of subsidizing such worthwhile pursuits as research and the growth of knowledge. Society has the uneasy feeling that it's for someone to care about such irrelevancies as the source of Shakespeare's plots or whether the gentleman above me"—nodding to the bust of Homer on the shelf above his head—"was responsible for the Homeric poems or if he was just one of a committee, or the influence of the Flemish weavers on the economy of England during the Middle Ages, or the effect of gamma rays on the development of spyrogyra.

"We're set apart in the grove of academe to fritter away our lives while the rest of the world goes about its proper business of making money or children or war or disease or pollution, or whatever the hell they're into. As for the students, they can look over our shoulders if they like and learn something. Or they can pay their tuition fees which help support us and hang around here for four years having fun. Personally, I don't give a damn which they do, as long as they don't interfere with my quite comfortable life, thank you."

He drew deeply on his pipe and, removing it from his mouth, blew the smoke in the rabbi's direction.

"And you don't feel you owe the students anything?" the rabbi asked quietly.

"Not a damn thing. They're just one of the hazards of the game, like a sandtrap on a golf course. As a matter of fact, we do do something for them. After four years, they are given that degree you were talking about which entitles them to apply for certain jobs. Or to go on to a higher degree which they can cash into money by becoming doctors, lawyers, accountants. Not the fairest arrangement from the point of view of those who can't afford college, but quite normal in this imperfect world. Hell, is it any different in the tight trades where you have to serve a useless apprenticeship before you can join a union?" He shook his head as if answering his own question. "The only trouble comes when the students catch on, as they have in recent years, and kick up a fuss or stage a demonstration as your class did today."

"But if the college is for the faculty, and the student is here merely to mark time, why should you care what he does?"

Hendryx smiled. "Actually, I don't. Not unless it kills the goose that laid the golden egg. And that what's been happening the last few years. The student sensed he was being had. Of course he'd known all along that what he was getting here wasn't worth what he was paying. I once figured out it costs him about ten dollars per lecture. God, my lectures aren't worth that. Are yours? How smart does a student have to be to figure it out for himself? Still, he went along because he had to have the degree to get any sort of a job or train for any sort of profession. But then they rang in the war on him, and it struck him as a bit much: this degree we were giving him turned out to be just a ticket, somethimes one way, to Vietnam. So he rebelled."

"It also gave him a four-year moratorium from the war," observed the rabbi.

"Yes, it did, but that's human nature. Things have quieted down a lot in the last year to two, what with the change in the draft law and winding down the war, and the students have quieted down correspondingly. But they acquired the habit of protest, even violence, and that we can't have."

QUESTION

In what ways is the teacher-student relationship beneficial to learning, and what kinds of problems are associated with that relationship?

Chapter 12

The Economic System

In every society there are some institutions through which the goods and services of the society are distributed. These structures can range from a single barter system to an elaborate industrialized economy. Regardless of the structure the main function of the economic system, that of distributing wealth within a society, is accomplished.

An attribute of economics is that there are various forms, and perhaps the most widely praised and criticized form is capitalism. According to Adam Smith, an early theorist of capitalism, it is the best of all possible economic systems because it allows the society and the individual to achieve the maximum or the minimum amount of wealth, the only limitations being the society's and/or the individual's talents and abilities. Smith would also argue that capitalism is good for the individual because it permits the greatest amount of freedom for the individual.

The question of freedom under capitalism has been attacked by many people, and one of the more maligned aspects is the assembly line. The assembly-line method of production has a worker doing the same task over and over, again and again, day after day. The monotony becomes extremely stifling on the worker, and *F.O.B. Detroit* reveals the impact of the assembly line on the worker.

Another feature of capitalism, particularly the American variety, that has been criticized is the Puritan ethic. First brought to the attention of scholars by the German sociologist Max Weber, the main tenet of the Puritan ethic is that success is the end result of hard work. People, then, should work as hard as they can so that they can get as much as they can, an idea which is very compatible with capitalism. Perhaps no other character in literature personifies the essence of the Puritan and capitalistic ethic better than George Babbitt in Sinclair Lewis's novel, *Babbitt*.

F.O.B. Detroit

Wessel Smitter

Under the economic system of capitalism, an emphasis is placed upon production: the more a person or company produces, the more the financial reward. Consequently, any means which increases individual or mass production and either maintains or lowers the cost of production is highly desirable.

One technique that modern capitalism has employed to increase production is the assembly line. Conceived by a master capitalist, Henry Ford, the main principle of the assembly line is to produce certain items as fast and efficiently as possible. One individual does the same task over and over again, passing his or her completed product to the next worker. By limiting the worker to a single task, a minimal amount of error will occur along with faster production, a goal of capitalism.

However, the assembly line overlooks one important item: the human cost. How much stimulation does a person get from installing left fenders over and over again for eight hours a day? The drudgery of the assembly line, the relentless running of the machines that the workers use, and their effect on the human workers is significant, and this selection from Wessel Smitter's book, *F.O.B. Detroit,* illustrates the point well.

One night, coming out of the factory after we'd been in motor assembly a little more than a month, we passed the bone-yard, and there, in with ten acres of other scrapped machinery, we saw the rig. One side was down in the mud; the boom was all screwy, and the big iron claw hung loose and open like an idiot's mouth.

"There's Old Betsy," said Russ. "Let's go in and see what they've done to her."

I didn't see the use, but I went, getting my feet wet and muddy. He went up to the rig and put his hand on the control box.

"Cold iron," he said, serious. "No static, even. But if you was to turn the juice into her she'd soon come to warm life again."

"She'll come to warm life," I said, "when they get the torches to work on her—cut her up and feed her to the open hearths. One of these days she'll be coming over the line in the shape of cylinder blocks and you'll be starting nuts on her."

"You know, Bennie," he said, sliding his hand back and forth along a drive-shaft, "there's something almost funny about the way this steel feels

From *F.O.B. Detroit* by Wessel Smitter, 1938.

to the touch. You get used to having a thing feel the same way, don't you? And when it doesn't—it's almost as though something was wrong. Even during the night she never got really cold. In the morning there was always some heat left in the metal. It must be that way when you feel the hand of someone you've known a long time and—"

"Must be," I said. "Let's get going. If the H.P.s see us fooling around here you'll have a hard time making 'em believe that you're preaching a funeral sermon and not trying to get away with some brass bearings."

"Don't rush me," he said. "What's the difference if we get outa this place a few minutes later than usual? This is probably the last time we'll see the old rig."

"Last time you get sentimental about it, I hope."

"To you," he said, "this machine here is just a pile of old iron—junk. But to me it's more than that, Bennie. To me—it's Old Betsy—still. To you, all machines are alike. Pieces of steel and iron put together—all alike. But they're not, Bennie. Machines do things to us—the men that work with them. Things the engineers never think about. Some machines build us up—help us to make the most of ourselves. Some tear us apart—grind us down. A machine geared to a man—is one thing. A man geared to a machine—is something else. One's human, gives you a chance to be your best self. The other works on you like a gear-cutter—whittling you down, chiseling at you, cutting grooves in you, making you like all the other small gears that work on the line."

He stood there fingering a winged nut on a brakerod, just the bare hint of a smile near the corner of his mouth, that smile that I never knew quite how to take.

"I don't know what you're thinking about," I said, "but I guess it's all right."

"I'm not sentimental," he said, in his quiet way. "At least, I don't think I am. I see things for what they are worth—to me. When I was in the drop forge I had a man's job and did a man's work. It was fun. Remember how I used to stay after the bell rang and try to work out ideas for getting the work done faster, better? I had a chance to use the brains I was born with. Old Betsy, here, gave me a chance to get the most out of myself. When a job was done, I looked it over. Took some of the credit, if it was good. Took some of the blame, if it wasn't. Tried to figure out how to do it better the next time. Old Betsy was geared to my brain—did what I wanted it to do. Gave its strength to my hand, gave its power to my will. I was the boss.

"But in the motor assembly, Bennie, it's different. There the machine is the boss. The machine does the nice work—the hard work—the part that takes skill. The machine's everything and gets credit for the work done. You're nothing until you've learned to be a gear—a small part of the big machine—until there's nothing left of you but a very small cog without any will. You start and stop when the machine's ready—go slow or fast as the machine tells you. The machine counts—you don't. And why should you? You don't furnish the brains. You don't furnish the skill. All you do is fasten a nut, put on a washer, stamp on a number. The machine does the real job. It's the big boss standing over your head—grinding you down—wasting your strength—whittling away at your brain. Making you a small part of its dead, mechanical self."

"Come on," I said, "it's late. Supper will be waiting for us. We haven't cleaned up yet."

"That's right," he said, picking his way through the mud, "we haven't cleaned up. In the drop forge—we used to clean up every night before leaving. Used to change our clothes and wash the dirt from our faces. Walk out of the gate looking decent. Now we don't—ever. Nobody does. When it's time for the bell we don't think about anything except getting out— getting out. Getting away from the machines. We lay our tools just so—roll our sleeves down—untie the knots in our aprons. We get set for the bell. We get ready to rush out when the bell rings, thinking we'll get rid of the machines for a spell—the machines that eat into us like gear-cutters. But we don't, Bennie. We don't—ever. It's there when we hurry out—there on the river of dead faces streaming out through the gate. And in the morning, when we come back to the machines—it's still there. We go home and use water and soap but we never clean up. The work of the machines that keep whittling and chiseling at us is too deep."

QUESTION

What are some of the effects working in a factory or on an assembly line has had on the individual and society?

Babbitt

Sinclair Lewis

In his novel *Babbitt,* Sinclair Lewis created a character, George Babbitt, who is the personification of two ideas: the capitalistic and Puritan ethics. Although the former deals with economics and the latter with religion, both stress the value of hard work and the belief that only through hard work can a person be deemed a productive member of society. If people do not produce to the utmost of their ability, the capitalistic and Puritan ethics hold that these people are to be despised.

In this selection, George Babbitt, a real estate promoter, is having a conversation with his family. During the course of their discussion, Babbitt reveals the basic premises of both capitalism and the Puritan ethic.

Relieved of Babbitt's bumbling and the soft grunts with which his wife expressed the sympathy she was too experienced to feel and much too experienced not to show, their bedroom settled instantly into impersonality.

It gave on the sleeping-porch. It served both of them as dressing-room, and on the coldest nights Babbitt luxuriously gave up the duty of being manly and retreated to the bed inside, to curl his toes in the warmth and laugh at the January gale.

The room displayed a modest and pleasant color-scheme, after one of the best standard designs of the decorator who "did the interiors" for most of the speculative-builders' houses in Zenith. The walls were gray, the woodwork white, the rug a serene blue; and very much like mahogany was the furniture—the bureau with its great clear mirror, Mrs. Babbitt's dressing-table with toilet-articles of almost solid silver, the plain twin beds, between them a small table holding a standard electric bedside lamp, a glass for water, and a standard bedside book with colored illustrations—what particular book it was cannot be ascertained, since no one had ever opened it. The mattresses were firm but not hard, triumphant modern mattresses which had cost a great deal of money; the hot-water radiator was of exactly the proper scientific surface for the cubic contents of the room. The windows were large and easily opened, with the best catches and cords, and Holland roller-shades guaranteed not to crack. It was a masterpiece among bedrooms, right out of Cheerful Modern Houses for Medium Incomes. Only it had nothing to do with the Babbitts, nor with any one else. If people

had ever lived and loved here, read thrillers at midnight and lain in beautiful indolence on a Sunday morning, there were no signs of it. It had the air
of being a very good room in a very good hotel. One expected the chamber-
maid to come in and make it ready for people who would stay but one
night, go without looking back, and never think of it again.

Every second house in Floral Heights had a bedroom precisely like
this.

The Babbitts' house was five years old. It was all as competent and
glossy as this bedroom. It had the best of taste, the best of inexpensive rugs,
a simple and laudable architecture, and the latest conveniences. Throughout, electricity took the place of candles and slatternly hearth-fires. Along
the bedroom baseboard were three plugs for electric lamps, concealed by
little brass doors. In the halls were plugs for the vacuum cleaner, and in the
living-room plugs for the piano lamp, for the electric fan. The trim dining-
room (with its admirable oak buffet, its leaded-glass cupboard, its creamy
plaster walls, its modest scene of a salmon expiring upon a pile of oysters)
had plugs which supplied the electric percolator and the electric toaster.

In fact there was but one thing wrong with the Babbitt house: It was
not a home.

Often of a morning Babbitt came bouncing and jesting in to breakfast.
But things were mysteriously awry to-day. As he pontifically tread the upper hall he looked into Verona's bedroom and protested, "What's the use of
giving the family a high-class house when they don't appreciate it and tend
to business and get down to brass tacks?"

He marched upon them: Verona, a dumpy brown-haired girl of twenty-two, just out of Bryn Mawr, given to solicitudes about duty and sex and
God and the unconquerable bagginess of the gray sports-suit she was now
wearing. Ted—Theodore Roosevelt Babbitt—a decorative boy of seventeen. Tinka—Katherine—still a baby at ten, with radiant red hair and a
thin skin which hinted of too much candy and too many ice cream sodas.
Babbitt did not show his vague irritation as he tramped in. He really disliked being a family tyrant, and his nagging was as meaningless as it was
frequent. He shouted at Tinka. "Well, kittiedoolie!" It was the only pet
name in his vocabulary, except the "dear" and "hon." with which he recog-
nized his wife, and he flung it at Tinka every morning.

He gulped a cup of coffee in the hope of pacifying his stomach and his
soul. His stomach ceased to feel as though it did not belong to him, but
Verona began to be conscientious and annoying, and abruptly there re-

turned to Babbitt the doubts regarding life and families and business which had clawed at him when his dream-life and the slim fairy girl had fled.

Verona had for six months been filing-clerk at the Gruensberg Leather Company offices, with a prospect of becoming secretary to Mr. Gruensberg and thus, as Babbitt defined it, "getting some good out of your expensive college education till you're ready to marry and settle down."

But now said Verona: "Father! I was talking to a classmate of mine that's working for the Associated Charities—oh, Dad, there's the sweetest little babies that come to the milk-station there!—and I feel as though I ought to be doing something worth while like that."

"What do you mean 'worth while'? If you get to be Gruensberg's secretary—and maybe you would, if you kept up your shorthand and didn't go sneaking off to concerts and talkfests every evening—I guess you'll find thirty-five or forty bones a week worth while!"

"I know, but—oh, I want to—contribute—I wish I were working in a settlement-house. I wonder if I could get one of the department-stores to let me put in a welfare-department with a nice rest-room and chintzes and wicker chairs and so on and so forth. Or I could—"

"Now you look here! The first thing you got to understand is that all this uplift and flipflop and settlement-work and recreation is nothing in God's world but the entering wedge for socialism. The sooner a man learns he isn't going to be coddled, and he needn't expect a lot of free grub and, uh, all these free classes and flipflop and doodads for his kids unless he earns 'em, why, the sooner he'll get on the job and produce—produce—produce! That's what the country needs, and not all this fancy stuff that just enfeebles the will-power of the working man and gives his kids a lot of notions above their class. And you—if you'd tend to business instead of fooling and fussing— All the time! When I was a young man I made up my mind what I wanted to do, and stuck to it through thick and thin, and that's why I'm where I am today."

QUESTION

What are the key ideas of the Puritan ethic, and how have they affected the individual and American society?

Chapter 13

Politics

Conflict is a normal human interaction, and in order to keep conflict from becoming too pervasive, institutions have been created in order to resolve conflict. Conflict resolution is the primary function of politics or the political process.

Of critical concern to any political process is public opinion, because it defines the boundaries in which politics can operate. If politicians go beyond the limits set by public opinion, the people will let their leaders know how they feel through various means, either peaceful or violent. The influence of public opinion on political leaders is quite visible in the chapter from Leon Uris's *Exodus*.

Another problem for the political process is the amount of support that the people give to it. A political system cannot continue to exist without support, and if the people begin to distrust the system, then the political process is hampered. In America alienation or distrust and aloofness from the political process has been increasing, and it has not gone unnoticed. In *The Drifters* James Michener has captured the mood of the people, among the young and the old alike.

Exodus

Leon Uris

Every political system wants to perpetuate itself. No regime has willingly given up and, consequently, institutions have been established so that political change can occur. If the system does not cope with its various problems, it will subsequently go out of existence.

One way in which a political system can perpetuate itself is through public opinion. By knowing what the people are thinking and to what extent, political leaders can react in a positive manner to try to alleviate any discord. Public opinion is a channel through which the people can funnel information and, it is hoped, readjust the system.

The power of public opinion and its effect on political leaders is portrayed in this chapter from the novel *Exodus.* Set in the post–World War II period, a shipload of European Jews is bound for Palestine but is detained by British officials who are limiting Jewish migration to that area. The Jewish leaders, particularly Ari Ben Canaan, want to end the stalemate and start a hunger strike among the children in order to dramatize their demands. British officials are then subject to world public opinion and have to make a difficult decision, as the chapter indicates.

HUNGER STRIKE
CALLED ON EXODUS!

Children Vow Starvation Rather than Return to Caraolos.

After allowing the story to build up over a two-week period, Ari Ben Canaan fooled everyone by launching an offensive. It was no game of "wait and see" now; the children were forcing a decision.

A huge sign was tied to the sides of the *Exodus* with lettering in English, French, and Hebrew. The sign read:

Hunger Strike/Hour #1

Hunger Strike/Hour #15

Two boys and a girl, aged ten, twelve, and fifteen, were brought on the forward deck of the *Exodus* and laid out, unconscious.

Hunger Strike/Hour #20

Ten children were stretched out on the forward deck.

"For Christ's sake, Kitty, stop pacing and sit down!"

"It's over twenty hours now. How much longer is he going to let this go on? I just haven't had the courage to go to the quay and look. Is Karen one of those children unconscious on deck?"

"I told you ten times she wasn't."

"They aren't strong children to begin with and they've been cooped up on that ship for two weeks. They have no stamina left." Kitty pulled nervously at a cigarette and tugged at her hair. "That man is a beast. An inhuman beast."

"I've been thinking about that," Mark said. "I've been thinking about it a lot. I wonder if we really understand what is driving those people so hard. Have you ever seen Palestine? It's worthless desert in the south end and eroded in the middle and swamp up north. It's stinking, it's sunbaked, and it's in the middle of a sea of fifty million sworn enemies. Yet they break their necks to get there. They call it the Land of Milk and Honey . . . they sing about water and sprinklers and irrigation ditches. Two weeks ago I told Ari Ben Canaan that the Jews don't have a patent on suffering but I'm beginning to wonder. I swear I wonder. I wonder how something can hurt so badly that can drive them so hard."

"Don't defend them, Mark, and don't defend those people."

"Try to remember one thing. Ben Canaan couldn't do this without the support of those kids. They're behind him one hundred per cent."

"That's what hurts," Kitty said, "this loyalty. This fantastic loyalty they have for each other."

The phone rang. Mark answered, listened, and hung up.

"What is it? I said what is it, Mark!"

"They've brought some more kids up on the deck unconscious. A half dozen of them."

"Is . . . is . . . Karen . . . ?"

"I don't know. I'm going to find out."

"Mark."

"What?"

"I want to go on the *Exodus.*"

"That's impossible."

"I can't take it any more," she said.

"If you do this you're finished."

"No, Mark . . . it's different. If I knew she were alive and well I could bear it. I swear I could. I made myself know that. But I can't just sit idly and know she's dying. I can't do that."

"Even if I can get Ben Canaan to let you on the *Exodus* the British won't let you."

"You must," she said fiercely, "you must."

She stood with her back to the door and blocked his exit. Her face determined. Mark lowered his eyes. "I'll do what I can," he said.

Hunger Strike/Hour #35

Angry crowds in Paris and Rome demonstrated before the British embassies. Fierce oratory and placards demanded the release of the *Exodus.* Police clubs and tear gas were used in Paris to disperse the mob. In Copenhagen and in Stockholm and in Brussels and in The Hague there were other demonstrations. These were more orderly.

Hunger Strike/Hour #38

A spontaneous general strike swept over the island of Cyprus in protest against the British. Transportation stopped, businesses shut down, and ports closed, theaters and restaurants locked their doors. Famagusta, Nicosia, Larnaca, and Limassol looked like morgues.

Hunger Strike/Hour #40

Ari Ben Canaan stared at his lieutenants. He looked into the somber faces of Joab, David, Zev, and Hank Schlosberg.

Zev, the Galilee farmer, spoke up first. "I am a soldier, I cannot stand by and watch children starve to death."

"In Palestine," Ari snapped, "youngsters this same age are already fighters in Gadna."

"It is one thing to fight and it is another to starve to death."

"This is only another way of fighting," Ari said.

Joab Yarkoni had worked with Ari for many years and had served with him in World War II. "I have never gone against you, Ari. The minute one of those children dies this whole thing is liable to boomerang on us."

Ari looked over to Hank Schlosberg, the American captain. Hank shrugged. "You're the boss, Ari, but the crew is getting jittery. They didn't bargain for this."

"In other words," Ari said, "you want to surrender."

Their silence confirmed it.

"David, what about you? I haven't heard from you."

David, a scholar, was steeped in the Torah and in the holy books. He had a closeness to God that none of the rest of them had and they respected it.

"Six million Jews died in gas chambers not knowing why they died," he said. "If three hundred of us on the *Exodus* die we will certainly know why. The world will know too. When we were a nation two thousand years ago and when we rebelled against Roman and Greek rule we Jews established the tradition of fighting to the last man. We did this at Arbela and

Jerusalem. We did this at Beitar and Herodium and Machaerus. At Masada we held out against the Romans for four years and when they entered the fort they found us all dead. No people, anywhere, have fought for their freedom as have our people. We drove the Romans and the Greeks from our land until we were dispersed to the four corners of the world. We have not had much opportunity to fight as a nation for two thousand years. When we had that opportunity at the Warsaw ghetto we did honor to our tradition. I say if we leave this boat and willingly return to the barbed-wire prisons then we have broken faith with God."

"Are there any further questions?" Ari said.

Hunger Strike/Hour #42

In the United States, South Africa, and England mass prayer meetings were being held in synagogues, and in many churches there were prayers for the safety of the children on the *Exodus*.

Hunger Strike/Hour #45

The Jews in Argentina began to fast in sympathy with the children aboard the *Exodus*.

Hunger Strike/Hour #47

It was getting dark as Kitty boarded the *Exodus*. The stench was over-powering. All over the deck, in the lifeboats, on the superstructure she saw the crush of humanity. Everyone was lying down and absolutely motionless to conserve energy.

"I want to see those children who have passed out," she said.

David led her to the bow of the ship where there were three rows of unconscious children, sixty in number. David knelt and held his lantern close to the bodies as Kitty moved from one to the other, feeling their pulses and looking into the pupils of their eyes. Half a dozen times she thought she would faint as her heart pounded and she rolled over a child who looked like Karen.

David led her around the packed deck, stepping over the prostrate bodies. The children stared listlessly at her with dazed eyes. Their hair was matted and dirt caked their faces.

David led her down the steep ladder onto the hold. She nearly vomited as the stink enveloped her. In the half light she saw the ghastly sight of the children packed in shelves one atop the other.

On the deck of the hold they lay piled against each other. She found Karen in a corner, enmeshed in a tangle of arms and legs. Dov was asleep next to her. They lay on a pile of rags and the deck was slimy beneath them. "Karen," she whispered. "Karen, it's me, Kitty."

Karen's eyes fluttered open. There were huge black circles beneath them and her lips were caked dry. She was too weak to sit up.

"Kitty?"

"Yes, it's me."

Karen held her arms open and Kitty held her tightly for many moments. "Don't leave, Kitty. I'm so frightened."

"I'll be near," Kitty whispered, releasing the girl.

She went to the hospital and examined the limited supply of drugs and sighed despondently. "There is very little that can be done," she said to David. "I'll try to make them as comfortable as possible. Can you and Joab work with me?"

"Of course."

"Some of those unconscious are in serious condition. We'll have to try to sponge them to get their fevers down. It is chilly up on deck. We'll keep them covered. Then I want everyone who is capable of working to get this ship clean."

Kitty labored feverishly for hours to ward off death. It was like trying to fill an ocean with a thimble. As soon as one child was brought under control three more became seriously ill. She hadn't the drugs, water, or other facilities to do very much. Food, the one weapon, could not be used.

Hunger Strike/Hour #81

Seventy children in coma lay on the deck of the *Exodus.*

On the quay of Kyrenia harbor there were angry grumbles of insubordination from the British ranks. Many of the soldiers could stand it no longer and asked to be removed, even at the risk of court-martial. The eyes of Cyprus fastened on Kyrenia.

Hunger Strike/Hour #82

Karen Hansen Clement was carried to the bow of the ship, unconscious.

Hunger Strike/Hour #83

Kitty walked into the wheelhouse and slumped exhausted into a chair. She had worked for thirty-five straight hours and her mind was muddled and dazed. Ari poured her a stiff brandy.

"Go on and drink," he said. "You aren't on strike."

She swallowed it down, and a second drink brought her to her senses. She stared at Ari Ben Canaan long and hard. He was a powerful man. He showed almost no effects of the siege. She looked into his cold eyes and wondered what thoughts, what plots, what tricks were running through his brain. She wondered if he was frightened or even knew fear. She wondered if he was sad or shaken.

"I was expecting you to come up here to see me much sooner," he said.

"I won't beg you, Ari Ben Canaan. Ben Canaan and God . . . in that order . . . isn't that right? Well, there are a dozen children on the verge of death. I am merely reporting to you like a good Palmachnik. They're going to die, Mr. Ben Canaan. How do you rule?"

"I've been insulted before, Kitty. It doesn't bother me. Is this humanity of yours so great that it cries out for all these children or does it appeal for the life of one child?"

"You have no right to ask that."

"You are begging for the life of one girl. I am begging for the lives of a quarter of a million people."

She rose. "I had better get back to work. Ari, you knew why I wanted to come on board the *Exodus*. Why did you let me?"

He turned his back to her and looked from the window out to sea where the cruiser and destroyers stood watch. "Maybe I wanted to see you."

Hunger Strike/Hour #85

General Sir Clarence Tevor-Browne paced up and down Sutherland's office. The smoke from his cigar clouded the room. He stopped several times and looked out the window in the direction of Kyrenia.

Sutherland tapped out his pipe and studied the array of sandwiches on the tray on the coffee table. "Won't you sit down, Sir Clarence, and have a bite to eat and a spot of tea?"

Tevor-Browne looked at his wrist watch and sighed. He seated himself and picked up a sandwich, stared at it, nibbled, then threw it down. "I feel guilty when I eat," he said.

"This is a bad business to be in for a man with a conscience," Sutherland said. "Two wars, eleven foreign posts, six decorations, and three orders. Now I've been stopped in my tracks by a band of unarmed children. A fine way to end thirty years of service, eh, Sir Clarence?"

Tevor-Browne lowered his eyes.

"Oh, I know you've been wanting to talk to me," said Sutherland.

Tevor-Browne poured some tea and sighed, half embarrassed. "See here, Bruce. If it were up to me . . ."

"Nonsense, Sir Clarence. Don't feel badly. It is I who feel badly. I let you down." Sutherland rose and his eyes brimmed. "I am tired. I am very tired."

"We will arrange a full pension and have the retirement as quiet as possible. You can count on me," Tevor-Browne said. "See here, Bruce. I stopped over in Paris on my way here and I had a long talk with Neddie. I told her about your predicament. Listen, old boy, with some encouragement from you, you two could get together again. Neddie wants you back and you're going to need her."

Sutherland shook his head. "Neddie and I have been through for years. All we ever had between us that was meaningful was the Army. That's what held us together."

"Any plans?"

"These months on Cyprus have done something to me, Sir Clarence, especially these past few weeks. You may not believe this, but I don't feel that I've suffered a defeat. I feel that I may have won something very great. Something I lost a long time ago."

"And what is that?"

"Truth. Do you remember when I took this post? You told me that the only kingdom that runs on right and wrong is the kingdom of heaven and the kingdoms of the earth run on oil."

"I remember it well," Tevor-Browne said.

"Yes," Sutherland said, "I have thought so much about it since this *Exodus* affair. All my life I have known the truth and I have known right from wrong. Most of us do. To know the truth is one thing. To live it . . . to create the kingdom of heaven on earth is another. How many times in a man's life does he do things that are repulsive to his morality in order to exist? How I have admired those few men in this world who could stand up for their convictions in the face of shame, torture, and even death. What a wonderful feeling of inner peace they must have. Something that we ordinary mortals can never know. Gandhi is such a man.

"I am going to that rotten sliver of land that these Jews call their kingdom of heaven on earth. I want to know it all . . . Galilee, Jerusalem . . . all of it."

"I envy you, Bruce."

"Perhaps I'll settle down near Safed . . . on Mount Canaan."

Major Alistair entered the office. He was pale and his hand shook as he gave Tevor-Browne a note to read. Tevor-Brown read it and reread it and could not believe his eyes. "Great God, save us all," he whispered. He passed the note to Bruce Sutherland.

URGENT

Ari Ben Canaan, spokesman for the Exodus, *announced that beginning at noon tomorrow ten volunteers a day will commit suicide on the bridge of the ship in full view of the British garrison. This protest practice will continue until either the* Exodus *is permitted to sail for Palestine or everyone aboard is dead.*

Bradshaw, with Humphrey Crawford and half a dozen aides, sped out of London to the quiet of a peaceful, isolated little house in the country. He had fourteen hours to act before the suicides on the *Exodus* began.

He had badly miscalculated the entire thing. First, the tenacity and determination of the children on the ship. Second, the powerful propaganda the incident created. Finally, he had not imagined that Ben Canaan would take the offensive and press the issue as he had. Bradshaw was a stubborn man but he knew when he was defeated, and he now turned his efforts to making a face-saving settlement.

Bradshaw had Crawford and his aides cable or phone a dozen of the top Jewish leaders in England, Palestine, and the United States to ask them to intervene. The Palestinians, in particular, might possibly dissuade Ben Canaan. At the very least they could stall the action long enough to enable Bradshaw to come up with some alternate plans. If he could get Ben Canaan to agree to negotiate then he could talk the *Exodus* to death. Within six hours, Bradshaw had his answers from the Jewish leaders. They answered uniformly: WE WILL NOT INTERCEDE.

Next Bradshaw contacted Tevor-Browne on Cyprus. He instructed the general to inform the *Exodus* that the British were working out a compromise and to delay the deadline for twenty-four hours.

Tevor-Browne carried out these instructions and relayed Ben Canaan's answer back to England.

URGENT

Ben Canaan informed us there is nothing to discuss. He says either the Exodus *sails or it doesn't sail. He further states that complete amnesty to the Palestinians aboard is part of the conditions. Ben Canaan summarized: Let my people go.*

Tevor-Browne

Cecil Bradshaw could not sleep. He paced back and forth, back and forth. It was just a little over six hours before the children of the *Exodus* would begin committing suicide. He had only three hours left in which to make a decision to hand to the Cabinet. No compromise could be reached.

Was he fighting a madman? Or was this Ari Ben Canaan a shrewd and heartless schemer who had deftly led him deeper and deeper into a trap?

LET MY PEOPLE GO!
Bradshaw walked to his desk and flicked on the lamp.

URGENT

Ari Ben Canaan, spokesman for the Exodus, *announced that beginning at noon tomorrow ten volunteers a day will commit suicide . . .*

Suicide . . . suicide . . . suicide . . .
Bradshaw's hand shook so violently he dropped the paper.

Also on his desk were a dozen communiqués from various European and American governments. In that polite language that diplomats use they all expressed concern over the *Exodus* impasse. He also had notes from each of the Arab governments expressing the view that if the *Exodus* were permitted to sail for Palestine it would be considered an affront to every Arab.

Cecil Bradshaw was confused now. The past few days had been a living hell. How had it all begun? Thirty years of formulating Middle Eastern policy and now he was in his worst trouble over an unarmed salvage tug.

What queer trick of fate had given him the mantle of an oppressor? Nobody could possibly accuse him of being anti-Jewish. Secretly Bradshaw admired the Jews in Palestine and understood the meaning of their return. He enjoyed the hours he had spent arguing with Zionists around conference tables, bucking their brilliant debaters. Cecil Bradshaw believed from the bottom of his heart that England's interest lay with the Arabs. Yet the Mandate had grown to over half a million Jews. And the Arabs were adamant that the British were fostering a Jewish nation in their midst.

During all the years of work he had been realistic with himself. What was happening? He could see his own grandchildren lying on the deck of the *Exodus*. Bradshaw knew his Bible as well as any well-brought-up Englishman and like most Englishmen had a tremendous sense of honor although he was not deeply religious. Could it be that the *Exodus* was driven by mystic forces? No, he was a practical diplomat and he did not believe in the supernatural.

Yet—he had an army and a navy and the power to squash the *Exodus* and all the other illegal runners—but he could not bring himself to do it.

The Pharaoh of Egypt had had might on his side too! Sweat ran down Bradshaw's face. It was all nonsense! He was tired and the pressure had been too great. What foolishness!

LET MY PEOPLE GO!

Bradshaw walked to the library and found a Bible and in near panic began to read through the pages of Exodus and about the Ten Plagues that God sent down on the land of Egypt.

Was he Pharoah? Would a curse rain down on Britain? He went back to his room and tried to rest, but a staccato rhythm kept running through his tired brain . . . let my people go . . . let my people go . . .

"Crawford!" he yelled. "Crawford!"

Crawford ran in, tying his robe. "You called?"

"Crawford. Get through to Tevor-Browne on Cyprus at once. Tell him . . . tell him to let the *Exodus* sail for Palestine."

QUESTION

In what ways can public opinion define the boundaries in which the political leaders of a society act?

The Drifters

James Michener

For any government to continue to exist, it must have a minimal amount of support from the people. Thus, laws are made in such a manner that people believe that the laws are right and therefore should be obeyed. If, however, the people lost confidence or trust in their leaders, this could undermine the operation of the government.

One phenomenon that can undermine a government is alienation. Alienation or the feeling of estrangement and disillusionment with one's government is a major factor in American society, for it crosscuts all sectors of society: class, sex, race, nationality, and age. Many people are dissatisfied with the government and want to change it but do not know how. Consequently, their trust in the government is dwindling.

In his novel *The Drifters*, James Michener captures this feeling of alienation not only from the young people, the most common source of alienation, but also from the older generation. George Fairbanks, the narrator of the story, and Henry Holt, a technical representative for a large overseas company, come to realize that they have the same values as the young Americans they have met. The only difference is that Fairbanks and Holt have "copped out" in a socially acceptable manner,

while the youth have expressed their disillusionment in one that is unac-
ceptable.

Often as I walked back to my hotel at night I reflected on the discussions I
had heard in Inger's and I was amazed at how vocal the young people were
in stating their opinions and how little they read to support them. This was
a generation without books. Of course, everyone has handled volumes by
Herbert Marcuse and Frantz Fanon, but I found no one who had actually
read the more easily understood works like *Essay on Liberation* or *Toward
the African Revolution* or *The Wretched of the Earth*. It was also true that
most of the travelers had read newspaper reports of Marshall McLuhan's
theories, and hardly a day passed but someone would proclaim, 'After all,
the medium is the massage,' but I met no one who had read the book of
which this taut summary was the title or who knew what it meant.

There was always a dog-eared copy of the *I-Ching* somewhere in the
hotel, and many had dipped into it, but no one had read it, not even Claire
from Sacramento. The strong books of the age were unknown to this group,
and I often wondered how they had got as far along in college as they had.
On the other hand, their verbal knowledge was considerable and they could
expatiate on almost any topic. Six pronouncements I noted one night were
typical of the conclusions reached every night.

'We have entered what Walter Lippmann terms the New Dark Age.'

'Before 1976 an armed showdown between races will be inevitable in
American cities.'

'The military-industrial complex rules our nation and dictates a contin-
uance of the Vietnam war.'

'A permanent unemployment cadre of seven million must be anticipated.'

'By the year 2000 we will have seven billion people on earth.'

'Universities are prisoners of the Establishment.'

But in spite of these statements, I found that most Americans overseas
were hard-line conservatives; of the many in Marrakech, the majority had
supported the Republican party in 1968 and would do so again in 1972. I
took the trouble to check the six young people I had seen unconscious on
the floor of the Casino Royale; Claire took me back one morning, and I
found that four were solid Republicans, one was a neo-Nazi, and Moor-
man, the honor student from Michigan who sang ballads with Gretchen,
said 'I don't know what I am.'

I found more than a few supporters of George Wallace, and Constitutionalists, and crypto-fascists, and backers of other ill-defined movements. The basic ideas of the John Birch Society were often voiced, but I met no one who admitted membership.

Most older people who visited Marrakech were surprised to find that among the young Americans, there were practically no oldstyle American liberals. This was true for obvious reasons. To get as far as Marrakech required real money, so that those who made it had to come from well-to-do families of a conservative bent, and throughout the world children tend to follow the political attitudes of their fathers. A boy of nineteen might rebel against Harvard University, country-club weekends and the dress of his father, and run away to Marrakech to prove it, but his fundamental political and social attitudes would continue to be those his father had taught him at age eleven. In my work I constantly met conservative adult Americans who, when they saw the young people with long hair and beards, expected them to be revolutionaries; they were pleasantly gratified to find that the young people were as reactionary as they were.

Harvey Holt exemplified this response. When he first met the gang at Pamplona he was positive they must be revolutionaries, but after several long discussions involving politics, he told me 'You know, apart from Vietnam and this nonsense about brotherhood between the races, these kids are pretty solid.' Later he said, 'You could be misled if you listened to their songs. You'd think they were going out to burn down New York. But when you talk to them about economics and voting, you find they're just as conservative as you or me . . . but they do it in their own way.' I asked him how he thought I voted, and he said, 'Oh, you sympathize a lot with the young people, but I'm sure that in a pinch you can be trusted.'

'To vote Republican?'

'How else can a sensible man vote?' he asked.

I was constantly appalled by the poverty of language exhibited by many of the young people, and these from our better colleges. Claire, as I have said, sometimes talked for a whole hour saying little but 'you know' and 'like wow,' but this had a certain cute illiteracy. More intolerable was the girl from Ohio who said at least once every paragraph, 'You better believe it.' Whenever one of the boys from the south agreed with one of my opinions, he said, 'You ain't just whistlin' "Dixie," bub.' A college girl from Missouri introduced every statement with: 'I just want you to know,' while a young man from Brooklyn related everything to André Gide—he seemed quite incapable of any other comparison.

Two aspects of the intellectual life of these young Americans surprised me. The first was politics. Not one person I knew ever mentioned the name

Richard Nixon; they rejected Lyndon Johnson and ridiculed Hubert Humphrey, charging these men with having betrayed youth, but Nixon they dismissed. They would have voted for him, had they bothered to vote, and would vote for him in 1972, if they happened to be registered, but he played no role in their lives. A whole segment of American history was simply expunged by these people; they had opted out with a vengeance.

I say that they would vote Republican in 1972, if they voted, and by this I mean that of all the young Americans I met over the age of twenty-one, not one had ever bothered to vote, and it seemed unlikely to me that any would do so much before the age of thirty-two or thirty-three. To hear them talk, you would think they were battering down the barricades of the Establishment, and some few I suppose would have been willing to try, but they were not willing to vote; in fact, I met none who were even registered.

In spite of this seeming indifference, there were those few I reflected upon that morning when I stood in the Casino Royale amid the stenches and the fallen forms, the few who were painfully carving out an understanding of their world, and their place in it. Because they came from families with income and advantage, they tended to be Republican, and when they settled down, they were going to be good Republicans. Some, like Gretchen, had worked for Senator Eugene McCarthy, but not because he was a Democrat; they would quickly return to creative Republicanism and the nation would profit from the forging process they had gone through.

But when I have said this about politics, I have still not touched upon the mighty chasm that separated them from me: they honestly believed that their generation lived under the threat of the hydrogen bomb and that consequently their lives would be different from what mine had been. They were convinced that no man my age could comprehend what the bomb meant to them, and even when I pointed out that a man of sixty-one like me had been forced to spend nearly half his adult life under the shadow of nuclear bombs and had adjusted to it, they cried, 'Ah, there it is! You'd enjoyed about half your life before the bomb fell. We haven't'. It seemed there could be no bridge of understanding on this point, and after several futile attempts to build one, I concluded that on this topic we could not talk together meaningfully.

QUESTION

What is alienation, and how extensive and pervasive is it in American society today?

Chapter 14

Change

If any one idea about the nature of society can safely be labeled constant, it is the thesis that society is never constant; it's always changing. Change is an in-built norm of society, albeit in many different forms. It can be major or minor, immediate or slow, violent or peaceful, temporary or permanent. Regardless of what form it takes, change is inevitable.

Change, its inevitability and its impact on society, has been the subject of many sociological studies, and Alvin Toffler's *Future Shock* is a good example of one which tries to understand the nature of change so that society can learn to cope with change. Unfortunately, the necessary formula has not been found yet.

It is precisely this point that the famous operant-conditioning psychologist B. F. Skinner had in mind when he wrote his utopian novel, *Walden Two*. Skinner wanted to demonstrate that there are ways in which change, its form, and its impact can be minimized through planning. Thus he wrote this novel to prove his idea. In the following excerpt, a director of Walden Two tries to explain to some visitors just how the community works.

Walden Two

B. F. Skinner

We found space near the windows of a small lounge and drew up chairs so that we could look out over the slowly darkening landscape. Frazier seemed to have no particular discussion prepared and he had begun to look a little tired. Castle must have been full of things to say, but he apparently felt that I should open the conversation.

"We are grateful for your kindness," I said to Frazier, "not only in asking us to visit Walden Two but in giving us so much of your time. I'm afraid it's something of an imposition."

"On the contrary," said Frazier. "I'm fully paid for talking with you. Two labor-credits are allowed each day for taking charge of guests of Walden Two. I can use only one of them, but it's a bargain even so, because I'm more than fairly paid by your company."

"Labor-credits?" I said.

"I'm sorry. I had forgotten. Labor-credits are a sort of money. But they're not coins or bills—just entries in a ledger. All goods and services are free, as you saw in the dining room this evening. Each of us pays for what he uses with twelve hundred labor-credits each year—say, four credits for each workday. We change the value according to the needs of the community. At two hours of work per credit—an eight-hour day—we could operate at a handsome profit. We're satisfied to keep just a shade beyond breaking even. The profit system is bad even when the worker gets the profits, because the strain of overwork isn't relieved by even a large reward. All we ask is to make expenses, with a slight margin of safety; we adjust the value of the labor-credit accordingly. At present it's about one hour of work per credit."

"Your members work only four hours a day?" I said. There was an overtone of outraged virtue in my voice, as if I had asked if they were all adulterous.

"On the average," Frazier replied casually. In spite of our obvious interest he went on at once to another point. "A credit system also makes it possible to evaluate a job in terms of the willingness of the members to undertake it. After all, a man isn't doing more or less than his share because of the time he puts in; it's what he's doing that counts. So we simply assign different credit values to different kinds of work, and adjust them from time to time on the basis of demand. Bellamy suggested the principle in *Looking Backward.*"

"An unpleasant job like cleaning sewers has a high value, I suppose," I said.

"Exactly. Somewhere around one and a half credits per hour. The sewer man works a little over two hours a day. Pleasanter jobs have lower values—say point seven or point eight. That means five hours a day, or even more. Working in the flower gardens has a very low value—point one. No one makes a living at it, but many people like to spend a little time that way, and we give them credit. In the long run, when the values have been adjusted, all kinds of work are equally desirable. If they weren't, there would be a demand for the more desirable, and the credit value would be changed. Once in a while we manipulate a preference, if some job seems to be avoided without cause."

"I suppose you put phonographs in your dormitories which repeat 'I like to work in sewers. Sewers are lots of fun,' " said Castle.

"No, Walden Two isn't that kind of brave new world," said Frazier. "We don't *propagandize.* That's a basic principle. I don't deny that it would be possible. We could make the heaviest work appear most honorable and desirable. Something of the sort has always been done by well-organized governments—to facilitate the recruiting of armies, for example. But not here. You may say that we propagandize *all* labor, if you like, but I see no objection to that. If we can make work pleasanter by proper training, why shouldn't we? But I digress."

"What about the knowledge and skill required in many jobs?" said Castle. "Doesn't that interfere with free bidding? Certainly you can't allow just anyone to work as a doctor."

"No, of course not. The principle has to be modified where long training is needed. Still, the preferences of the community as a whole determine the final value. If our doctors were conspicuously overworked *according to our standards,* it would be hard to get young people to choose that profession. We must see to it that there are enough doctors to bring the average schedule within range of the Walden Two standard."

"What if nobody wanted to be a doctor?" I said.

"Our trouble is the other way round."

"I thought as much," said Castle. "Too many of your young memebers will want to go into interesting lines in spite of the work load. What do you do, then?"

"Let them know how many places will be available, and let them decide. We're glad to have more than enough doctors, of course, and could always find some sort of work for them, but we can't offer more of a strictly medical practice than our disgustingly good health affords."

"Then you don't offer complete personal freedom, do you?" said Castle, with ill-concealed excitement. "You haven't really resolved the conflict between a *laissez-faire* and a planned society."

"I think we have. Yes. But you must know more about our educational system before I can show you how. The fact is, it's very unlikely that anyone at Walden Two will set his heart on a course of action so firmly that he'll be unhappy if it isn't open to him. That's as true of the choice of a girl as of a profession. Personal jealousy is almost unknown among us, and for a simple reason: we provide a broad experience and many attractive alternatives. The tender sentiment of the 'one and only' has less to do with constancy of the heart than with singleness of opportunity. The chances are that our superfluous young premedic will find other courses open to him which will very soon prove equally attractive."

"There's another case, too," I said. "You must have some sort of government. I don't see how you can permit a free choice of jobs there."

"Our only government is a Board of Planners," said Frazier, with a change of tone which suggested that I had set off another standard harangue. "The name goes back to the days when Walden Two existed only on paper. There are six Planners, usually three men and three women. The sexes are on such equal terms here that no one guards equality very jealously. They may serve for ten years, but no longer. Three of us who've been on the Board since the beginning retire this year.

"The Planners are charged with the success of the community. They make policies, review the work of the Managers, keep an eye on the state of the nation in general. They also have certain judicial functions. They're allowed six hundred credits a year for their services, which leaves two credits still due each day. At least one must be worked out in straight physical labor. That's why I can claim only one credit for acting as your Virgil through *il paradiso.*"

"It was Beatrice," I corrected.

"How do you choose your Planners?" said Rodge.

"The Board selects a replacement from a pair of names supplied by the Managers."

"The members don't vote for them?" said Castle.

"*No,*" said Frazier emphatically.

"What are Managers?" I said hastily.

"What the name implies: specialists in charge of the divisions and services of Walden Two. There are Managers of Food, Health, Play, Arts, Dentistry, Dairy, various industries, Supply, Labor, Nursery School, Advanced Education, and dozens of others. They requisition labor according to their needs, and their job is the managerial function which survives after they've assigned as much as possible to others. They're the hardest workers among us. It's an exceptional person who seeks and finds a place as Manager. He must have ability and a real concern for the welfare of the community."

"*They* are elected by the members, I suppose?" said Castle, but it was obvious that he hoped for nothing of the sort.

"The Managers aren't honorific personages, but carefully trained and tested specialists. How could the members gauge their ability? No, these are very much like Civil Service jobs. You work up to be a Manager—through intermediate positions which carry a good deal of responsibility and provide the necessary apprenticeship."

"Then the members have no voice whatsoever," said Castle in a carefully controlled voice, as if he were filing the point away for future use.

"Nor do they wish to have," said Frazier flatly.

"Do you count your professional people as Managers?" I said, again hastily.

"Some of them. The Manager of Health is one of our doctors—Mr. Meyerson. But the word 'profession' has little meaning here. All professional training is paid for by the community and is looked upon as part of our common capital, exactly like any other tool."

"*Mr.* Meyerson?" I said. "Your doctor is not an M.D.? Not a real physician?"

"As real as they come, with a degree from a top-ranking medical school. But we don't use honorific titles. Why call him *Doctor* Meyerson? We don't call our Dairy Manager *Dairyman* Larson. The medical profession has been slow to give up the chicanery of prescientific medicine. It's abandoning the hocus-pocus of the ciphered prescription, but the honorific title is still too dear. In Walden Two—"

"Then you distinguish only Planners, Managers, and Workers," I said to prevent what threatened to be a major distraction.

"And Scientists. The community supports a certain amount of research. Experiments are in progress in plant and animal breeding, the control of infant behavior, educational processes of several sorts, and the use of some of our raw materials. Scientists receive the same labor-credits as Managers—two or three per day depending upon the work."

"No pure science?" exclaimed Castle with mock surprise.

"Only in our spare time," said Frazier. "And I shan't be much disturbed by your elevated eyebrows until you show me where any other condition prevails. Our policy is better than that of your educational institutions, where the would-be scientist pays his way by teaching."

"Have you forgotten our centers of pure research?" I said.

"Pure? If you mean completely unshackled with respect to means and ends, I challenge you to name five. It's otherwise pay-as-you-go. Do you know of any 'pure' scientist in our universities who wouldn't settle for two hours of physical labor each day instead of soul-searching work he's now compelled to do in the name of education?"

I had no ready answer, for I had to consider the cultural engineering needed to equate the two possibilities. My silence began to seem significant, and I cast about for a question along a different line.

"Why should everyone engage in menial work?" I asked. "Isn't that really a misuse of manpower if a man has special talents or abilities?"

"There's no misuse. Some of us would be smart enough to get along without doing physical work, but we're also smart enough to know that in the long run it would mean trouble. A leisure class would grow like a cancer until the strain upon the rest of the community became intolerable. We might escape the consequences in our own lifetime, but we couldn't visualize a permanent society on such a plan. The really intelligent man doesn't want to feel that his work is being done by anyone else. He's sensitive enough to be disturbed by slight resentments which, multiplied a millionfold, mean his downfall. Perhaps he remembers his own reactions when others have imposed on him; perhaps he has had a more severe ethical training. Call it conscience, if you like." He threw his head back and studied the ceiling. When he resumed, his tone was dramatically far-away.

"That's the virtue of Walden Two which pleases me most. I was never happy in being waited on. I could never enjoy the fleshpots for thinking of what might be going on below stairs." It was obviously a borrowed expression, for Frazier's early life had not been affluent. But he suddenly continued in a loud, clear voice which could leave no doubt of his sincerity, "Here a man can hold up his head and say, 'I've done my share!'"

He seemed ashamed of his excitement, of his show of sentiment, and I felt a strange affection for him. Castle missed the overtones and broke in abruptly.

"But can't superior ability be held in check so it won't lead to tyranny? And isn't it possible to convince the menial laborer that he's only doing the kind of work for which he's best suited and that the smart fellow is really working, too?"

"Provided the smart fellow is really working," Frazier answered, rallying himself with an effort. "Nobody resents the fact that our Planners and Managers could wear white collars if they wished. But you're quite right: with adequate cultural design a society might run smoothly, even though the physical work were not evenly distributed. It might even be possible, through such engineering, to sustain a small leisure class without serious danger. A well-organized society is so efficient and productive that a small area of waste is unimportant. A caste system of brains and brawn could be made to work because it's in the interest of brains to make it fair to brawn."

"Then why insist upon universal brawn?" said Castle impatiently.

"Simply because brains and brawn are never exclusive. No one of us is all brains or all brawn, and our lives must be adjusted accordingly. It's fatal to forget the minority element—fatal to treat brawn as if there were no brains, and perhaps more speedily fatal to treat brains as if there were no brawn. One or two hours of physical work each day is a health measure. Men have always lived by their muscles—you can tell that from their physiques. We mustn't let our big muscles atrophy just because we've devised superior ways of using the little ones. We haven't yet evolved a pure Man Thinking. Ask any doctor about the occupational diseases of the unoccupied. Because of certain cultural prejudices which Veblen might have noted, the doctor can prescribe nothing more than golf, or a mechanical horse, or chopping wood, provided the patient has no real need for wood. But what the doctor would like to say is 'Go to work!'

"But there's a better reason why brains must not neglect brawn," Frazier continued. "Nowadays it's the smart fellow, the small-muscle user, who finds himself in the position of governor. In Walden Two he makes plans, obtains materials, devises codes, evalutes trends, conducts experiments. In work of this sort the manager must keep an eye on the managed, must understand his needs, must experience his lot. That's why our Planners, Managers, and Scientists are required to work out some of their labor-credits in menial tasks. It's our constitutional guarantee that the problems of the big-muscle user won't be forgotten."

We fell silent. Our reflections in the windows mingled confusingly with the last traces of daylight in the southern sky. Finally Castle roused himself.

"But four hours a day!" he said. "I can't take that seriously. Think of the struggle to get a forty-hour week! What would our industrialists not give for your secret. Or our politicians! Mr. Frazier, we're all compelled to admire the life you are showing us, but I feel somehow as if you were exhibiting a lovely lady floating in mid-air. You've even passed a hoop about her to emphasize your wizardry. Now, when you pretend to tell us how the trick is done, we're told that the lady is supported by a slender thread. The explanation is as hard to accept as the illusion. Where's your proof?"

"The proof of an accomplished fact? Don't be absurd! But perhaps I can satisfy you by telling you how we knew it could be done before we tried."

"That would be something," said Castle dryly.

"Very well, then," said Frazier. "Let's take a standard seven-day week of eight hours a day. (The forty-hour week hasn't reached into every walk of life. Many a farmer would call it a vacation.) That's nearly 3000 hours per year. Our plan was to reduce it to 1500. Actually we did better than that, but how were we sure we could cut it in half? Will an answer to that satisfy you?"

"It will astonish me," said Castle.

"Very well, then," said Frazier quickly, as if he had actually been spurred on by Castle's remark. "First of all we have the obvious fact that four is more than half of eight. We work more skillfully and faster during the first four hours of the day. The eventual effect of a four-hour day is enormous, provided the rest of a man's time isn't spent too strenuously. Let's take a conservative estimate, to allow for tasks which can't be speeded up, and say that our four hours are the equivalent of five out of the usual eight. Do you agree?"

"I should be contentious if I didn't," said Castle. "But you're a long way from eight."

"Secondly," said Frazier, with a satisfied smile which promised that eight would be reached in due time, "we have the extra motivation that comes when a man is working for himself instead of for a profit-taking boss. That's a true 'incentive wage' and the effect is prodigious. Waste is avoided, workmanship is better, deliberate slowdowns unheard of. Shall we say that four hours of oneself are worth six out of eight for the other fellow?"

"And I hope you will point out," I said, "that the four are no harder than the six. Loafing doesn't really make a job easier. Boredom's more exhausting than heavy work. But what about the other two?"

"Let me remind you that not all Americans capable of working are now employed," said Frazier. "We're really comparing eight hours a day on the part of *some* with four hours on the part of practically *all*. In Walden Two we have no leisure class, no prematurely aged or occupationally disabled, no drunkenness, no criminals, far fewer sick. We have no unemploy-

ment due to bad planning. No one is paid to sit idle for the sake of maintaining labor standards. Our children work at an early age—moderately,
but happily. What will you settle for, Mr. Castle? May I add another hour
to my six?"

"I'm afraid I should let you add more than that," said Castle, laughing
with surprising good nature.

"But let's be conservative," said Frazier, obviously pleased, "and say
that when every potential worker puts in four hours for himself we have the
equivalent of perhaps two-thirds of all available workers putting in seven
out of eight hours for somebody else. Now, what about those who are
actually at work? Are they working to the best advantage? Have they been
carefully selected for the work they are doing? Are they making the best use
of labor-saving machines and methods? What percentage of the farms in
America are mechanized as we are here? Do the workers welcome and
improve upon labor-saving devices and methods? How many good workers
are free to move on to more productive levels? How much education do
workers receive to make them as efficient as possible?"

"I can't let you claim much credit for a better use of manpower," said
Castle, "if you give your members a free choice of jobs."

"It's an extravagance, you're right," said Frazier. "In another generation we shall do better; our educational system will see to that. I agree. Add
nothing for the waste due to misplaced talents." He was silent a moment, as
if calculating whether he could afford to make this concession.

"You still have an hour to account for," I reminded him.

"I know, I know," he said. "Well, how much of the machinery of
distribution have we eliminated—with the release of how many men? How
many jobs have we simply eliminated? Walk down any city street. How
often will you find people really usefully engaged? There's a bank. And
beyond it a loan company. And an advertising agency. And over there an
insurance office. And another." It was not effective showmanship, but Frazier seemed content to make his point at the cost of some personal dignity.
"We have a hard time explaining insurance to our children. Insurance
against what? And there's a funeral home—a crematory disposes of our
ashes as it sees fit." He threw off this subject with a shake of the head. "And
there and there the ubiquitous bars and taverns, equally useless. Drinking
isn't prohibited in Walden Two, but we all give it up as soon as we gratify
the needs which are responsible for the habit in the world at large."

"If I may be permitted to interrupt this little tour," I said, "what are
those needs?"

"Well, why do you drink?" said Frazier.

"I don't—a great deal. But I like a cocktail before dinner. In fact, my company isn't worth much until I've had one."

"On the contrary, I find it delightful," said Frazier.

"It's different here," I said, falling into his trap. Frazier and Castle laughed raucously.

"Of course it's different here!" Frazier shouted. "You need your cocktail to counteract the fatigue and boredom of a mismanaged society. Here we need no antidotes. No opiates. But why else do you drink? Or why does anyone?—since I can see you're not a typical case."

"Why—to forget one's troubles—" I stammered. "Of course, I see what you will say to that. But to get away, let's say, or to get a change—to lower one's inhibitions. You do have inhibitions, don't you? Perhaps someone else can help me out." I turned tactlessly to Barbara, who looked away.

Frazier chuckled quietly for a moment, and struck out again.

"Let me point out a few businesses which we haven't eliminated, but certainly streamlined with respect to manpower," he said. "The big department stores, the meat markets, the corner drugstores, the groceries, the automobile display rooms, the furniture stores, the shoe stores, the candy stores, all staffed with unnecessary people doing unnecessary things. Half the restaurants can be closed for good. And there's a beauty parlor and there a movie palace. And over there a dance hall, and there a bowling alley. And all the time busses and streetcars are whizzing by, carrying people to and fro from one useless spot to another."

It was a bad show but a devastating argument.

"Take your last hour and welcome," said Castle when he saw that Frazier was resting from his labors. "I should have taken your word for it. After all, as you say, it's an accomplished fact."

"Would you like to see me make it *ten* hours?" said Frazier. He smiled boyishly and we all laughed. "I haven't mentioned our most dramatic saving in manpower."

"Then you still have a chance to get away from the book," I said. "I must confess that I'm not quite so impressed as Mr. Castle. Most of what you have said so far is fairly standard criticism of our economic system. You've been pretty close to the professors."

"Of course I have. Even the professors know all this. The economics of a community are child's play."

"What about those two extra hours?" I said, deciding to let the insinuation pass.

Frazier waited a moment, looking from one of us to another.

"*Cherchez la femme!*" he said at last. He stopped to enjoy our puzzlement. "The women! The women! What do you suppose they've been doing all this time? There's our greatest achievement! We have industrialized housewifery!" He pronounced it "huzzifry" again, and this time I got the reference. "Some of our women are still engaged in the activities which would have been part of their jobs as housewives, but they work more efficiently and happily. And at least half of them are available for other work."

Frazier sat back with evident satisfaction. Castle roused himself.

"I'm worried," he said bluntly. "You've made a four-hour day seem convincing by pointing to a large part of the population not gainfully employed. But many of those people don't live as well as you. Our present average production may need only four hours per day per man—but that won't do. It must be something more than the average. You'd better leave the unproductive sharecropper out of it. He neither produces *nor consumes*—poor devil."

"It's true, we enjoy a high standard of living," said Frazier. "But our personal wealth is actually very small. The goods we consume don't come to much in dollars and cents. We practice the Thoreauvian principle of avoiding unnecessary possessions. Thoreau pointed out that the average Concord laborer worked ten or fifteen years of his life just to have a roof over his head. We could say ten weeks and be on the safe side. Our food is plentiful and healthful, but not expensive. There's little or no spoilage or waste in distribution or storage, and none due to miscalculated needs. The same is true of other staples. We don't feel the pressure of promotional devices which stimulate unnecessary consumption. We have some automobiles and trucks, but far fewer than the hundred family cars and the many business vehicles we should own if we weren't living in a community. Our radio installation is far less expensive than the three or four hundred sets we should otherwise be operating—even if some of us were radioless sharecroppers.

"No, Mr. Castle, we strike for economic freedom at this very point—by devising a very high standard of living with a low consumption of goods. We consume *less* than the average American."

It was now quite dark outside, and very still. Only the faint rhythmic song of frogs and peepers could be heard through the ventilating louvers. The building itself had grown quiet. No one else had been in the lounge for some time, and several of the lights had been frugally turned off. A pleasant drowsiness was creeping over me.

"You know, of course," Frazier said with a frown, "that this is by far the least interesting side of Walden Two." He seemed to have been seized with a sudden fear that we were bored. "And the least important, too—absolutely the least important. How'd we get started on it, anyway?"

"You confessed that you would be paid for talking to us," I said. "And very much underpaid, I may add. I don't know what the dollars-and-cents value of one labor-credit may be, but it's a most inadequate measure of an enjoyable evening."

The others murmured assent, and Frazier smiled with obvious delight.

"While you're in that mood," he said, "I should tell you that you'll be permitted to contribute labor-credits while you're here, too. We ask only two per day, since you're not acquiring a legal interest in the community or clothing yourselves at our expense."

"Fair enough," I said, but rather taken aback.

"We don't begrudge you the food you consume or the space you occupy, nor are we afraid of the effect of idleness upon the morale of our members. We ask you to work because we should feel inhospitable if you didn't. Be frank, now. No matter how warmly we welcomed you, wouldn't you soon feel that you ought to leave? But a couple of hours a day will fully pay for the services the community renders and incidentally do you a lot of good. And you may stay as long as you like with no fear of sponging. And because I receive a credit each day for acting as your guide, you needn't feel that you're imposing on me."

"What's to prevent some visitor—say, a writer—from putting in his two hours and staying on for good?" I asked. "He would find ample time for his trade and buy his own clothes and secure his own future without being a member."

"We've no objection, but we should ask that one half of any money made during his stay be turned over to Walden Two."

"Oh ho!" cried Castle. "Then it would be possible for a member to accumulate a private fortune—by writing books, say, in his spare time."

"Whatever for?" Frazier said. It seemed like genuine surprise, but his tone changed immediately. "As it happens, it isn't possible. All money earned by members belongs to the community. Part of our foreign exchange comes from private enterprises of that sort."

"Rather unfair to the member as compared with the guest, isn't it?" said Castle.

"What's unfair about it? What does the member want money for? Remember, the guest doesn't receive medical services, clothing, or security against old age or ill-health."

Frazier had risen as he was speaking, and we all followed his example promptly. It was clear that we had had enough for one day.

"I shouldn't be acting in the interests of the community," said Frazier, "if I kept you from your beds any longer. We expect a full day's work from you tomorrow morning. Can you find your way to your rooms?"

We made arrangements to meet at ten the next day and parted. Castle and I led the way down the silent, dimly lighted Walk. Presently we found that we were alone. Our companions, for reasons best known to themselves, had turned off and gone outside.

"I wonder what their two hours will be worth tomorrow?" said Castle. "Enemies of the people, I suppose you'd call them."

QUESTION

In what ways can society try to cope with change, and how effective are they?

Acknowledgments

From *A Man for All Seasons* by Robert Bolt. Copyright © 1960, 1962 by Robert Bolt. Reprinted by permission of Random House, Inc.

From *The Stranger* by Albert Camus, translated by Stuart Gilbert. Copyright 1946 and renewed 1974 by Alfred A. Knopf, Inc. Reprinted by permission of Alfred A. Knopf, Inc.

From *The Ox-Bow Incident* by Walter Van Tilburg Clark. Copyright 1940 and renewed 1968 by Walter Van Tilburg Clark. Reprinted by permission of Random House, Inc.

From *The Boy Who Painted Christ Black* by John Henrik Clarke. Copyright 1940 by John Henrik Clarke and copyright renewed 1968.

Reprinted by permission of Coward, McCann & Geoghegan, Inc., from *Lord of the Flies* by William Golding. Copyright © 1954 by William G. Golding.

From *The Inheritors,* copyright © 1955, by William Golding. Reprinted by permission of Harcourt Brace Jovanovich, Inc.

From *The Dune Messiah* by Frank Herbert. Reprinted by permission of